'Andrew Monaghan's compact and stimulating monograph is well worth reading.'

International Affairs

'Andrew Monaghan presents a convincing analysis of the strategic dissonance between the West and Russia. In this well-written book, which targets policymakers more than the scholarly community, he not only clearly lays out the problem but also points to a solution.'

Europe-Asia Studies

'As Monaghan so forcefully argues, "getting Russia right" matters so that misunderstandings do not escalate into conflict, and might eventually lead to fruitful cooperation. His book is an important start to a renewed debate on Russia and essential reading for anyone who needs to understand the country.'

RUSI Journal

'This is a masterful book and a refreshing read. It's valuable both to those newer to studying Russia and to anyone who finds it hard to navigate between claim and counter-claim (most of us, including myself!). It has gone straight on my student reading list.'

Luke March, *FORUM*

'In this lucid and important book, Andrew Monaghan argues that the West's capacity to understand Russia has been gravely run down. When Russia started reasserting itself in uncomfortable ways, we seized on Putin's personal role as an over-simple explanation. Our response has inevitably been overexcited and muddled.'

**Sir Rodric Braithwaite, British Ambassador
to the USSR/Russia 1988–1992**

'After years of less than benign neglect, this study places the "Russian question" front and center as substantively and objectively as possible. A must-read for those interested in foreign policy, experts and laymen alike, but especially for junior and senior policy-makers.'

**David Glantz, Editor-in-Chief, *Journal of
Slavic Military Studies***

T0283988

'A timely and sober corrective to the often ill-informed and contradictory analyses of Russia that are dominant today. This book cuts through hysteria and conventional wisdom, and is essential reading for those seeking to understand the challenges of dealing with Russia.'

Richard Connolly, Director of Eastern Advisory Group

'...offers a concise but thorough review of the key issues that have spurred a growing "strategic dissonance" between the West and Russia over the past twenty-five years and which have been amplified recently with Russia's intervention in Ukraine.'

John A. Pennell, Mission Director for USAID/Caucasus

'Those with an existing interest in Russia should read this book. Those without an existing interest, even more so: you have found the place to start. Dr Monaghan's excellent book is lucid, accessible and could not have come at a better time.'

Megan Edwards, Defence Specialist, Defence Select Committee

'*The new politics of Russia* expertly dismantles the way the West views Russia. The book is a refreshing addition to the literature on Russian-Western relations.'

Paul Robinson, Irrussianality blog

'Finally, the debate has been taken beyond a polarised discussion of the reasons behind the deterioration in Russia-Western relations. Monaghan gets to the heart of the most complex questions as to why many Western policymakers have struggled to understand Russia's actions and do more than simply react. A must-read for Western decision-makers.'

Sarah Lain, Associate Fellow, Royal United Services Institute

The new politics of Russia

Manchester University Press

RUSSIAN STRATEGY AND POWER

SERIES EDITORS

Andrew Monaghan and Richard Connolly

PREVIOUSLY PUBLISHED

Germany's Russia problem: The struggle for balance in Europe
John Lough

Russian Grand Strategy in the era of global power competition
Andrew Monaghan (ed.)

The sea in Russian strategy
Andrew Monaghan and Richard Connolly (eds)

Russian strategy in the Middle East and North Africa
Derek Averre

The new politics of Russia

Interpreting change

Revised and updated edition

ANDREW MONAGHAN

Manchester University Press

The right of Andrew Monaghan to be identified as the author of this work has been asserted in accordance with the Copyright, Designs and Patents Act 1988.

First edition published 2016 by Manchester University Press
This edition published 2024 by Manchester University Press
Oxford Road, Manchester, M13 9PL
www.manchesteruniversitypress.co.uk

British Library Cataloguing-in-Publication Data
A catalogue record for this book is available from the British Library

ISBN 978 1 5261 7805 3 hardback
ISBN 978 1 5261 5561 0 paperback

This edition first published 2024

The publisher has no responsibility for the persistence or accuracy of URLs for any external or third-party internet websites referred to in this book, and does not guarantee that any content on such websites is, or will remain, accurate or appropriate.

Typeset by Out of House Publishing
Printed in Great Britain by Bell & Bain Ltd, Glasgow

'We've moved on', Senior British official, 2011.

'I don't understand why you don't understand', Senior Russian official in discussion with Western officials, 2009.

'We often come up against the failure to understand our position and sometimes even an unwillingness to understand', Vladimir Putin, 'Direct line with Vladimir Putin', 17 April 2014. http://en.kremlin.ru/events/president/news/20796.

'One of the biggest delusions of the West has been that Russians are white. If we were black or blue, or dots, the West couldn't misunderstand Russians so much. But because we're white by race, they think we're the same as Europeans', Andrey Konchalovsky, 'A meeting with Andrey Konchalovsky: Part II', 27 June 2011. www.opendemocracy.net/node/60162/author/gerard-toal.

'Evropa ne znaet nas, potomu shto ne khochet znat; ili luchshe skazat znaet tak, kak znat khochet' [Europe does not know us, because it does not want to know; or better to say, it knows us as it wants to], Nikolai Danilevsky quoted in L. Kostromin, *Moya zhizn – razvedka* [*My Life as a Spy*] (Moscow: Detektiv Press, 2014), p. 284.

'I have a feeling that the situation which really exists in this country and the interpretations of the situation from the outside exist in some different, parallel worlds', Dmitri Medvedev, 22 January 2014; Interview with Ammanpour, http://government.ru/news/9868.

Contents

Preface: Russia matters

To many Western observers, Russia and the Russians defy logic. Russia appears as a country of incongruity, and the actions and decisions of its leaders can seem irrational, whether they be about providing succour and support for the leaderships of Iran or Syria when it would appear more logical for Russia's development to improve partnership with the West, or holding the Winter Olympic Games in the Black Sea resort of Sochi.

This 'defying of logic' tends to be emphasised by the high drama, even epic nature of the Russian story. Against the backdrop of the collapse of the Soviet Union and the widespread hope for a more democratic Russia and partnership with the West, a struggle has played out between heroes and villains, saints and sinners, embellished by extraordinarily wealthy oligarchs and the Committee of State Security (KGB), protesting liberals against established authorities, and of conspiracy theories, scandals, spies and war.[1]

At the same time, as one American observer has stated, the West has a 'painfully uneven track record of interpreting, let alone navigating developments in Russia during the Putin era'.[2] This is true: Western observers often fail to 'get Russia right',[3] and there is a persistent sense of surprise as expectations are confounded and the Russian leadership keeps the West guessing about its intentions and actions.

This can be attributed – partly – to the point that Russia is a 'museum of contradictions'.[4] Observers must navigate the ambiguity created by simultaneous Russian strength and weakness, tradition and novelty, wealth and poverty, freedom and restrictions: all the complications and complexity with which Russia has emerged – with some difficulty – from the rubble of the USSR. They must also try to grasp the balance and implications of a formal state with an informal style of leadership.[5]

These arguments are valid. Russia is difficult to understand, let alone 'get right'. But Western observers often get Russia wrong because of the way they approach it. Many apparent contradictions are instead paradoxes: the seemingly absurd or self-contradictory to a Western eye may be consistent if pursued through Russian logic. For this to be understood, however, expertise is required: a sophisticated, empathetic understanding of Russia and how it works. Yet since the end of the Cold War there has been a degradation of expertise, and the growth of an 'enormous foundation of ignorance' about Russia in the West.[6]

When attention is paid to Russia, it often suffers from a strong ethnocentrism – the imposition of Western national points of reference onto Russia – combined with a sense of the progressive march of history.[7] These problems emerge from a long debate about Russia's nature, about whether it is European or Asian; or whether Russia is 'a part of Europe or apart from it'.[8] As historians have pointed out, Russia serves to catalyse Western hopes and fears, aspirations and frustrations for the development of mankind. Indeed, it catalyses the broader antithesis of West and East, civilisation and barbarism.[9] Many in the Western political community hoped that the USSR's collapse validated the 'end of history' argument, the victory of Liberalism, and marked the beginning of Russia's progressive transition to democracy and return to the Western family of nations. One Western commentator has suggested that a 'single narrative about Russia has prevailed': 'openly or subconsciously, since 1991, Western leaders have acted on the assumption that Russia is a flawed Western country', one that, given Russia's forward progress, would sooner or later join the Western club.[10]

Consequently, Western observers often find themselves bound by 'Russian contradictions' of their own making, and their discussion about Russia has become lost in a series of confusing mazes and dead ends. Russia has appeared simultaneously to be resurgent and declining, a partner and a competitor; there is confusion over the Russian leadership, particularly whether Putin's leadership is strong and likely to last for a long time, or weak and likely to come to an end soon. Russia becomes abstracted to 'Russia', framed by Western points of reference – with the result that the Western officials and observers often get Russia wrong.

Getting Russia 'right', however, matters. It matters because of Russia's status as a permanent member of the United Nations Security Council, its great natural resource wealth, and its evolving military capability (particularly its nuclear weapons). This array of assets is accentuated by Russia's great size, which makes it a ubiquitous player in regions across the world in Europe, the Caucasus, Central Asia, Asia-Pacific and the Arctic, and by the efforts of the Russian leadership to turn Russia into an 'indispensable partner', one without whose participation major international questions, from conflict management and arms control to energy security and the architecture of international relations, cannot be addressed. To this end, the Russian leadership is investing vast resources to address its many internal problems and to retool its military, and to reach out across the world to establish or reinvigorate relationships with states and multilateral organisations from the Asia-Pacific region to Latin America.

Russia matters specifically to the West because since the mid 1990s, it has become a major partner, both as an energy supplier to the EU and for Western businesses. Additionally, as often stated by senior Western leaders, the West and Russia face many common problems and questions, from international terrorism to conflict resolution and the spread of weapons of mass destruction. Given its political influence and geographical location, Russia has an important role to play in many of the regional political and security questions that the West faces.

To be sure, there are serious long-term problems in Russia, including a struggling economy that relies on natural resources exports and demographic problems. Some critics argue that Russia is in strategic decline and that Russia's strategic outlook to 2050 is a negative one. And some suggest that the numerous disagreements between the West and Russia mean that the West should look elsewhere to develop partnerships to address solutions to international problems. Russia, the argument goes, does not matter because it does not act like a partner, nor does it demand prioritisation as a problem: it is merely a declining regional power.

These objections, though debatable, are important. But they miss the point. It is a one-eyed strategic outlook that only addresses the distant (and unpredictable) future: strategy is a dialogue with the current context and the immediate future.[11] And it is in this regard that Russia matters to Western policy-makers, given the scale of its assets and the explicit intentions of its leadership.[12] This is all the more true for the EU and NATO and many of their member states, given that they neighbour Russia.

Russia matters whether it is a partner, or, as seems more likely, a competitor. Indeed, the war in Ukraine that began in 2014 has illustrated that Russia matters because of the influence it wields on Euro-Atlantic security: senior NATO officials suggested that it has 'created a new strategic reality in Europe', and that Russia is speaking and behaving 'not as a partner but as an adversary'.[13] Philip Breedlove, NATO's Supreme Allied Commander Europe, suggested that 'Russia has managed to use its military, political and economic forces to fundamentally destabilise a European nation and change internationally recognised borders by illegally annexing Crimea'. The sudden shift, Breedlove suggested, 'carries significant implications for the future and seriously challenges how Europe has developed its stability and security since the end of the Cold War'.[14]

For the foreseeable future, therefore, Russia matters more to the West than any other single international question, not least because it weaves together questions of the evolution of wider international affairs, as well as specific issues of security, energy and economics. Indeed, it raises many wider questions about the end of the Cold War (and perhaps the post-Cold War) eras, the nature of Europe in the twenty-first century and how the West – including NATO and the EU – approaches the wider world. A better understanding of how Russia approaches international questions and how it is evolving domestically is necessary. This book takes a step in this direction by exploring Western interpretations of Russia and why many in the West, particularly in political and media circles, so often 'get Russia wrong' – and by exploring ways of how to 'get it right'.

Notes

1 R. Braithwaite, *Across the Moscow River: The World Turned Upside Down* (London: Yale University Press, 2002).
2 A. Weiss, 'Winter has come', *Democracy*, 30 (Fall 2013), www.democ racyjournal.org/30/winter-has-come.php?page=all. All links in the text were checked 3–7 August 2015.
3 D. Trenin, *Getting Russia Right* (Washington, DC: Carnegie Endowment, 2007).
4 J. Sherr, 'Russia: managing contradictions', in R. Niblett (ed.) *America and a Changed World. A Question of Leadership* (London: Chatham House and Wiley/Blackwell, 2010), p. 162.
5 R. Sakwa, 'Can Putinism solve its contradictions?', *OpenDemocracy* (27 December 2013), www.opendemocracy.net/od-russia/richard-sakwa/ can-putinism-solve-its-contradictions.
6 Personal correspondence with State Department official, September 2013.

7 K. Booth, *Strategy and Ethnocentrism* (London: Croom Helm, 1979), H. Butterfield, *The Whig Interpretation of History* (London: G. Bell and Sons, 1931).

8 V. Baranovsky, 'Russia: a part of Europe or apart from Europe?', *International Affairs*, 76:3 (2000), pp. 443–458.

9 M. Malia, *Russia Under Western Eyes: From the Bronze Horseman to the Lenin Mausoleum* (London: Belknap Press, 2000); J. Gleason, *The Genesis of Russophobia in Great Britain: A Study of the Interaction of Policy and Opinion* (Cambridge, MA: Harvard University Press, 1950).

10 A. Applebaum, 'A need to contain Russia', *Washington Post* (21 March 2014).

11 H. Strachan, *The Direction of War: Contemporary Strategy in Historical Perspective* (Cambridge: Cambridge University Press, 2014).

12 J.W. Parker and M. Kofman, *Russia Still Matters: Strategic Challenges and Opportunities for the Obama Administration*, INSS Paper SF-280 (Washington, DC: National Defence University, March 2013), http://inss.dodlive.mil/2013/03/01/strategic-forum-280/.

13 A. Vershbow, 'A new strategic reality in Europe', NATO (4 April 2014), www.nato.int/cps/en/natolive/opinions_108889.htm; Anders Fogh Rasmussen, 'De-escalations starts on the ground', NATO (13 April 2014), www.nato.int/cps/en/natolive/opinions_109102.htm.

14 P. Breedlove, 'The meaning of Russia's military campaign against Russia', *Wall Street Journal* (16 July 2014).

Preface to the updated edition

On 24 February 2022, Moscow launched a major military assault on Ukraine, driving deep into eastern and southern Ukraine, and attacking Kyiv from the north. The assault ended months of speculation, rumour, information releases by the USA and denials from the Russian authorities. After months of fighting, including faltering Russian offensives and setbacks, and Ukrainian counter-attacks, in September Moscow announced first a 'partial' mobilisation, calling up 300,000 men, then the annexation of the Donetsk, Lugansk, Zaporizhe and Kherson regions. In October, President Putin moved Russia onto a war footing.

By the winter, then, Europe was witnessing not just the largest-scale and most intense combat since 1945, but scenes and language very reminiscent of the two world wars. If the fighting had become attritional, with Russia and Ukraine digging networks of trenches, sowing extensive minefields and firing thousands of artillery rounds each day, the language also evoked those wars. Although Moscow had launched the invasion in what it called a 'special military operation', the language senior Russian officials used recalled the 'Fatherland'-type wars against Napoleon and Hitler. Dmitry Medvedev, former president and prime minister, and now head of the United Russia party in the parliament and a senior figure in the national Security Council, stated that the war was about Russia's 'survival'. Sergei Kirienko, first deputy head of the Presidential Administration, emphasised that Russia would win if the war became a 'people's war'.[1] Although the combat was in Ukraine, Moscow also pointed the finger at the Euro-Atlantic community, accusing it of waging a proxy war against Russia. For Putin, Moscow's military assault was 'pre-emptive'.[2]

The Euro-Atlantic community rejects all of Moscow's claims. The USA, the UK and some allies had repeatedly warned of an invasion and threatened severe repercussions if Moscow went ahead. So, when the attack started, the Euro-Atlantic community largely severed political contact with Russia and sought (and won) international diplomatic condemnation of Russia's actions. The United Nations voted to condemn the invasion as illegal in a resolution on 2 March 2022 and the humanitarian situation caused by the invasion on 24 March. A third resolution in April suspended Russia's membership of the UN's human rights council. In October the UN called on Russia to reverse its 'attempted illegal annexation' of the four territories,[3] and in February 2023 it called for an immediate end to the war and Russia's withdrawal from Ukraine.

The Euro-Atlantic community has also imposed a wide range of severe sanctions on Russia and provided extensive political, economic and military support to Kyiv. Western observers and officials have asserted the need to ensure Russia's defeat and humbling; commentators foresaw the collapse of the Russian economy, the end of Putin and even the disintegration of Russia. Once again, the Euro-Atlantic community and Russia are not just firmly divided into two opposing camps, with the shadow of war looming over a structural strategic contest, but appear to live in different worlds.

This edition offers an occasion to reflect on how far we have – and have not – come in nearly a decade since the book was written. It offers a chance to re-visit and re-emphasise the central arguments in the original book and to reflect on comments and questions by reviewers and readers who have contacted me. This edition seeks to emphasise the points of departure and main questions of the first edition, then, rather than attempting to offer a blow-by-blow update of all the many developments and events that have happened since its first publication. What is the longer-term trajectory of the Euro-Atlantic community's relationship with Russia? What does the evolution of Russian domestic politics and power look like, and what are the key themes? What have we seen before, and what is new? How might we think about Russia in the twenty-first century?

So, this edition offers a concise 'backstory' for what has again emerged as one of the most serious and pressing crises facing Western governments. It presents a benchmark for observing continuity and change across a generation and in the build-up to Russian presidential elections currently scheduled for 2024, not only in what is happening inside Russia and in relations with it but also in terms of how we think about Russia. Certainly, a great deal has changed, but there is also a strong sense of déjà vu not only in the Euro-Atlantic community's relationship with Russia, but also in much of the Western discussion about Russia.

I have only added the lightest of polishing touches to the original main text, removing some repetition and updating some specific points of detail. Instead, I have added a substantive epilogue, in which I have brought up to date some aspects of both foreign policy and relations between the West and Russia, and Russian domestic politics, and elaborated on some of the questions that have emerged since Moscow's renewed assault on Ukraine in 2022. I have also added an update about how Russia studies is evolving as a discipline, since it has again gone through a major period of self-reflection in the wake of the war.

Thanks are, as always, due to many people for their support and kindness while I have worked on this book. Some things do not change: I remain very grateful to all those I acknowledged in the original text. This was my first book, and I remain indebted to those who helped me through the learning process, including, of course, my publishers at Manchester University Press. The first edition was written while I was an Academic Visitor at St Antony's College, Oxford, and I am still grateful to all my hosts there for the friendly and stimulating environment in which to concentrate to write, also for the opportunity to present the book once it was published and debate it with the scholars there. Since then, though, I have moved on, and now also offer my thanks to the Royal United Services Institute in London and the Wilson Center's Kennan Institute in Washington, DC for their support.

Notes

1 D. Medvedev, 'Nashi Lyudi, nasha zemlya, nasha Pravda' [Our people, our land, our truth], *Rossiiskaya Gazeta* (25 December 2022); 'Kirienko: Rossiya vyigraet voinu, esli ona stanet narodnoi' [Kirienko: Russia will win the war if it becomes a people's war], *Kommersant* (22 October 2022), www.kommersant.ru/doc/5631885?from=top_main_3.

2 'Parad pobedy na Krasnoi ploshchadi' [Victory parade on Red Square] (9 May 2022), http://kremlin.ru/events/president/news/68366.
3 'Ukraine: UN General Assembly demands Russia reverse course on "attempted illegal annexation"', *UN News* (12 October 2022), https://news.un.org/en/story/2022/10/1129492.

Acknowledgements

Thanks are due to many people. First, this book was written during my time at St Antony's College, Oxford, and I am grateful to Alex Pravda and Roy Allison for their support. It is also the product of my work over a longer period, and it draws on and develops work done at the NATO Defence College, Rome, and in the Russia and Eurasia Programme at Chatham House. Particular thanks therefore go to Dieter Löser, Grant Hammond, Rich Hooker and participants in the Roman Baths Advisory Group for their support and friendship in Rome, and to James Nixey, Lubica Pollakova and all my colleagues at Chatham House.

I have benefited from the support, patience and courtesy of many librarians, and would like to thank Simon Blundell, Richard Ramage at St Antony's, the library team at the NDC, and David Bates and his team at Chatham House. I am also grateful to Jan Techau at Carnegie Europe, Caroline Soper at *International Affairs* and Amanda Moss at Chatham House, the Royal Institute for International Affairs, for permission to draw on and develop material already published.

Caroline Wintersgill commissioned and encouraged the book, and I am grateful to her and to my publishers, Manchester University Press for their skilful support in seeing the book through to publication.

Many individuals have also helped to shape the thinking that lies behind this book. I have enjoyed and benefited from discussions with many Western officials in the UK, USA, NATO and EU, and also many Russians. I greatly appreciate the frank terms on which of these exchanges were held. Similarly, discussions with Florence Gaub, Nazrin Mehdiyeva, David Hamon, Patrick Porter, Beatrice Heuser, David Glantz, Wayne Allensworth, Hew Strachan and Rob Johnson, among many others, have stimulated my thinking. Particular thanks go to three anonymous peer reviewers, Jake Kipp,

Dov Lynch, Julian Cooper, Silvana Malle, L.-J. O'Neill, Rob Dover, Keir Giles, Henry Plater-Zyberk, Don Jensen and Emily Ferris for taking the time to discuss the book's themes and read drafts of parts or all of the text. Their comments have been invaluable, and for the most part incorporated into the text. Where I have failed to do so, and for any remaining errors, I have only myself to blame.

In Russia, I have benefited from much warmth and hospitality. I would like to thank Boris Mikhailovich, Mikhail Borisovich, Viktor Nikolaevich and Ekaterina Vladimirovna for their kindness and generosity in looking after me in various ways. The book would not have been the same without the work of Arkadiy Zvezdin and Lazar Vaysbeyn.

Finally, most of all, my thanks and love go to my family, Charles and Dorothy Monaghan and Yulia, for their patient and unfailing support and encouragement. Without them the book could not have been written, and so it is dedicated to them, and to Lara Andreevna whose happy presence is eternally felt.

Abbreviations

ASI	Agency of Strategic Initiatives
CAI	Cooperative Airspace Initiative
CC	Coordination Council
CFE	Treaty on Conventional Forces in Europe
EU	European Union
FSB	Federal Security Service
IFOR	Implementation Force
JR	Just Russia
KGB	Committee of State Security
KPRF	Communist Party of the Russian Federation
LDPR	Liberal Democratic Party of Russia
MG	Molodaya Gvardia
MoD	Ministry of Defence
NATO	North Atlantic Treaty Organisation
NGO	Non-Governmental Organisation
NRC	NATO–Russia Council
ONF	All-Russian Popular Front
OECD	Organisation for Economic Cooperation and Development
OSCE	Organization for Security and Cooperation in Europe
PJC	Permanent Joint Council
PPC	Permanent Partnership Council
STANDEX	Stand-off Detection of Explosives and Suicide Bombers
UN	United Nations
UR	United Russia
WTO	World Trade Organization

Introduction: 'we've moved on'

'We've moved on.' This apparently simple phrase, often uttered by officials and commentators on both sides since 1991, captures the evolving ambiguity of the relationship between the West and Russia. One (early) interpretation offered the more positive view that both sides have moved on from the confrontation of the Cold War: Russia is very different from the USSR, the West is much changed, and the relationship between them greatly altered. Despite numerous points of friction, there was no systemic ideological conflict with military confrontation – the West and Russia 'no longer peer at each other through binoculars', as one Western official observed in late 2013.[1] Indeed, since the start of the 1990s, significant cooperation has taken place between the West and Russia in terms of business, but also in sensitive areas including in the military and intelligence domains.

Another interpretation draws attention to the persistent friction between the West, particularly in its institutional forms such as the European Union (EU) and North Atlantic Treaty Organisation (NATO) and Russia, whether over questions of wider Euro-Atlantic security, such as that caused by the Kosovo crisis in 1998/9 and the Russo-Georgia War in 2008, or bilaterally, such as the crisis in UK–Russia relations caused by the murder of Alexander Litvinenko in 2006. The various 'resets' and 'reloads' conducted in relations, most recently between 2009 and 2013, reflect attempts to draw a line under these problems and 'move on' from them.

But at a deeper level, this simple phrase reflects a conceptual gap in how Russia and the West interpret international affairs. When used by Western officials and observers, this phrase has often indicated Russia fatigue: 'we've moved on' has meant that the West has moved on from the political and security priorities of the Cold War era, and Russia, seen by many to be a declining power, is no longer among the new priorities – not least because it has not moved on towards the hoped-for democracy and partnership with the West. Even with the emergency in Ukraine continuing into 2015, and then the Russian deployment to Syria, which together have led some senior military officials in the West to suggest that Russia poses the main threat to NATO and the USA, consensus on prioritisation has been difficult to achieve. Secretary of State John Kerry, for instance, disagreed with the military analysis of Russia, and suggested that Russia is a state with which the USA has disagreements, but not as an existential threat,[2] and there has been a tendency to focus instead on other problems such as Islamic State and counter-terrorism.

When the phrase is used by Russian officials and observers, on the other hand, it is to suggest that the post-Second World War international architecture led by the West no longer works, that Western political, economic and security frameworks are obsolete (and even create problems) and Western, especially Anglo-Saxon, influence in international affairs is declining. Indeed, the asymmetry of 'we've moved on' is thus echoed by a different symmetry: the West and Russia view each other as declining and decreasingly relevant powers that are morally bankrupt at home and pursue reckless and dangerous international policies abroad. This gap, set in the foundations of relations between the West and Russia in the early 1990s, has grown and is the font of the strong sense of strategic dissonance that increasingly characterises the relationship.

The war in Ukraine that began in 2014, the most serious emergency in relations for many years, threw the emphasis very much onto the dissonance inherent in this latter interpretation. But it also highlighted the inability to move on from the Cold War in terms of how both sides perceive the other. This book explores this gap, focusing on the Western difficulties in interpreting Russia.

This chapter sketches out the book's underlying themes, beginning by reflecting on some of the problems that are set in the foundations of Russia's post-Cold War relationship with the West. The chapter then points to problems that emerge from linguistic and historical 'interpretation', before laying out the structure of the book.

Russia's post-Cold War emergence

Under Vladimir Putin's leadership, Russia has emerged from the rubble of the USSR, getting up 'off its knees' and become increasingly active on the international stage. Moscow has reached out to establish or enhance relationships with states and multilateral international organisations both in Eurasia and further afield, from Europe to China to Latin America, and sought to play a role in many of the major international questions of our time. At the same time, Russian domestic affairs and foreign policies have often surprised Western partners, officials and observers alike.

These surprises take different forms. They have come in 'active' forms, such as unexpected actions taken – the Russo-Georgia War in 2008, the energy crises in 2006 and 2009, the annexation of Crimea in 2014, and Russia's intervention in Syria in September 2015 and then its partial withdrawal from Syria in March 2016 being perhaps the most obvious examples. And they come in 'passive' forms, such as expected developments that did not take place, such as the anticipated rescinding of Russia's recognition of the states of South Ossetia and Abkhazia, which came as a surprise to many in NATO and had a chilling effect on NATO–Russia relations at the time of the NATO Chicago summit in May 2012.[3] Such surprises often have important ramifications for the West's relations with Russia. Change comes where it is not expected, and does not come where it is, and Russian policies and politics appear to change when they do not, and do evolve in ways that are not seen or anticipated – all creating dissonance in the relationship.

This sense of surprise is largely because post-Cold War Russia is poorly understood in the West – Russia has not conformed to Western expectations and hopes for its transformation, nor have senior Western officials been able effectively to interpret Russian language and actions. Often the interpretation of Russia has been based on *Western* assumptions rather than Russian ones. For much of the post-Cold War era, Russia has not been a political priority either for organisations such as NATO, or for member states such as the USA, UK and others, and so official expertise on it has been wound down or dispersed, and a gap has grown between policy-making and what remains of expertise on Russia in other areas such as academia.

This has allowed the emergence of a mainstream discussion about Russia that tends to dominate Western public policy and headlines but that suffers from numerous problems. It tends to be reactive and to focus on a small number of narrow and simplistic questions that are supposed to offer the skeleton key to unlocking the puzzle of Russia. These often focus on single issues and the crisis of the day, and offer a simplified binary picture that produces a one-dimensional discussion of Russia, such as whether Russia is a democracy or authoritarian state, or whether Russia's relations with the West are cooperative or confrontational.

This is not new. In 1947, British author Edward Crankshaw emphasised the 'astonishingly limited and repetitive' nature of questions in the USA and UK. These included 'is Russia out to dominate the world? Is Russia a democracy *or* (always *or*) is Stalin a dictator? Is the N.K.V.D. really a Gestapo?'[4] The central questions today directly echo those that Crankshaw sketches out, and the responses too often degenerate into a form of positional trench warfare, dominated by partisan factual bombardments of lists of violations (such as human rights) and confirmations of known sins (for example corruption), and counter-bombardments of lists of extenuating contextual reasons and circumstances between those who are critical of Russia and those who advocate greater understanding and cooperation respectively.

This has generated a discussion dominated by worn out clichés and stereotypes and exotic myths and fantasies about Russian life, often bolstered by the repetition of quotes from Western historical figures such as Winston Churchill, George Kennan and the Marquis de Custine. Perhaps the most pervasive (and abused) is the reference to Churchill's statement 'I cannot forecast to you the action of Russia. It is a riddle wrapped in a mystery inside an enigma.' The quote is usually incomplete, however, omitting the continuation 'but perhaps there is a key. That key is Russian national interest.'

These clichés and stereotypes are amplified by speculative reflections and predictions that draw selectively on Russian grapevine whispers about the informal and obscure aspects of Russian political life. The resulting commentary is often dramatised and hyperbolic – and misleading – and, taken all together, the smoke and noise from the bombardments and speculation obscure our vision of already complex and difficult to understand developments in Russia.

Partly as a result of these problems, much Western analysis of Russia seems to be locked into cycles of hope, optimism and anticipation, followed by disappointment, frustration and anger. Again, this is not new: Crankshaw noted this 'dire and inflexible rhythm' of the 'monotonous and gloomy regularity with which the birth and recurrent rebirth of goodwill between [the UK and Russia] has been succeeded by the resurrection of suspicion, hardening quickly into hostility open or concealed'.[5]

Such cycles have been visible throughout the post-Soviet era.[6] Optimism about relations between Russia and the West during the early 1990s moved towards crisis, even towards breaking point during the NATO campaign against Serbia in 1999, but subsequently underwent an improvement over the next few years leading to the Rome Declaration in May 2002 and the establishment of the NATO Russia Council. By 2008 and the Russo-Georgia War, however, relations had again reached crisis point before undergoing a series of 'resets' and 'reloads' in 2009 and 2010.

Similar cycles have been visible regarding hopes for Russia's development. With Boris Yeltsin came hope for Russia's change and transition to democracy. But, as Russia faced numerous economic and social problems and as Yeltsin's own health deteriorated, including public displays of drunkenness, Yeltsin became a figure of mockery in the West. When Vladimir Putin came to power in 2000, he was hailed as a sober, effective, even reformist leader. But this too turned first to disappointment and then, in some sections of officialdom and the wider commentariat, to an almost visceral dislike from 2003. When Dmitri Medvedev became president in 2008, he too was hailed by many as a figure who could modernise and liberalise Russia. Yet with the announcement in September 2011 that it would be Putin who ran for the presidency in 2012, the attitude of many in the West was to write Medvedev off with a mixture of almost tangible contempt and disappointment. Even though he moved to the position of prime minister, he was either spoken of by many Western commentators in the past tense or ignored.

In 2012, with Putin's return to the presidency, the cycle entered another downturn. Indeed some officials and observers suggested that it was worse even than before, and commentators pointed to the final death of the 'reset' as a bilateral meeting between Presidents Obama and Putin was cancelled in autumn 2013 amid fractious debates over Western intervention in Libya, the ongoing civil war in Syria and another round of spy scandals – this time Moscow's offer of asylum to Edward Snowden. Articles in high-profile media suggested that Putin's third term as president was being defined by a newly confrontational attitude in Moscow, as the Russian leadership was simultaneously increasingly in conflict with the West and aggressive at home. *The Economist* suggested that 'hostility to the West' had become a 'hallmark of Putin's third presidential term' and was leading to a 'cold climate' of 'ill-concealed' mutual resentment between the West and Russia.[7] And all this came before the war in Ukraine that led to mutual recriminations, a suspension of partnership formats, and the imposition of sanctions first by the USA and EU on Russia, and then by Russia on Western states that support sanctions against it – effectively the start of economic war.

The result of these points is that the mainstream view of Russia in the West among many political leaders and observers is narrow, simplistic and repetitive: with each new crisis, the same terms, phrases, analogies and images are repeated. A one-dimensional and increasingly automatic view of Russia has thus emerged, emphasised by the often hyperbolic tone of the discussion.

The shadow of the Cold War

For many, the war in Ukraine has created a crisis in relations between Russia and the West, one that is often presented as a new and deeply negative stage in relations, a 'new Cold War'. The Cold War provides comfortable mental furniture, particularly when describing Putin's Russia, which many have described as 'going back to the USSR', or the establishment of the 'USSR 2.0'. Strobe Talbott, deputy Secretary of State from 1994 to 2001 and special advisor to the Secretary of State for former Soviet affairs and now president of the Brookings Institute, has suggested, for instance, that the 'defining theme' of Putin's presidency was 'turning back the clock'.[8]

This 'new Cold War' theme is not new. Since the mid 2000s, observers have increasingly framed tensions between Russia and the West in terms of whether or not they marked the start of a 'new Cold War'. The debate was given lasting impulse when Vladimir Putin observed in a speech in 2005 that the collapse of the USSR was the 'greatest geopolitical catastrophe of the twentieth century', in the process providing a quote often casually (but wrongly) deployed ever since to illustrate his apparent desire to re-establish the USSR.[9] This sense was enhanced by Putin's speech at the Munich security conference in February 2007, widely reported as the Russian leadership rekindling the Cold War, emphasised by Russian moves such as its suspension of the Treaty on Conventional Forces in Europe (CFE) and the resumption of Russian strategic bomber flights in 2007.[10]

The Cold War also informs the discussion – and policies – in Russia. In 2004, Vladislav Surkov, then first deputy head of the presidential administration, suggested that international groups continued to live with Cold War phobia and consider Russia an adversary. During a speech in Berlin in June 2008, then president Dmitri Medvedev stated that it was 'hard to escape the conclusion that Europe's architecture still bears the stamp of an ideology inherited from the past'.[11] He thus emphasised Moscow's attempt to advance a new European security treaty to overcome this. Indeed, these proposals and other elements of Russian foreign policy during the Putin era can be understood as attempts to revise the results of the Cold War.[12]

But if the debate about a 'new Cold War' has increasingly featured in the discussion about the West's relationship with Russia, it is by returning to the end of the Cold War and early 1990s that we find the original gaps in the interpretation of events through which the current tensions have developed. The difference in understanding of the role of Mikhail Gorbachev, the last General Secretary of the Central Committee of the Communist Party of the Soviet Union, symbolises this gap. In the West, Gorbachev is seen as an heroic figure, one who brought democracy and freedom to the USSR and first eased tensions in the USSR's relations with the West, and then brought a 'bloodless' end to the Cold War. He was awarded the Nobel Peace Prize in 1990. This positive (albeit only partially accurate) view echoes today, where his views are still treated with respect.

In Russia, however, Gorbachev is cast, even reviled, by many as the villain of the collapse of the USSR and Russia's subsequent problems. Catherine Merridale reminds us that the terms so appealing to the West – 'glasnost' and 'perestroika' – were interpreted very differently in the USSR. To some, in the wake of the Chernobyl accident, the openness of 'glasnost' represented the threat of an internal witch-hunt against incompetent managers through the exposure of their mistakes. To others, the restructuring involved in 'perestroika', represented a threat to the wages and benefits of the working class. So while the idea of reform appealed to all, the practicalities of what that meant did not. Thus, as Andrei Grachev suggested, few ask about the number of *coups d'état* Gorbachev actually managed to avoid in six and a half years of reform.[13] Today in Russia he is broadly ignored, though feelings still run deep: one retired counter-intelligence colonel even recently referred to him as 'the number one German': ie. a traitor,[14] and others recently published a book entitled *Gorbachev: Anatomy of Betrayal*.[15]

Beyond this illustrative symbol, however, a series of founding myths and misunderstandings began with the end of the Cold War that provide the basis for today's dissonant relations. In the West, it was a time of optimism, excitement and hope that Russia would enjoy a positive transition to democracy and return to the

Western family of nations as a partner on the international stage. In Russia, too, it was a time of optimism, though the Russian leadership sought recognition and greater assistance from the West for the sacrifices and contribution it had made to the peaceful ending of the Cold War.[16] But a prolonged debate has raged about specific aspects of the post-Cold War era such as the lack of sufficient Western help for Russia (the failure to introduce a Marshall Plan for Russia, for instance), and yet too much ineffective or damaging 'help' for Russia (Western advisers giving bad advice), and then whether Russia's development into a 'normal country' had stalled and who was responsible for this.[17]

Here is not the place to reprise those arguments. Suffice it to say that from the first, misperceptions and disagreements were woven into the foundations of the relationship: both the West and Russia believe that they 'won' the Cold War, and both sides blame the other for having missed opportunities after that to shape a more positive 'post-Cold War' environment. In the West, many see the 1990s as a dark era for Russia, but nevertheless a missed opportunity in terms of Russia's transition to democracy. In Russia, a narrative, officially promoted and supported but not without substance, has evolved that points to the disastrous 1990s and the negative role the West played in those years, both misleading Russia with unfulfilled promises and inflicting damage on Russian interests while Russia was weakened after the collapse of the USSR.

A second important and long-lasting debate is over NATO's alleged 'no enlargement' promise. This has become a central point of disagreement between the West and Russia. This question was raised by Putin in his Munich speech in February 2007, and has regularly re-emerged, most recently and obviously during the war in Ukraine in 2014. Indeed, senior Russian officials have long asserted that assurances were given by Western leaders to the Soviet leadership that any NATO enlargement following the Soviet withdrawal would be limited to the reunified Germany. This has led to a prolonged series of exchanges in which Western officials and observers have denied that such promises were made on one hand, and accusations by Russian officials and observers that NATO is an organisation that says one thing but does another – and so cannot be trusted. When there are moments of crisis or dispute, such as during the Libya and Ukraine crises, the NATO non-enlargement promise dispute resurfaces.[18]

But this disagreement again reflects the small gaps in the foundations of relations caused by misinterpretation. As some have pointed out, the question is more ambiguous. Officials familiar with the discussions at the time suggest that spoken indications may have been given to Soviet officials – and then wrongly interpreted in Moscow as a promise. Rodric Braithwaite, UK ambassador to the USSR from 1988 to 1992, has subsequently suggested that

> The assurances which Western politicians gave about the future of NATO were not binding, they were not written down, and they were given by people in a hurry, intent on achieving more immediate objectives. They were not intended to mislead. But the Russians inevitably interpreted them to mean that there would be no further expansion of NATO beyond Germany's new Eastern boundary.[19]

Similarly, Mary Sarotte suggests that, contrary to the arguments of many in the West, the matter of NATO enlargement arose early and included discussions about both East Germany and Eastern Europe. Senior Western figures gave speeches and hinted that there would not be enlargement. However, contrary to Russian assertions, no promise was given that NATO would not enlarge. She suggests that Bush's senior advisors had 'a spell of internal disagreement in early February 1990 which they displayed to Gorbachev', before uniting and not offering such a promise.[20]

These are some of the 'original sins' on which today's relations between Russia and the West rest.[21] They are well known in the Russia-watching community, and often remarked upon. But there are other important gaps that contribute to problems in relations and also Western misunderstanding of Russia that are less often remarked upon.

Linguistic 'false friends'

The first is a strong linguistic dissonance, both in terms of translation and different interpretation of terminology. Swedish analysts have suggested that the Ukraine crisis has revealed that the West and Russia are 'speaking different dialects' on security.[22] And there are certainly visible gaps in terminology that reflect divergences: in Western terms, for instance, Crimea was 'annexed' by Russia, but in Russian terms, Crimea was 'reunified' with Russia. Similarly, NATO's policy is one of 'open door' or 'enlargement', whereas the Russian term is 'expansion'.

As important are the similar sounding words and phrases that act as 'false friends' that appear to offer commonality of meaning, but that are understood differently in Western capitals and Moscow with important implications for how Russia is understood in the West and also for the development of the relationship. Western concepts and terms are often imposed on the Russian situation with misleading results. The rise of a Russian middle class, for instance, was a central aspect of the mainstream Western understanding of the protest demonstrations in 2011 and at the heart of hopes for Russia's transition towards democracy. In the West, the Russian middle class is understood to be a driver of political change, part of an evolving entrepreneurial private sector and civil society increasingly free and independent from the state. In Russia, however, the middle class, while reflecting some of the trappings of a Western middle class, is understood to be those who are 'budjetniki' – in other words, financed by the state budget and so not free from it. This changes the picture of the Russian middle class and its role in important ways, and Russian commentators suggest that 'there is little reason to believe that the middle class will react to the ongoing financial and economic crisis with protests or renewed calls for change'.[23]

Once again, such problems are not new. During the Cold War, there were numerous linguistic divergences in which the same words were very differently understood. For instance, there was dissonance between the understanding of peace, détente and deterrence: such terms created false expectations based on the assumption that they meant something similar to both sides. As Peter Vigor observed, peace in the West has a positive connotation, embodied in the idea of freedom from, or cessation of, hostilities. The Soviet understanding, however, was different, having a more negative connotation, as 'peace as the absence of war or conflict'. Vigor suggested that these could be compared as Western 'peace and good will' and Soviet 'peace and ill will'. Similarly, in the West, deterrence was depicted as (mutual) vulnerability through the idea of mutually assured destruction. But in Moscow deterrence was understood as sufficiently strong war fighting capacity to impress an opponent and maintain strategic stability.

These differences had important ramifications as each side accused the other of hypocrisy when in fact they were acting within their own definitions. Different understandings of peace were translated into how each side viewed the processes of 'détente' and 'peaceful coexistence', and defence. Deterrence and defence were incompatible in the West, since improved defence would undermine the mutual vulnerability at the heart of deterrence, whereas in Russia improved defence was entirely compatible with deterrence.[24] As Ken

Booth noted, both Westerners and Soviets failed to get the other to accept and understand their understandings of such concepts.[25]

Clumsy interpretation and consequent linguistic misunderstanding endures, and plays an important role in the relationship, as official meetings can embark on two separate, unintentionally conflicting discussions as a result of interpretation.[26] One example was during a meeting in late 2011 between senior Russian military officers and their Western counterparts. During a question and answer session, Western officers posed questions about Russian counter-terrorism in Chechnya. The word 'terrorist' was interpreted as 'rebel',[27] however, leading initially to confusion, then frustration, then increasing anger on the Russian side, before the interpreter's error was recognised. Though on this occasion the misunderstanding was resolved, the linguistic gap here is important, and, as discussed in Chapter 2, these differences continue to resonate at the highest political levels in Russia.

Problems in interpretation also reveal instances of 'false friend' differences. One example was the attempt in 2009 by the Obama administration to place its relationship with Russia on a better footing in the wake of the rising tension and the Russo-Georgia War. Hillary Clinton presented a souvenir 'reset' button to Russian Foreign Minister Sergei Lavrov, asking him if the Russian was correct, and assuring him that her staff had worked hard to ensure it was. But instead of using the Russian word for 'reset', the US interlocutors used the Russian term for 'overload'. The Russian newspaper *Kommersant* ran it as a front-page story, with a photo of the exchange of the souvenir, with the caption 'difficulties in translation again hinder Russo-American relations'.[28]

Beyond the embarrassment caused, this linguistic error reflected deeper conceptual divergences in how the two sides saw the 'reset'. As Angela Stent noted, the question of the reset was both 'a literal and a philosophical question ... the metaphorical possibilities for interpreting reset were as extensive as the policy implications'. Did the reset mean pressing the button and returning the relationship to the status quo ante? If so, which status quo? For the USA, it appeared that the reset was an attempt to improve relations – to stem the deterioration, and, despite ongoing disagreements, 'revisit the many areas' in which the USA could and should be working with Russia.[29]

For Moscow, rather than offering an opportunity for cooperation on common issues, the 'reset' appeared as Washington correcting its political course. Lavrov stated that the 'deterioration of relations was not Russia's choice' and that it was the previous (George W. Bush) administration which had soured relations through its pursuit of the ballistic missile defence programme, 'unjustified NATO expansion' and the refusal to ratify the Adapted CFE Treaty. Before any reset of relations could go ahead, 'we must get rid of the toxic assets inherited from recent years'.[30] And, as Stent has suggested, the Russians never took ownership of the 'reset', while the term 'reset' was neither in the Russian style nor language.[31]

The publication of the Russian military doctrine in 2010 offers another illustration of the importance of linguistic precision. The document was reported to suggest that NATO was seen as a 'threat' to Russia. Yet this was to miscast the nature of a difficult relationship. The doctrine actually posits NATO as a 'danger'. It also clearly defines the distinction between 'threat' and 'danger': a 'threat' is defined as the realistic possibility of an armed conflict arising, while a 'danger' is a situation with the potential under certain circumstances to develop into a threat. While Moscow certainly has problems with the Alliance, particularly on issues such as NATO enlargement, the 2010 doctrine did not define NATO in the category of realistic possibilities of armed conflict; indeed it made the distinction clear.

Some might suggest that this definitional difference is merely splitting hairs, since Russian officials often refer to NATO in terms that effectively equate to a 'threat' – and because in the West the terms 'threat' and 'danger' are often used largely interchangeably.[32] But this is to miss the point. First, in the wake of the publication of the doctrine, much effort was spent on both sides attempting to clarify that Moscow did *not* see NATO as a threat, or with senior Western officials clarifying that NATO did not pose a threat to Russia, and that Moscow was wrong to think that it might – in effect a discussion about something that was not said and thus muddying an already complex and contentious question further. Interestingly, despite the rhetoric, this terminology did not change in the revised military doctrine published in late 2014.

Furthermore, as Keir Giles has pointed out, this distinction in the Russian military lexicon points to a more subtle perception of international affairs – and allows Russian officials to complain about NATO without being forced to do something such as re-orienting the military to counter the supposed threat posed by NATO.[33] Furthermore, by overlooking this subtle argument, the Western audience becomes insensitive to alterations made by Moscow in either previous or future iterations of the doctrine.

The wrong side of history?

The second strong dissonance relates to different understandings of history, and the way progressive understandings of history have underpinned Western interpretations of Russia. Swedish researcher Gudrun Persson has correctly suggested that history is an important element of state building in Russia today, as suggested by official statements, in official documents, and moves such as the establishment of a working group to develop a single interpretation of Russian history and the creation of a unit in the Ministry of Defence (MoD) to combat the falsifications of history.

If the focus on the centrality of the Great Patriotic War is explicit, the sense of dissonance with others in the international arena is unmistakable. The National Security Strategy and Foreign Policy Concept both state Moscow's intention to counteract attempts to revise international history and Russia's place in it, and use history to provoke confrontation and revanchism in international affairs. Furthermore, Persson notes that while the Russian approach to history – focused on greatness and military history – is not unusual, it reflects a nineteenth-century methodology and is at odds with the one prevalent in the West that adopts a 'more critical approach to sources and historical events'.[34]

There is a tendency among many Western observers and senior public policy figures – implicitly or explicitly – to discuss Russia in terms of being on the 'right' or 'wrong' side of history, of the 'progressive' nature of history and applying certain methods of assumption and inference as a result. Again, there are echoes of the late 1980s and early 1990s, since this builds on an optimistic vision of Francis Fukuyama's 'End of History' argument, the view that the end of the Cold War reflected the 'triumph of the West, of the Western idea' in the victory of liberalism, and the 'total exhaustion of viable systematic alternatives to Western liberalism'. (Many assumed that Fukuyama meant victory was complete. He did not, and stressed that it would be in the long run and that much of the world remained 'mired in history' – and, importantly for this discussion, 'Russia and China are not likely to join the developed nations of the West as liberal societies any time in the foreseeable future.')[35]

On this assumption is based the view that Russia – particularly under the leadership of Vladimir Putin – is on the 'wrong side of history' as 'shown' by the protest demonstrations in Russia in 2011, and the Russian state's position regarding the war in Syria. The US leadership returned to this theme after the Russian annexation of Crimea in March 2014, with President Obama stating that international criticism of Russian actions placed Russia on the 'wrong side of history', and John Kerry that Putin 'may have his version of history, but I believe that he and Russia … are on the wrong side of history'. 'I must say I was really struck and somewhat surprised and even disappointed by the interpretations in the facts as they were presented by (Putin)', he continued.[36]

Russian points of reference in history are also different. This was well illustrated by a discussion that Vladimir Putin had with Russian historians in November 2014. Western reportage of the meeting emphasised Putin's apparent 'rehabilitation' of the Molotov–Ribbentrop Pact.[37] Putin, however, pointed to the West's unreliability towards, even 'betrayal' of, its Eastern European allies, such as Poland in the Second World War, and contended that Western historians 'hush up' the Munich agreement and, in focusing on the Molotov–Ribbentrop Pact and the division of Poland, overlook how Poland invaded and annexed part of Czechoslovakia when the Germans annexed the Sudentenland in 1938.[38]

It is not surprising, therefore, that the Russian leadership does not see 'sides' of history in the same way, not least because Russia did not begin the same 'end of history' discussion that took place in the West. Lavrov has stated that 'many politicians, particularly in the West' enjoy using 'bright slogans' such as the 'right side of history', but these are 'extreme' and 'emotional'. He then suggested that those who had followed Russia's role in the arrangements for the destruction of Syrian chemical weapons, would recognise that Russia, with others, was on the 'right' side of history, while their (Western) partners had 'flip-flopped'.[39]

Nevertheless, ideas of the 'end of history' and the assumption that history can be interpreted in a progressive form has underpinned much of the Western understanding of Russia in the post-Cold War era. The entwining of ideas of 'progress' in history, and the comparison of Russian development with ourselves and Russia's 'return' to the Western family of nations through transition to democracy, offers an easy, even irresistible, rule of thumb by which points of emphasis can be selected and rejected, and imposes a certain form in which a particular scheme of historic transformation emerges, allowing the classification of people into those who either furthered progress or tried to hinder it.

Those who oppose Vladimir Putin, for example, have been easily classified into recognisable agents of change, because observers see similarities with a 'modern', Western society – and can be catego-rised as a 'rising urban middle class' – while the Russian leader-ship, especially Vladimir Putin, are categorised as those hindering progress.[40] This frames the discussion in a series of false delinea-tions and definitions of 'liberals' and 'conservatives': some senior Russian figures are understood to be 'liberals', it seems, mostly on the basis of what they are not, rather than what they actually are.

This emphasis on the principle of 'progress' standing paramount as the scheme of history encourages the drawing of simple lines of causation and change through events, in the search for a desirable trajectory.[41] This generates an outlook which acts with a gravita-tional pull on our inquiries – support is lent to those who appear to represent progress and is combined with the vilification of those who are seen to oppose it; and attention is focused on events, such as examples of popular protest against oppressive leaders, as a stage in the inevitable march of progress and liberty. On this basis observers adopt the role of participant and seek to deliver a moral judgement.

Second, this sense of transition builds on a series of abridg-ments that strips events and people of complexity and nuance. Furthermore, abridgments are based on a liberal Western perspec-tive of progress. Conflicting context and detail are removed, on the assumption that the essentials can be told through a series of gen-eralisations with apparently relevant examples. The abbreviation of complications and qualifications out of existence generates an unwarranted sense of certainty: abridgment builds on abridgment to oversimplify understanding, and, in doing so generates infer-ences rather than inquiry and concentrates the focus on our own questions. But these inferences are from the organisation we have given to our knowledge, from a particular series of abstractions, rather than developments in Russia. This serves to confirm and even imprison us in our biases, begging fewer questions about Russia and only drawing out the things we are looking for, while remov-ing troublesome elements in the complexity to make the crooked straight and the story fit.

The third point is the combination of these two features: with the sense of transition and the abridgment comes the concentration on and magnification of similarities and differences in reference to the West. There is a particular tendency to write – explicitly or implicitly – on the side of, or in praise of the opposition in Russia, on the assumption that it is more analogous to the West's own con-ditions. This tends to load the evidence in one direction, making the opposition seem more prominent, united and 'Western' than it is. In drawing on the more accessible, more readily appreciable, Western-oriented evidence, it is hard to keep in mind the differences and diversity in Russia. It is easy to forget that opposition figures may oppose policies we support, or endorse policies we oppose, and to overlook or dismiss opposition forces that do not equate to our understanding of how developments should evolve. In sum, this 'progressive', transitional interpretation of Russia from communism to liberal democracy allows easy dramatisation with the pleasure of the apparent recognition of some of the participants and the plausibility of wider links and comparisons with an outcome that is earnestly desired.

Structure of the book

This book takes the form of an essay about Russia and how it is understood in the West. The central theme linking these aspects is that mainstream Western public policy and media views of Russia are dominated by a strong blend of ethnocentrism and a 'progressive' historical template, and that the expectation of Russia's convergence with the West, its 'return to the Western family of nations' as a democratic state that acts as a partner on the international stage, is both flawed and has distorted Western understanding of post-Cold War Russia.

The chapters each take one aspect of this theme, and examine it from different angles. While Chapter 1 reflects in depth on specifically Western aspects of this question, Chapters 2, 3 and 4 initially link to the central theme of the West's anticipation of Russian transition, but each then turns towards more detailed exploration of the Russian views of the international environment and domestic developments, and thus offer different ways of interpreting Russian foreign policy and domestic politics.

Beginning with the idea of the prevalent sense of surprise, Chapter 1 looks first at the impact of Russia's decline as a political priority for the West since the end of the Cold War and the practical impact this has had. It then reflects on the rising influence, especially, but not only, in public policy and media circles, of 'transitionology' (the conviction that post-communist states were moving towards democracy) as the main lens through which developments in Russia were interpreted. Finally, it sketches out a series of problems such as the prevalence of 'Putinology' and historical analogies.

Chapter 2 examines the evolution of the West's relationship with Russia since the end of the Cold War, focusing particularly on the

NATO–Russia relationship. Practical cooperation has taken place and a deep and wide institutional framework established, but dissonance has become increasingly obvious – and increasingly systematic. It sketches out some background, returning to the founding myths of the 1990s, especially the idea that Russia will return to the Western family of nations, before framing the chronological development of relations and the emergence of strategic dissonance from 2003.

Strategic dissonance refers to the increasing sense of disharmony and friction between the West and Russia over major questions both in bilateral relations and in how the world is understood – a disharmony that reflected the trend away from hopes for a 'strategic partnership' that dominated the 1990s and even continued into the 2000s, but that stopped short of being open conflict. It then explores the differing interpretations of international affairs that mean that 'common' problems are are not 'shared' or even compatible.

Chapter 3 turns to look at Russian domestic politics, particularly the Western belief in and search for a particular kind of change in Russia – a transition to democracy. Taking as its focal point the election cycle of 2011–2012, the chapter begins by sketching the scene as often depicted in the West – the emergence of a largely middle class, liberal 'white ribbon' opposition in 'unprecedented' demonstrations, and the essentially reflexive sense that the Putin era was coming to a close. The term 'reflexive transitionology' suggests that, in responding to the (unanticipated) protest demonstrations in December 2011, the Western debate about Russia was an automatic return to the hopes, even ideals, of the earlier debates about Russia's transition to democracy: the rise of an affluent, technologically advanced and politically liberal urban middle class instigating progressive political change towards liberal democracy in Russia.

The chapter explores the protest demonstrations, notes the ongoing importance of the role of the political left in Russia, and sets out the leadership's response. Although many have emphasised the more repressive actions such as the imprisonment of protest leaders, the focus is on other significant developments that took place, including the establishment of para-institutional organisations such as the All-Russian Popular Front (ONF).

Chapter 4 continues the exploration of domestic politics, but turns to address the theme of 'Putinology', the focus on Putin as the central figure in Russian politics.[42] Though he is undeniably important, 'Putinology' and 'Putin's Russia' increasingly appears as a means of attempting to label Putin in the totalitarian tradition and a vivid symbol of the development of Russia in the 'wrong direction'. Furthermore, many other figures, both well established and emergent, have been either ignored or blanked out into abstract groupings such as 'siloviki' (those from the power structures) and 'liberals' (those suggested to be more Western leaning). They thus appear merely as ciphers, and, though subject to certain conditions and capable of certain desires, remain faceless, un-individualistic and asocial symbols. It has led to many errors in the general understanding of the nature of power and politics in Russia, not least the generational aspects of the leadership, the difficulties of power creation and the emergence of new figures. The chapter explores the nature of 'manual control' and the need for effective managers, and offers a brief overview of some of the prominent and emerging figures and their roles.

The conclusion briefly draws the threads together. In sum, this book offers an appraisal of how and why Russia has been misinterpreted in the West since the early 1990s and seeks to initiate a refocus. This is important because the next few years are likely to see the continuation of a dissonance and competition, the intractability of old problems and doubtless the emergence of new ones – whether they be on international affairs questions such as the ballistic missile defence programme and unresolved Euro-Atlantic security questions (not least the consequences of the war in Ukraine), or disagreements over developments in Russia itself, such as the parliamentary and presidential elections, scheduled respectively for 2016 and 2018.

Some caveats are necessary. First, the increasingly troubled nature of Russia's relationship with the West is such that certain terms have become politically loaded. The terms 'understanding' and even 'interpreting' require clarification about what they do *not* mean in this book. Discussion about Russia has become more partisan as a result of the war in Ukraine, and in this context, 'understanding' is often equated with compromise with, and the appeasement of, Putin, and applied to apologists for him ('Putin understanders'). To be clear from the outset, the terms 'interpreting' and 'understanding' are not used here as synonyms for 'accommodating', 'compromising with' or 'accepting' Russia, nor are they used as basis for 'apologies for' Russia or arguing that Western observers must be more politically 'fair' to Russia by overlooking the many problems, or ascribing extenuating circumstances.

Instead, the focus is on exploring the linguistic and conceptual gaps that have emerged between the West and Russia and how Russia works. In other words, it asserts that the route to a better understanding of Russia and thus a better ability to decipher

Russian politics and foreign policy takes into consideration Russian history and political landscape and language, and a clearer under-standing of the individuals and groups involved. This requires curiosity and empathy – the capacity to understand what another person is experiencing from within the other person's frame of ref-erence, in effect putting oneself in another's shoes. But empathy is not synonymous with sympathy, and the book illustrates clearly the disagreements between Russia and the West.

The second caveat concerns what is referred to in the book as a 'mainstream Western' view of Russia that has interpreted Russia in terms of 'transition' towards or away from democracy. This raises two points for clarification. First, the West is not as united as it was during the Cold War, and there are important distinctions within the West in terms of how Russia is seen and relations with it. Therefore, to be clear, the primary focus of the analysis of Western debate is on the debate in the Anglo-Saxon sphere. Thus attention is paid pre-dominantly to US and British debates, though it also includes the debate at institutional level particularly in NATO, but also the EU.

Since there is also debate about what 'transitology' means, how it has evolved and the extent to which it dominated the academic debate, second, it is worth setting out what is meant here. Some, such as Gans-Morse, have argued that 'transitology' had only very limited influence in Russia studies. His analysis reflects a quanti-tative and qualitative examination of specifically academic litera-ture. However, he does not reflect on the public policy and media influence on this debate, where the transition paradigm was at its strongest. Nor does he explore the deeper and more implicit influence of the transition approach that evolved into the 'regime question'.[43] Indeed, there is an extensive literature on post-Soviet transition, particularly relating to Russia, but also to other former Soviet states, including Georgia and Ukraine.[44] This literature offers the core of what is understood here as 'the mainstream', prominent as it is in public policy, think tank and media circles. In attempting to delineate this from other political science and academic 'transi-tion' paradigms, Stephen Cohen coined the term 'transitionology'.[45] Although it is imperfect, given its linguistic clumsiness, 'transitionol-ogy' is the term used below to describe the transition paradigm and the search for 'progress' in Russia.

The third caveat relates to what the book does not attempt to address. Despite its focus on transition and democratisation, the book does not directly address questions of Russian democracy or authoritarianism. The various questions these themes raise have been thoroughly examined by many others, indeed, it has been the central theme of analysis, though it is important to say here that critiquing the Western transition paradigm does not imply that Russia meets Western democratic standards. Equally, many other important issues are touched upon or raised tangentially, such as, in foreign policy terms, the Russo-Georgia war, the energy disputes between Gazprom and Naftogaz Ukraini (in 2006 and 2008–2009), or even the war in Ukraine, or domestically, flaws in the electoral process and corruption, but are not dealt with in depth. These, too, are covered elsewhere.

The fourth and final caveat is that the book focuses on Russia, and it does not explore whether the criticisms made of Western Russia studies are comparable to Western interpretations of other states or regions, either historically or currently, though there are some indications that they might be.[46] Some fine work was carried out during the Cold War era on the lack of empathy and fallacies of imposing Western conceptual, linguistic, political and societal frames of reference on to the USSR and the Middle East and making the false assumptions that Soviet decision-makers were operating on much the same principles and much the same view of the strategic situation as their Western counterparts.

Though they are not explored, many of the points made are also relevant in terms of Western understandings of other states of the former Soviet Union – beyond small handfuls of experts, there were very few who could claim expertise on Georgia or Ukraine until the wars in 2008 and 2014 respectively, and much of the discussion about them has been conducted along the lines of their transition to democracy. Western policy-makers and observers were often surprised by the responses of Tbilisi and Kyiv during these crises and misread their actions. Similarly, Western capitals were surprised by the so-called 'Arab Spring', and the discussion and responses to it likewise showed the hallmarks of optimistic assumptions about a transition to democracy.

This has also been a theme in the context of the West's military interventions in Afghanistan and Iraq, in which critics have argued that the West suffers from similar problems, including a lack of awareness of the environment in which they were operating – and the attempt to exercise influence without deeming it necessary to learn about those whom they are seeking to influence.[47] It is sobering to hear senior US and British officials observe that, even after such long experience at war in Iraq and Afghanistan there are still too few people who know the regions intimately enough to be able to frame the questions clearly enough to learn appropriate lessons from them, and to reflect on the potential implications of the contrasting lack of resources dedicated to Russia over the same period for the belated scramble to try to correct this from 2014. While additional resources are necessary, however, what is more important is a fresh way of thinking about Russia.

Notes

1 Correspondence with State Department official, October 2013.

2 'Kerry doesn't view Russia as an existential threat: State Department', *Reuters* (15 July 2015), www.reuters.com/article/us-usa-defense-dunford-state-idUSKCN0PK27120150710.

3 Correspondence with senior NATO official, May 2012. NATO summit declaration, paragraph 30, www.nato.int/cps/en/natolive/official_texts_87593.htm?mode=pressrelease.

4 E. Crankshaw, *Russia and the Russians* (London: Macmillan and Co. Ltd., 1947), p. 6. Emphasis in original.

5 Crankshaw, *Russia and the Russians*, p. 3.

6 Philip Hanson has suggested that Western commentary on Russia since the early 1990s has been 'prone to surges of great optimism on one hand and deep gloom on the other', with both proving exaggerated. P. Hanson, *Russia to 2020*. Occasional Paper, Finmeccanica (November 2009), p. 43. Angela Stent also explored these cycles in the US–Russia relationship in her book *The Limits of Partnership: US-Russia Relations in the Twenty First Century* (Princeton: Princeton University Press, 2014).

7 'Russia and the West: cold climate', *The Economist* (31 August 2013).

8 S. Talbott, 'The making of Vladimir Putin', *Politico* (19 August 2014), www.politico.com/magazine/story/2014/08/putin-the-backstory-110151.html#.VQLB3r7JvL8.

9 This quote competes with the Churchill reference noted above for the most common reference used in the Western discussion about Russia. 'Annual address to the Federal Assembly of the Russian Federation' (25 April 2005), http://archive.kremlin.ru/eng/speeches/2005/04/25/2031_type70029type82912_87086.shtml.

10 'Back to the Cold War?', BBC (10 February 2007), http://news.bbc.co.uk/1/hi/world/europe/6350847.stm; E. Lucas, *The New Cold War: How the Kremlin Menaces both Russia and the West* (London: Bloomsbury, 2008).

11 'Speech at meeting with German political, parliamentary and civic leaders' (5 June 2008), http://archive.kremlin.ru/eng/speeches/2008/06/05/2203_type82912type82914type84779_202153.shtml.

12 D. Trenin, 'Vneshnaya politika' [Foreign policy], *Kommersant Vlast* (28 January 2008).

13 C. Merridale, *Red Fortress: The Secret Heart of Russia's History* (London: Allen Lane, 2013), pp. 352–353, 358.

14 A.S. Tereshchenko, *Marshal Voennoi Razvedki* [Marshal of Military Intelligence] (Moscow: Akva-term, 2012), p. 352. The author is grateful to Henry Plater-Zyberk for drawing this to his attention.

15 B. Oleinik, V. Pavlov and N. Ryzhkov, *Gorbachev: Anatomia predatelstva* [Gorbachev: Anatomy of Betrayal] (Moscow: Algoritm, 2013).

16 D. Trenin, *Getting Russia Right* (Washington, DC: Carnegie Endowment, 2007).

17 S. Graubard, 'The next debate: who lost Russia? A major debacle looms abroad while American policy makers ponder their domestic navels', *Los Angeles Times* (11 January 1994), http://articles. latimes.com/1994-01-11/local/me-10540_1_american-foreign-policy. The debate rumbled on for years: see J. Stiglitz, *Globalisation and its Discontents* (London: W.W. Norton and Co, 2002), chapter 5; the review article by J. Kaplan, 'Who lost Russia?', *New York Times* (8 October 2000), www.nytimes.com/2000/10/08/books/who-lost-russia.html?pagewanted=all&src=pm; V. Ivanenko, 'The importance of being normal', *Russia in Global Affairs*, 3:4 (October 2005); and 'Putin's victory and the limits of the "who lost Russia" debate' (5 March 2012), http://open.salon.com/blog/don_rich/2012/03/05/putins_victory_and_limits_of_the_who_lost_russia_question. It morphed into the Russia as a 'normal country' debate. See A. Shleifer and D. Treisman, 'A normal country', *Foreign Affairs* (March–April 2004); A. Schleifer and D. Treisman, 'A normal country: Russia after communism', *Journal of Economic Perspectives*, 19:1 (winter 2005), pp. 151–174; S. Rosefielde, 'Russia: an abnormal country', *The European Journal of Comparative Economics*, 2:1 (2005), http://eaces.liuc.it/18242979200501/182429792005020101.pdf. A similar debate has taken place in the Western discussion about China and Japan.

18 O. Lungescu, 'NATO expansion and the Ukraine conflict', *Guardian* (5 March 2015); M. Kramer, 'The myth of a no-NATO enlargement pledge to Russia', *Washington Quarterly*, 32:2 (April 2009); M. Ruhle, *NATO Enlargement and Russia: Die Hard Myths and Real Dilemmas*, NDC Research Report (15 May 2014); E. Primakov, *Gody v bolshoi politike* [Years in Big Politics] (Moscow: Sovershenno sekretno, 1999), pp. 232–233.

19 R. Braithwaite, *Across the Moscow River: The World Turned Upside Down* (London: Yale University Press, 2002), p. 134.

20 M. Sarotte, 'A broken promise? What the West really told Moscow about NATO expansion', *Foreign Affairs* (September/October 2014).

21 There are others, such as NATO's campaign in Kosovo in 1999.

22 N. Granholm, J. Malminen and G. Persson (eds), *A Rude Awakening: Ramifications of Russian Aggression Towards Ukraine* (Stockholm: FOI, June 2014), p. 11.

23 Nikolai Svanidze, 'Diletanty: pastukh i stado: kak menyalis otnosheniya naroda i glav gosudarsvta' [Dilettantes: the shepherd and flock: how relations between people and state leaders changed], *Radio Ekho Moskvy* (14 August 2014), http://echo.msk.ru/programs/Diletanti/1379172-echo/#element-text; A. Kolesnikov, 'The Russian middle class is a besieged fortress', Carnegie Centre, Moscow (6 April 2015), http://carnegie.ru/publications/?fa=59655.

24 P. Vigor, *The Soviet View of War, Peace and Neutrality* (London: Routledge and Kegan Paul, 1975), chapter 3, pp. 160–165.

25 K. Booth, *Strategy and Ethnocentrism* (London: Croom Helm, 1979), chapter 3.

26 It is a tangential but interesting point that Western and Russian approaches to linguistic interpretation differ: in the West, the preference is for L1 interpretation, the interpreter translating the foreign language into their own native language. From the Soviet period, Russian interpreting has tended to be L2 – the interpreter translates from their native language into a second language.

27 The Russian term used – повстанец (povstanets) – suggests a more romanticised image of a rebel with a cause. Unsurprisingly, this image is particularly provocative when dealing with serving Russian military officers who have fought in the Chechen campaigns.

28 'Sergei Lavrov i Khillary Klinton zagruzili povestku dnya' [Sergey Lavrov and Hillary Clinton loaded the day's agenda], *Kommersant* (7 March 2009), www.kommersant.ru/doc/1131090; 'Button gaffe embarrasses Clinton', *BBC News* (7 March 2009), http://news.bbc.co.uk/1/hi/7930047.stm.

29 Remarks by Vice President Biden at the 45th Munich Security Conference (7 February 2007), www.whitehouse.gov/the_press_office/RemarksbyVicePresidentBidenat45thMunich ConferenceonSecurityPolicy/.

30 S. Lavrov, 'Russia-US relations: perspectives and prospects for the new agenda', speech at the Carnegie Endowment for International Peace (7 May 2009), http://carnegieendowment.org/2009/05/07/foreign-minister-lavrov-on-russia-u.s.-relations-perspectives-and-prospects-for-new-agenda/1scd.

31 A. Stent, *The Limits of Partnership: US-Russia Relations in the Twenty First Century* (Princeton: Princeton University Press, 2014), pp. 211–212. Nevertheless, it is worth noting that, as discussed in Chapter 3, the Russian term for 'reset' is being used in a domestic political context.

32 'Sir John Sawers, ex-MI6 chief, warns of Russia "danger"', BBC's Today Programme (28 February 2015), www.bbc.co.uk/news/uk-31669195.

33 K. Giles, *The Russian Military Doctrine of the Russian Federation 2010*, NATO Defence College Review (February 2010), www.ndc.nato.int/research/series.php?icode=9.

34 G. Persson, *Russian History: A Matter of National Security*, RUFS Briefing No. 19 (August 2013).

35 F. Fukuyama, 'The End of History?', *The National Interest* (Summer 1989).

36 'Obama: Russia on the wrong side of history', *Associated Press* (3 March 2014), www.youtube.com/watch?v=-zUTcQB7SGE; Kerry cited in 'Russia on the wrong side of history says Kerry', *First Post* (19 March 2014), www.firstpost.com/world/russia-on-wrong-side-of-history-says-john-kerry-1440151.html. The Obama administration has often used the phrase 'the wrong side of history', also in contexts other than Russia.

37 T. Snyder, 'Russia: Putin defends Soviet-Nazi pact', *New York Times* (7 November 2014).

38 'Meeting with young academics and history teachers' (5 November 2014), http://eng.kremlin.ru/transcripts/23185.

39 Lavrov cited in 'U nashikh partniorov buili sharakhanya' [Our partners have been flip-flopping], *Kommersant* (30 September 2013), www.kommersant.ru/doc/2308493.

40 J. Yaffa, 'Reading Putin', *Foreign Affairs* (July/August 2012), www.foreignaffairs.com/articles/137728/joshua-yaffa/reading-putin.

41 For a critical examination of such an interpretation of history, see H. Butterfield, *The Whig Interpretation of History* (London: G. Bell and Sons, 1931). In some ways, Butterfield's book provides a model for this one.

42 Apart from some brief media profiles, the only major English language biographies of political figures in the post-Soviet period are of Boris Yeltsin and Vladimir Putin. Fiona Hill and Clifford Gaddy's book *Mr Putin: Operative in the Kremlin* is perhaps one of the best for offering detail on some of the other important figures. F. Hill and C. Gaddy, *Mr. Putin: Operative in the Kremlin* (Washington, DC: Brookings, 2012); T. Colton, *Yeltsin: A Life* (New York: Basic Books, 2008). A number of biographies of Vladimir Putin were published to coincide with the presidential elections in 2012: M. Gessen, *The Man Without a Face: The Unlikely Rise of Vladimir Putin* (London: Granta, 2012); C. Hutchins and A. Korobko, *Putin* (Leicester: Matador, 2012); R. Sakwa, *Putin Redux: Power and Contradiction in Contemporary Russia* (London: Routledge, 2014). Media profiles of individuals such as Alexei Navalniy tend to be hagiographical, one-dimensional and repetitive. J. Ioffe, 'Net impact: one man's crusade against Russian corruption', *The New Yorker* (4 April 2011), www.newyorker.com/reporting/2011/04/04/110404fa_fact_ioffe?currentPage=all. There are some biographical sketches of well-established business figures: C. Freeland, *Sale of the Century: The Inside Story of the Second Russian Revolution* (London: Abacus, 2005); D. Hoffman, *The Oligarchs: Wealth and Power in the New Russia* (New York: Public Affairs, 2002); C. Erickson, *The Oligarchs: Money and Power in Capitalist Russia* (Stockholm: Text, 2012).

43 J. Gans-Morse, 'Searching for transitologists: contemporary theories of post-communist transitions and the myth of a dominant paradigm', *Post-Soviet Affairs*, 20:4 (2004), pp. 320–349. For the 'regime question', see R. Sakwa, '"New Cold War" or twenty years' crisis?', *International Affairs*, 84:2 (March 2008).

44 M. McFaul, *Post Communist Politics: Democratic Prospects in Russia and Eastern Europe* (Washington, DC: Carnegie Endowment for International Peace, 1993); M. McFaul, N. Petrov and A. Ryabov (eds), *Between Dictatorship and Democracy: Russian Post-Communist Political Reform* (Washington, DC: Carnegie Endowment for International Peace, 2004); A. Aslund and M. McFaul (eds), *Revolution in Orange: The Origins of Ukraine's Democratic Breakthrough* (Washington, DC: Carnegie Endowment, 2006); T. Bjorkman, *Russia's Road to Deeper Democracy* (Washington, DC: Brookings Institution Press, 2003); L. Shevtsova, *Russia – Lost in Transition: The Yeltsin and Putin Legacies* (Washington, DC: Carnegie Endowment for International Peace, 2007); M.S. Fish, *Democracy Derailed in Russia: The Failure of Open Politics* (New York: Cambridge University Press, 2005); *Russia's Wrong Direction: What the United States Can and Should Do*, Council on Foreign Relations Report No. 57 (2006), www.cfr.org/iran/russias-wrong-direction/p9997.

45 S. Cohen, *Failed Crusade: America and the Tragedy of Post Communist Russia* (London: W.W. Norton and Co., 2000), p. 23.

46 B. Chu, *Chinese Whispers: Why Everything You Know about China is Wrong* (London: Weidenfeld & Nicolson, 2013); M. Todorova, *Imagining the Balkans* (London: Oxford University Press, 1997); F. Gaub, *Arab Transitions: Late Departure, Destination Unknown*, EUISS Brief, Paris (July 2014); K. Booth, *Strategy and Ethnocentrism*, (London: Croom Helm, 1979); E. Kedourie, *The Chatham House Version and Other Middle Eastern Studies* (Chicago: Ivan Dee, 1970).

47 F. Ledwidge, *Losing Small Wars: British Military Failure in Iraq and Afghanistan* (London: Yale University Press, 2011), pp. 11–12.

1

Russia: the state of surprise

Rude awakenings

The eruption of war in Ukraine in 2014 illustrated the strong and prevailing sense of surprise, even astonishment, that has pervaded post-Cold War Western public policy and mainstream media commentary in response to Russian actions. Perhaps the sharpest point was Russia's unexpected annexation of Crimea: one US observer suggested that the US administration was 'not prepared for the contingency that Putin would act so brazenly'.[1] William Hague, then British Foreign Secretary, had reassured the House of Commons that Russia was unlikely to intervene militarily in Crimea. Reflecting on Russian military actions, Breedlove stated that the Russians had demonstrated 'unexpected flexibility' in handling their forces in the Ukraine crisis.[2] Swedish analysts thus captured the sense of surprise perfectly as a 'rude awakening'.[3] Yet if the military surprises were widely acknowledged, others, even when the tension of the already aggravated situation should have sharpened awareness of Russian actions, escaped much mention: Russia's retaliatory imposition of sanctions on Western agricultural produce, for instance, was also largely unanticipated, as for many was the Russian military deployment to Syria in autumn 2015.

More precisely, however, it is *another* rude awakening. Since the 'founding surprise' of the collapse of the USSR – still for many the exemplary failure of expert political prediction[4] – Western officials and observers have been repeatedly surprised by developments in Russian domestic politics and Russian actions on the international stage, as expectations have been confounded and unanticipated developments emerged. They include a mix of longer-term trends and sudden developments, including Russia's economic recovery after the financial crisis of 1998, the Russian 'dash to Pristina' airport in June 1999, which created panic in NATO, Vladimir Putin's rise to the leadership in 1999/2000, the gas disputes in 2006 and (again) in 2009, the Russo-Georgia war in 2008 (which David Miliband, then British Foreign Secretary, called a 'rude awakening'),[5] and the eruption of protest demonstrations in 2011.

Surprises can be attributed to cultural differences and the difficulties of political prediction, especially for outside observers of an environment such as Russia's in which institutions are weak and informal networks render decision-making processes and factional interests opaque, and in which there is simultaneously a lack of important information and a 'scarcely comprehensible overflow' of often deceptive and misleading information.[6] Indeed, one of the reasons why interpreting Russia has proved so difficult is the increasingly obvious inability to distinguish between information which is important and that which is irrelevant, or between what may be called 'the signal and the noise'.[7]

Similarly, those who are trying to interpret the actions of others can fall prey to deliberate deception. Deception and surprise are consequences of a culture of opacity and a deliberate feature of Russian life – in politics, but particularly, of course, in terms of military affairs. So central to Soviet thinking was it, that one observer concluded in the mid 1980s that 'NATO's senior commanders would do well to plan on the basis that they will (not may) be the victims of strategic surprise'.[8] This is still relevant, as illustrated by the infiltration and occupation of Crimea during the war in Ukraine in 2014. This we might separate from 'surprise' by calling 'shock', in that it is intended to achieve mental paralysis in opponents. If the Crimea operation was a 'surprise', since Western officials and observers were not paying attention to Russia more broadly and did not know what to expect, it was also a 'shock', since the surprise was deliberate.

But such an extensive list of surprises suggests that there are problems in how senior Western decision-makers, politicians and observers interpret Russia. Three related groups of more 'culpable' surprise stand out. The first might be called 'unknown knowns':[9] the necessary information was available, and appropriate warnings given to senior decision-makers by officials and experts, but then went unheeded in the final analysis either because it was poorly understood or interpreted, or because it was ignored. Many of the surprises noted above fall into this category. Prior to the outbreak of the Russo-Georgia War, for instance, experts and officials were advising senior leaders of the increasingly tense situation in the South Caucasus. The Organization for Security and Cooperation in Europe (OSCE) had provided early warning in and around the conflict zone, and in the days before the conflict, the OSCE mission provided 'clear early warning of the escalation of hostilities'.[10] One Western official observed that all the relevant information was there, but senior decision-makers refused to believe that the Russians would resort to war – because they themselves would not have conceived of doing so. A similar situation prevailed in 2013 and 2014.

The second group may be called 'unknown unknowns', which are contingencies that have not been considered. These are the consequences of the serious decline in resources allocated to understanding Russia since the early 1990s. This has led to the degradation of institutional memory and a narrowed focus to only specific issues, and an inability to explore the wider picture beyond an often superficial grasp of the day's urgent headline. Again, this degradation can be illustrated by the war in Ukraine: only a very small handful of people had either the detailed and specific subject matter knowledge required to understand Russian military operations and thinking, particularly about Russian special operations forces, or evolving Russian threat perceptions that stretched back to the 1990s and through the Colour Revolutions in 2003 and 2004.

The third group of culpable surprises might be called 'assumed knowns'. These relate to the prevalence in the mainstream Western discussion of Russia of flawed predictions based on wishful thinking about Russia, the desire to see 'progress' and Russia's transition to democracy and acceptance of Western values. This created the basis for the orthodoxy of the ongoing 'crisis' of Putinism, with its corollaries of, for instance, the long-term misreading of the Putin–Medvedev tandem, especially the ongoing suspense over the anticipated split between the 'conservative' Putin and the 'liberal' Medvedev, and when Putin would fire Medvedev, and the repeated anticipations of the end of the Putin era.

This chapter explores the reasons for this state of surprise, sketching them out from the starting point of the significant (and ongoing) impact of the collapse of the USSR on Western understandings of Russia. First, it explores the practical ramifications for the decline of Russia as a political priority on the wider political stage: the West has not paid attention to developments in Russia unless they were part of an urgent and immediate crisis; in effect, the West 'moved on' from Russia, and since it was no longer a political (or security) priority, attention and resources were redirected elsewhere, and much of the practical capacity for understanding Russia has been dispersed. It then turns to look more specifically at Russia studies. Buoyed by a confidence in the 'end of history', many of those in the West who continued to focus on Russia and the former Soviet space believed that Russia was in transition from communism to democracy and the acceptance of Western values: it would 'move on' from the political ruins of the USSR to return to the Western family of nations and become a partner on the international stage. This progressive, transitional paradigm broadly replaced a more classical area studies style approach to understanding Russia. This provides the basis for the final part of the discussion which outlines some of the problems of the current mainstream discussion of Russia, which is drowning in a discourse of speculation and rumour, 'Putinology' and historical analogies. This creates a great deal of additional noise that blocks the signal.

Moving on from Russia

Russia has been prominent in a flood of editorials, media interviews and think tank publications first on the Sochi Winter Olympics and then the developing crises in Ukraine and Syria. There has been much debate about Vladimir Putin, his plans and goals, and his mental and physical health, as well as wider debates about corruption in Russia, the failings of the Russian economy, and Russian neo-imperial aggression.

As some observers suggested in spring 2014, however, this prominence has only obscured the 'slow death of Russian and Eurasian studies',[11] one that can be traced back to the collapse of the USSR. This argument that there is a lack of Russia expertise in the West has some merit, and was revisited in late December 2015 and January 2016.[12] Even in the early 1990s, Western governments were already looking beyond Russia and Eurasia to other priorities, such as the first Gulf War and Japan's rise. This sense that the West had 'moved on' from Cold War era priorities and the problems with which post-Soviet Russia is associated subsequently accelerated in the late 1990s and early 2000s for two main reasons. First, there was increasing disappointment at the highest political levels in the West about the problematic nature of Russia's transformation. This, combined with the Russian financial crisis in 1998, meant that, as one American observer suggested, 'by late 2000 the "forget Russia" school was in the ascendency' in the highest US official circles. Russia, weak at home and abroad, was no longer seen to matter, even as virtually irrelevant and not 'worth worrying about'.[13]

Second, the trend accelerated as a result of problems elsewhere. The conflicts in the Middle East, the terrorist attacks on the USA on 11 September 2001 and the subsequent protracted wars in Afghanistan and Iraq, and the rise of China: these have been the major themes dominating the Western political and security agenda since 2001. Even during the war in Ukraine, attention to Russia was diluted by the Ebola virus, the civil wars in Syria and Libya and migration across the Mediterranean Sea, and the emergence of the Islamic State, which most NATO member states asserted was the most serious threat to the West. This process was further accelerated by the wider conditions of economic austerity since the financial crisis of 2008 which have seriously affected state budgets, foundations and the media.[14]

Despite the numerous questions it poses, therefore, resources dedicated to understanding Russia were directed to other priorities and sharply decreased. Consequently, expertise on Russia across much of the Euro-Atlantic and 'G7' countries has either been redirected to other priorities or has atrophied and become both limited and fragmented as research centres have been wound down or closed.

As a result of this shift of attention, government support for Russia and Eurasia studies in the USA began a prolonged decline from the early 1990s. This continued into the 2000s, when the Bush administration conducted a review of Russia policy and reorganised the State Department, abolishing the Russia desk and sweeping it into the Bureau of European and Eurasian Affairs (which included 54 countries).[15] In late 2013, the State Department announced that it would withhold the budget for its Title VIII programme which provided support for policy relevant research and training on Eastern European and former USSR matters. One official suggested that 'in this fiscal climate, it just did not make it' (though Title VIII was resuscitated in 2015, it was at less than half its previous funding level and with its future unclear).[16] This has directly affected those institutions responsible for Russia-related research and teaching. Private funding for Russia-related research by grant making foundations has also considerably shrunk.

Russia expertise in the UK government has faced similar problems. Funding cuts led to a reduction in the number of Russian linguists in the armed forces, and the department with the relevant area expertise based at the Defence Academy of the UK was closed down in April 2010,[17] while Russia specialists were transferred to other desks, such as counter-terrorism. Speaking in September 2011, William Hague stated his surprise on discovering a shortage of skilled Russian speakers in the FCO and an institutional shift away from 'investment in geographical and regional knowledge towards a prioritisation of rather nebulous themes'.[18] This point was reinforced by Rory Stewart, MP, who emphasised the shift from awareness of international affairs to management competencies, and thus a 'loss of capacity and hollowing out of (government) institutions which meant that not enough people were available to analyse' Crimea and Ukraine.[19] Elsewhere in Europe the situation is similar – Poland is one of the few places in the Euro-Atlantic area in which Russia studies have comparatively thrived.

To be sure, expertise and experience does remain, both in public policy circles and in academia. The appointment of John Tefft, for instance, a career Foreign Service Officer, as US ambassador to Russia in autumn 2014 illustrates the remaining core of expertise in the USA.[20] Similarly there are those such as Celeste Wallander and Ashton Carter who have longer-term experience of dealing with Russia. In the UK, there are a small number of officials with real knowledge about Russia and how it works. Nevertheless, it is noteworthy that those with Russia expertise, including Tefft, are effectively being brought out of retirement; and, all told, the practical capacity to understand Russia is much reduced in policy-making circles. This has been recognised by Breedlove, who stated that his command's pool of Russia experts had 'shrunk considerably', and that 'Russian military operations in Ukraine and the region more broadly have underscored that there are critical gaps in our collection and analysis' of information about Russia. Thus, 'our textured feel for Russia's involvement on the ground in Ukraine has been quite limited'.[21] It was also underlined in a House of Lords report published in early 2015, which stated that EU member states had 'lost analytical capacity on Russia, with a concomitant decline in their ability to maintain oversight of the direction of the EU-Russia relationship', and 'weakened the ability to read political shifts and offer an authoritative response'. One consequence was that in the run up to the Ukraine crisis, 'important analytical mistakes were made', and warning signs 'were missed'.[22]

Beyond the immediate question of Ukraine, this decline in the practical capacity to understand the Russians is part of wider trends away from longer-term analysis and regional expertise (including developing a knowledge of those involved through the preparation of detailed personality reports on leading and emerging figures), and towards shorter-term crisis management approach. This has had a double impact for understanding Russia. First, few senior political or official careers have been built on Russian affairs since the 1990s, so there are very few experienced Russia specialists at the heart of high-level decision-making in the West. There are also few younger experts or officials building Russia-focused careers in government and public policy debates – so if there are currently large gaps in expertise about Russia in the middle and higher echelons of officialdom, academia and the media, this problem will remain at least over the short term and be exacerbated by imminent retirements. Career turnover means that most of the remaining Soviet and early post-Soviet era specialists will soon retire, and those officials with experience and expertise gained during the late Soviet era and early 1990s will be replaced at the top by those who have built their careers in the post-9/11 era of attention to the Middle East and Central Asia.

Second, those public policy bodies and think tanks that retained a Russia capacity were either understaffed or have run small programmes with only few analysts who attempt to cover wide regional and thematic portfolios – often one researcher or analyst attempting to cover the whole of the former Soviet space, including economic, political, social and military matters. This can only result in superficial work, particularly in the form of short-term responses to the current headlines or the immediate crisis. More wide-ranging or detailed research cannot be carried out, and subjects which require specialised knowledge, such as military or the security services, or even economics, do not receive sustained, sophisticated attention. In many cases, therefore, the research agenda has narrowed to specific questions relating to the trend towards liberal priorities such as the development of grassroots civil society and the politics of protest in Russia.

The situation in academia is similar. Peter Rutland, a professor of government and long-term Russia specialist, has noted that only three of eight Ivy League universities have appointed a tenured professor in Russian politics since the collapse of the USSR, and none have appointed any in economics or sociology. In Germany there are only three professors of Russian politics, and one each in Russian economics and sociology.[23]

These points tend to be emphasised by the way mass media or government agencies draw on a limited number of commentators who broadly fall into two camps: the growing number of pessimists who see Russia as a declining power that poses a threat to its neighbours and a destabilising international role, and the decreasing number of optimists who argue Russia's extenuating circumstances and that Russia is a 'normal country'. The result, Rutland suggests, is a superficial public policy and media discussion that is both further separated from what remaining expertise there is, and often little more than an exchange between these two camps divided along relatively primitive and binary 'good v. evil' lines.[24] This is further emphasised because the shrinking scale of expertise on Russia opens the field to pundits and pseudo-experts offering 'crunchy deductions' about Russia, which are often little more than threadbare metaphors and analogies, stereotypes and clichés.

In some ways, therefore, it is tempting to argue that the sense of surprise is due to the reduced capacity to understand Russia – there has been an emptying out of regional expertise (and the gap is often filled by non-experts offering opinions). The fracturing and loss of available institutional memory and expertise in the West about how Russian leaders perceive the world, what has happened and why in Russia, what has been tried in relations with Russia and why, and what has worked (and failed) and why, has had important consequences. Indeed, the knowledge of and capacity to understand the 'who is who' (and why) and 'what is what' (and why) of Russian politics has been considerably diminished.

Nevertheless, this is only part of the picture. It is highlighted because what remains of the expertise and experience is not well transmitted to – or received by – decision-makers, often because it has been overshadowed by attention to other questions or because it contradicts the prevailing political orthodoxy which has emphasised wishful 'end of history' thinking and Russia's transition to a democracy and attempts to build strategic partnership with Russia as a member of the 'Western family of nations'. The problems of 'unknown knowns' and 'assumed knowns' both illustrate the separation of expertise from politics and decision-making, and mean that even a substantial increase in analysts might not reduce surprise or help to 'get Russia right'. This leads to the second set of problems, the dominance of a misleading orthodoxy about Russia's domestic and international trajectory.

The rise of 'transitionology': Russia – moving on?

The collapse of the Warsaw Pact and the USSR led to a new confidence in the 'end of history' and the hope that Russia was in transition towards democracy and returning to the Western family of nations. This optimism provided the more theoretical basis of the view among many Russia watchers that Russia was 'moving on'.

In fact, the collapse of the USSR has had serious ramifications for the study of Russia in the West, resulting in a major reassessment of Soviet studies, often bitter and acrimonious.[25] Two sets of problems stand out, one more focused on the nature of the debate in the mid-to-late 1980s, the other reflecting a deeper question about how best to understand Russia.

First, David Engerman points to the political split in the 1980s among US Soviet experts over the role of Gorbachev, between those who were more 'totalitarian' and those who were more 'revisionist'. The groups were divided over whether Gorbachev really intended reform, or was just talking a good game, and, if he was serious, would he succeed? According to Engerman, this debate was largely framed on the basis of previously held ideological views of Russian and Soviet history, and developments in the USSR were used as point-scoring in internal debates, rather than as a means of understanding developments in the USSR itself. 'While Gorbachev stirred the USSR out of its Brezhnev era stagnation, his policies did little to stir Sovietologists out of theirs', Engerman suggested.[26]

Others have pointed to supplementary problems. Patrick Coburn noted the 'alarming multiplication' of the use of historical analogies in Soviet studies, a point echoed by others. Leo Labedz, too, suggested that analogies were 'produced like rabbits from a magician's hat on any occasion', that are as 'suggestive as they are misleading', strimming off of peculiarities, details and doubts about the progressive nature of history. Prominent analogies included comparing Gorbachev with Peter the Great and the rise and fall of Khrushchev. These allowed observers to draw comfortable implications that what was happening was not so original, and that recent reforms were continually vulnerable to conservative counter-attack, perhaps culminating – like the fate of Khrushchev in 1964 – in the overthrow of Gorbachev and the reversal of the changes he had introduced. Yet such analogies were misleading, because Soviet society had evolved enormously between 1964 and 1984, and because they often acted as substitutes for sober evaluation, he argued.[27]

In his 'post mortem' on Sovietology in 1993, Peter Rutland suggested that a preoccupation with current events at the expense of longer-term trends compounded this analytical weakness, suggesting that the 'role of media pundit and soothsayer proved all too attractive to well-placed Sovietologists', while careful empirical research offered only meagre rewards. Thus the discussion became dominated by those who 'could hardly find the Volga river on the map', but felt qualified to reflect publicly on the views of leading political figures.[28] As discussed below, all of these are problems that have continued – or resurfaced – in Russia studies today.

The second problem related to the best method of understanding Russia. During the late 1980s, Soviet studies was dominated by two main methodological approaches, the more 'area studies' approach often called 'Kremlinology', which focused on elite politics, and the more comparative social and political science approach that explored questions of wider civil society. Tension between the two approaches is long-standing. Kremlinology is often described as the 'careful, usually tedious study of who was up and who was down', through noting 'which stiff, unappetising looking man had been positioned closest to the leader at a state parade' because there was 'no other way to calibrate the hierarchy'.[29] Indeed, as historian Robert Conquest suggested in 1961:

> Kremlinology had long been seen as a 'somewhat disreputable' and eccentric approach that extrapolated too much from very limited available information. Its advocates appeared to speak 'absolute certainties on the basis of cloudy figures swirling in [their] crystal balls, sometimes going beyond what the evidence could stand and offering assertions instead of knowledge. It was thus considered by many to be an approach associated with the "black arts" and intelligence agencies, rather than scholarship'.[30]

By the 1980s, political and social science critics of Kremlinology asserted that it was merely dynastics and crypto-politics, and that its focus on bureaucratic processes and the leadership came at the expense of attention to wider civil and social phenomena. This critique became more pronounced in response to Gorbachev's perestroika, as some scholars of communism began to draw on modernisation theories to explain the fall of authoritarian regimes based on structural factors such as increased wealth, communications and education.

The revolutions and the failure of the majority of the Soviet studies community to foresee them intensified this critique. One of the main reasons for the failure to predict them, some suggested, was the excessive focus on the political leadership and bureaucracy instead of the relationship between the leadership and the population, and the obsession with endless succession struggles rather than the deeper trends in society.[31] In the wake of the revolutions, the social science based approach gained greater traction, as many in the West assumed that Russia was in transition to something better and higher, and the focus of their attention shifted away from studying the roles and relations of senior individuals towards a greater focus on civil society and Russia's movement towards liberal democracy.[32] This sense of transition, visible in parts of academia, was particularly strong in the public policy and the media, and the result was a turn away from understanding the functions of the main leadership organs towards a focus on democratisation and electoral processes, political parties, the influence of public opinion on Russian foreign policy, and public opinion forecasting and statistical modelling.[33]

The centre of attention was thus on indices of political competition and participation, human rights, corruption, the rule of law, and media freedom. These have remained the focal points of analysis, even as attention has drifted back to a narrower snapshot of the role of the Russian leadership. Echoing the waves of enthusiasm for democracy promotion in other regions in the 1980s, this approach became the core of the Western official and expert approach to Russia, and the basic premise that, however difficult the route might prove, Russia was in a process of reform from communism to capitalism and democracy became the new orthodoxy and prevailing way of posing questions about Russia.[34]

In some ways, hopes for Russia's transformation to democracy began to fade in the early 2000s. As Thomas Carothers noted in 2002, 'many countries that policy makers and aid practitioners persist in calling "transitional" are not in transition to democracy, and of the democratic transitions that are under way, more than a few are not following the model' (of transitionology).[35] But this represented an evolution rather than a change of approach, and if most officials and academic observers of Russia have become increasingly aware of the limitations of approaching Russia in terms of its progress towards democracy, the threads of transitionology/democratisation have remained dominant and re-emerge with regularity. Indeed, they have been sustained by a series of social movements in other countries, first in the 'Colour Revolutions' in the former USSR from 2003 to 2005,[36] then the so-called 'Arab Spring' and then protest demonstrations in Russia in 2011–2012, and most recently the Euro-Maidan in Ukraine.[37]

Regarding Russia more specifically, the question evolved from 'transitionology' to the 'regime question' – a different epithet for much the same series of issues – and adjectival democracy and qualified authoritarianisn, such as discussion of 'managed democracy'. Even as hopes for Russia's moves towards democracy faded during Putin's second term as president (2004–2008), mainstream media, academic, think tank and official analysis was still conducted pursuing questions of the roll-back of democracy and the lengthening list of sins against democratic standards carried out by the Russian leadership, and the desirability of supporting democratic change in Russia. This 'roll back of democracy' or 'de-democratisation' included the taming of independent media, decreasing the autonomy of regional governments and the appointment of regional governors, the emasculation of the Federal Assembly, and pressure on, even repression of, political parties not aligned with the Kremlin, with particular attention being given to the more liberal ones, such as Yabloko and the Union of Right Forces, who often sought support in the West.[38] The focus of mainstream Western attention narrowed to support for the (liberal) opposition to Putin and objections to the Kremlin's repressive measures against it, in effect the story of embattled and threatened democracy. As historian Stephen Kotkin noted, the narrative of Russia's 'overturned democracy unite(d) Cold War nostalgists who miss the enemy with a new generation of Russia watchers, many of whom participated earnestly in the illusory 1990s democracy building project in Russia and are now disillusioned (and tenured)'.[39]

And so periodic revitalisations of the hope for Russia's transition to democracy emerged, most obviously when Dmitri Medvedev replaced Vladimir Putin as president in 2008. Many Western officials and commentators saw him as a more liberal and Western-leaning figure, an independent alternative to Putin, a leader from the post-Soviet generation who attacked legal nihilism and the concept of sovereign democracy, promised reforms and reached out to the opposition. As discussed below, most of the mainstream debate about Russia during Medvedev's term as president (2008–2012) focused on whether the more 'liberal' Medvedev would succeed in stimulating Russia's internal transformation, and create a turning point in Russian history and pull away from the more conservative Putin, and an underlying sense that Medvedev was gradually leading Russia towards joining the international order.[40] This belief in the more liberal Medvedev underlay the 'reset' undertaken by the Obama administration in 2009.

Similarly, hopes for democratic transition re-emerged during the protest demonstrations in late 2011 and early 2012, widely seen in the West as an 'unprecedented re-politicisation' of Russian politics and society, and the emergence (at last) of an increasingly politically active liberal urban middle class led by a new wave of non-systemic opposition to Putin that used Western-style political campaigning and modern communications technology (particularly social media) to mobilise a support base. As a result, one Western journalist noted that the protesters were greeted with 'almost unanimous enthusiasm in the West as representatives of a new, freer generation of Russians'.[41]

Many of the theoretical concepts that had been applied in the late 1980s were (often unwittingly) dusted down and used to explain the protest demonstrations in 2011 and 2012: the importance of the leader–population relationship and the declining legitimacy of authoritarian rulers as a result of increasing popular wealth, education and improving communications. The demonstrations, as will be discussed in more depth in Chapter 3, were represented as Putin 'losing touch' with the population, particularly the part that had previously supported him (the middle classes who had become more wealthy during his first two terms in office) and their evolution into an increasingly wealthy urban middle class which demanded fair political representation. The 'beginning of the end of the Putin era' had begun, many believed, with some suggesting that the Putin regime might even collapse like the Soviet one had before it. (This theme returns regularly to the discussion, most recently during late 2014 when the Russian economy came under severe pressure, a crisis reported by some as heralding a collapse similar to the collapse of the USSR.)[42]

Even in Putin's third term, starting in 2012 and continuing through the 2014 Ukraine crisis, when there has been much more focus on increasing authoritarianism in Russia and particularly Putin himself (even to the extent, as discussed below, of the emergence of 'Putinology'), the threads of transitionology and the hopeful search for liberalism in Russia have remained strong. Interviewing Putin about amnesties he had granted in December 2013, one prominent British journalist wanted to know if they were 'real liberal efforts' that were part of Russian policy. When Putin asked what kind of answer Andrew Marr expected from him, Marr replied 'I'd like you to say "I am a real liberal and hold liberal views".'[43] Indeed, the underlying assumption of much mainstream analysis is that it is Putin himself (even Putin alone) who blocks Russia's transition, seeks to turn back the clock, and stops it from rejoining the West – and that when he leaves the stage, democratic transformation will succeed.[44]

This progressive, transition-based approach has placed significant limits on understanding Russia. It is inherently ideological: how to reform Russia in the model of the West and explain it through Western concepts. Such an approach has proved elliptical and very selective in its choice of emphasis – and, of course, of omission.

Indeed, as Stephen Cohen has suggested, by adopting a comparative approach and in the certainty of change, many 'overlooked Russia itself', instead offering 'virtual accounts' of a Russia they wanted to see, one that was becoming ever more like the West.[45]

The mainstream public and official discussion often begins from the point of view of what we would like to happen, ought to happen.[46] This has served as the means by which questions are shaped and evidence is chosen: ignoring some altogether, exaggerating desired evidence, and removing it from the Russian context and placing it onto a Western-shaped Procrustean bed in the confident assertion of the end of history and the inevitability of Russia's West-ward democratic change. At the same time, many who discuss Russia tend towards using a limited range of sources (including interviewing a limited circle of Russians) – most of which have a more liberal or Western orientation.[47] Together, this has created an understanding of Russia through 'mirror-imaging', the assumption that the Russians see the world in the same way and with the same points of reference and understandings.

As suggested above, it has progressively narrowed the range of questions posed of Russia to those which focus on the (liberal) opposition to Putin and the leadership's repressive responses, thus shining a distorting light on how Russia works, one which leaves many shadows and gaps, particularly in terms of how the state works, the 'who is who' and 'what is what'. The vertical of power, for instance, has been understood in democratic/authoritarian terms, rather than its effectiveness, allowing the perpetuation of the idea that it has worked well. But it does not work well, and the attempt to make it function more effectively, as discussed in Chapter 4, is one of the central themes of Russian political life. Similarly, reforms are considered along the spectrum of whether they leading towards a more Western, transitional model or not. This can miss the purpose behind the almost constant reforms ongoing in Russia, and also their failings (and occasional successes). The spotlight focus on the elections in 2011 and 2012 (and their flaws), and Putin's return to the presidency has meant that there has been little sophisticated attention directed to the shaping of his goals and policies – and the conspicuous failure to achieve them.[48]

Finally, the progressive, transition-based approach has drawn the discussion away from research and detailed analysis towards advocacy and partisan debate over this narrow range of questions. This has had two main results. First, as Marc Bennetts, a Western journalist based in Moscow, has suggested, the sins of Putin's regime were so apparent, even blatant, that it was tempting to support the opposition without examining too closely the convictions and ideologies of its figureheads: reformers and critics of the regime are assumed to be pro-Western and often hailed.[49] Alexei Navalniy, for instance, a young and photogenic figure, is often feted in the West as a 'blogger and anti-corruption campaigner', and 'a pro-democracy campaigner', a 'new figure' who emerged with the protests to unite the Russian opposition. His ten-year career as a politician is often ignored, as are many of his less palatable political views and actions which do not correspond to Western democratic standards.[50] Here it is also worth noting that in international affairs, too, participant sources are imported often wholesale without examination: during the Russo-Georgia War in 2008, and war in Ukraine that began in 2014, Georgian and Ukrainian sources were often not critically examined before being absorbed and deployed in assessments of Russia and Russian intentions.

Second, related to this, there is a tendency towards linguistic and numerical inflation and imprecision – again, often directly imported unchecked from opposition leaders themselves. Thus Putin's leadership is often described variously as authoritarian, autocratic, dictatorial or even despotic,[51] whereas those (particularly non-systemic) opposition figures who oppose him are championed as charismatic 'crusaders' and democratic – with characteristics that do not accord with this image either soft-pedalled or entirely ignored. As will be discussed in more depth in Chapter 3, the protest demonstrations offer a good example of numerical inflation, as estimates of the size of the protest demonstrations grew according to estimates given by the organisers (and supplemented by reportage of the calls by those organisers for 'million man marches'). Thus duly impressive numbers of demonstrators could be suggested to have emerged onto the streets of Russia – and it has now become standard to portray them as a 'wave of popular protest' of 'tens of thousands', or even 'tens, then hundreds of thousands'.[52]

Such an approach has its place. But many commentators appear to seek to play a part in 'the Russian play', partial to one side (the opposition), constructing a narrative to support its cause and delivering draconian moral verdicts, even seeking to exact some form of revenge on the other (Putin). Too often, therefore, advocacy and analysis become conflated: the story is drawn in straight lines and the classification of Russia into those who furthered the desirable cause of progress and the villains who hindered it, and the leaving out of the evidence that gets in the way of the moral judgement.

Drowning in discourse: the noise, but not the signal

Despite the dominance of transitological/regime question approach and the perceived eccentricity of Kremlinology, for many it has remained a truism of Russian political life that the final decisions are made behind the closed doors of the Kremlin. As a result, the mainstream discussion of Russia is peppered with exotic myths and anecdotal information and rumours about veiled, behind-the-scenes power often reflected in vague but compelling caricatures of 'grey cardinals'[53] and the 'return to power of the KGB'. Observers comment with great conviction about matters about which they cannot possibly know,[54] and unsubstantiated (and often misleading) rumours and opinions are often directly imported unchecked from the politicised and cynical Russian political and media discussion into the Western mainstream discussion. Masquerading as evidence, they are often recycled until they become laundered and established 'facts on the historical record'. Speculation and insinuation is widespread about reshuffles, infighting within and between clans, potential 'palace coups' in the Kremlin, and about the health,[55] sexuality or even criminality[56] of senior figures in the Russian leadership. This creates a discussion close to what Russian post-modern novelist Viktor Pelevin would call 'discourse-mongering',[57] which amplifies the noise, even to the exclusion of the signal.

Conspiracy theories

The roles of the KGB and its successor agencies, particularly the Federal Security Service (FSB), offer a broad canvas of historical and ideological conflict, political and commercial intrigue, sex and glamour and accusations of mass murder and international assassination.[58] The KGB and FSB are the subject of a number of conspiracy theories, perhaps the most prominent and recurring of which is a series of bombings in 1999, in which four explosions destroyed apartment blocks in cities across Russia, killing 293 people. Conspiracy theories were based initially on the discovery of the FSB in a fifth location, apparently preparing another attack, but this was fanned by a series of subsequent suspicious coincidences, including the deaths of two people who were investigating the explosions, the arrest of a third on dubious charges and finally a closed trial of two suspects.

Undoubtedly, the FSB handled the matter clumsily. But there was little substantial evidence to support the theory, and researchers have suggested that it is more likely that Chechens or Chechen-associated Wahhabi militants carried out the attacks.[59] The conspiracy theory has survived, however, largely due to the efforts of exiled political opponents of Vladimir Putin. The theory gained a new lease of life after the murder of Alexander Litvinenko in London in 2006, who had himself contributed to the theory, co-authoring a book on it. Indeed, Litvinenko's murder was another scandal spun into dark conspiracy theories, some tying the two events together, suggesting that he was murdered because of his whistle-blowing about the bombings.

The point here is that conspiracy theories thrive in a context of 'normalisation', where it is to be found everywhere, and conspiracy theories and normal politics in Russia have become entwined in mainstream Western thinking about Russia. This is important because the security services also loom large in the wider narrative of Russian politics, the broad threads of which are that Vladimir Putin, a former KGB officer, has led a return to power of the KGB to rule Russia. Thus the sense of conspiracy underpins the discussion of Russian politics as a whole, and often returns to the surface as 'fact'. Some suggested, for instance, that the FSB were behind the terrorist attacks in Volgograd in December 2013,[60] and conspiracy theories immediately proliferated with the murder of Boris Nemtsov in February and then with Putin's 'disappearance' in March 2015.

Signals signifying nothing? Putin v. Medvedev

Perhaps the most obvious illustration of speculation coming to dominate the mainstream discussion, however, relates to the relationship between Vladimir Putin and Dmitri Medvedev.[61] This reflected the influence of the 'transitionology' approach as officials and commentators sought (and often predicted) a split between the two men who were seen to represent different political camps. Putin, the former KGB agent, was seen to represent a reactive past, while Medvedev, the younger man, was seen to represent a post-Soviet outlook and more liberal future.

It is not entirely clear today where the sense of Medvedev's liberalism came from. It appears to have been built on a mix of negatives and assumptions: he is not Putin, and not KGB, but a lawyer who decried legal nihilism and corruption in Russia, and who appeared to adopt a more tolerant approach to individual rights. His domestic priorities were seen to suggest a preference for modern technology, innovation and modernisation, while his foreign priorities were seen to suggest a less confrontational approach to the West. This view was illustrated by Obama immediately prior to a visit to Russia in 2009, when he suggested that Putin kept 'one foot in the old ways of doing business', while Medvedev understood that 'cold war behaviour is outdated'.[62]

Medvedev's long-standing relationship with Putin, and other important aspects of his biography which might have cast doubt on his liberal credentials, such as his senior position in Gazprom, the Russian gas monopoly, rarely featured in the Western discussion. Nevertheless, on this somewhat unclear but hopeful basis, senior Western officials and commentators invested much hope in Medvedev as a man of the future (even if they believed him to be vulnerable in the shadow of Putin), and evidence of contradiction between the two men was sought on almost every issue. Indeed, the search became so prevalent that every speech or interview given by either individual was microscopically examined not so much for the thrust of what was said, but for hints of contradictions and indications of preparation for campaigning for the presidency. Increasingly absurd possibilities were voiced by observers: some suggested that Medvedev – who many asserted had only a weak team of supporters – could run against Putin, defeat him, and then set out his own more liberal agenda. Others posited that Putin and Medvedev, despite representing the same political leadership team, might decide to run against each other in the election.

Serious tensions between a state's president and prime minister are an important matter. The dominance of this question, however, posed more problems for the Western understanding of Russia than benefits offered. It served to distract Western attention and generate much inaccurate and often meaningless discourse. First, and perhaps most obviously, the predictions of Putin firing Medvedev that began in 2008 when Medvedev became president proved incorrect. Although they drew on Russian commentary, they ran counter to the views of senior Russian officials and political observers. As one prominent Russian commentator suggested, the differences between the two men are 'mainly in the minds of dreamer political analysts, rather than reality'.[63]

Regardless, for years this remained the lens through which Russian politics was viewed and explained in the mainstream Western discussion, and there has been surprisingly little retrospective reflection on this approach, either about the persistent failure of these expectations to take place, or in terms of possible alternative ways to view the Putin–Medvedev relationship: it often appeared to miss the important point that if Medvedev did not have a team of his own, he was still on Putin's team.

With the announcement in September 2011 that Putin would run for the presidency in 2012, predictions of a split between the men continued but in a different guise: Putin would not fulfil his (publicly announced) intention to appoint Medvedev as his prime minister, and would instead appoint Alexei Kudrin. When Putin did appoint Medvedev, the debate evolved again to focus on when Putin would fire Medvedev and his cabinet to be replaced by Kudrin. Again, this rested on a series of abridged assumptions – that Putin would appoint Kudrin, a successful finance minister for many years popular in the West, to the position of prime minister, and that Kudrin is a liberal figure.

These assumptions are tenuous, often running against important evidence, such as Putin's own statements, and reflect hopeful abstraction rather than political reality; they reflected the shifting of the liberal mantle Western observers had imposed on Medvedev onto Kudrin. They also fail to offer answers to questions important for understanding Russian politics: on what grounds would Medvedev be removed from the position of prime minister? To where would he, a close ally of Putin, be moved? How might Kudrin offer a substantial difference to Medvedev? Would he be any more able to implement an agenda than Medvedev?

'Putinology'

Since the mid 2000s, the mainstream Western discussion of Russia has progressively focused on Vladimir Putin as the means by which to understand Russia. As Stephen Kotkin has put it, this offers to explain Russia through the lens of a 'one man capture of the state', in which his KGB background, the lingering emotions and politics of the Cold War, and scandals and conspiracy theories are all mixed together and magnified.[64] This accelerated with the announcement in September 2011 that it would be Putin who would run for the presidency.

'Putinology' may appear as a form of Kremlinology, albeit a 'pale 21st-century successor' presenting an understanding of the leadership as the key to understanding current events.[65] It is not. As one observer has pointed out, it is usually a range of speculations about his personality and intentions, not a careful analysis of what he says.[66] Instead, despite its appearances, as noted above, 'Putinology' is more often a form of transitionology: the constant reiteration of Putin's KGB background offers a means of highlighting authoritarianism, and of suggesting that Putin, the 'anti-Yeltsin' and 'anti-Gorbachev', seeks to 'turn back the clock' and repudiate the transformational policies of his predecessors. Indeed, in many ways, particularly since 2011, 'Putinology' has appeared as 'demonology', a line in the struggle of 'good v. evil'.[67]

Two particular threads of 'Putinology' stand out. First, in depicting his creation of the 'vertical of power', Western observers have over-invented Putin as a strong, authoritarian leader. But such a story leaves many gaps, and fails to distinguish, for example, between his dominance of politics and his grip on power. This theme has remained resistant to considerable evidence to the contrary. The 'vertical of power' does not work effectively, however, except through direct manual control, and so if Putin has a broad 'grip on politics' in terms of his dominance of the political situation, his grip on power in terms of having policies implemented is less clear: his instructions are often ignored.

Second, 'Putinology' often degenerates into cod psychology: the attempt to 'read' Putin to understand Russia and Russian actions. Journalists and other observers 'diagnose' Putin with a range of psychological disorders, from his 'deep insecurity' to becoming 'unhinged' during the Ukraine crisis, from being arrogant and self-assured, yet paranoid and hypersensitive, to an authoritarian kleptocrat, a sufferer of pleonexia. He is 'stuck in the past', a neo-Soviet who 'sees the world as a KGB officer would', someone who believes his own propaganda and lies, and is afraid of the democratic breakthrough in Ukraine that exposes his own lack of legitimacy.[68] In February 2015, a US Pentagon-sponsored report surfaced suggesting that Putin suffered from autism – which could, some observers asserted, explain his 'authoritarian style' and 'obsession with "extreme control"'.[69]

Such an approach creates some serious problems in understanding Russia because it increasingly becomes an analytical dead-end. Observers and officials alike accuse Putin of lying or irrationality – but if he is lying (or 'crazy') then his views, which are certainly unappealing to many in the West, do not have to be listened to or entertained, let alone argued with. Thus it becomes 'Putinology without Putin' – since the undesirable 'substance' of Putin can be ignored.

'Putinology' has become ever more prominent – as illustrated by the discussion surrounding his 'disappearance' for a few days in March 2015, during which speculation and rumour spread quickly about his health (cancer, a stroke, even death), or had fallen victim to a coup led by 'hard-liners' such as Secretary of the Security Council Nikolai Patrushev or by Head of the Presidential Administration Sergei Ivanov, and that Prime Minister Dmitri Medvedev was calling the shots,[70] or that Putin was preparing a major political re-organisation, or that he had flown to Switzerland to attend the birth of his child.

Certainly Putin is the central figure of Russian political life, wielding substantial political power at the heart of the leadership team, and enjoying considerable popularity. But Putinology – often tantamount to demonology – has served as an alibi for the absence of a policy towards Russia,[71] and disguised the lack of wider knowledge about Russia and understanding of how it works. Not only are the micro-assessments of Putin and 'what he is thinking or really wants' often misleading, but Putin is not synonymous with Russia, nor is he all-powerful.

Indeed, nor is it clear that 'Putinology' has helped to understand Putin. Though he has been the focus of the West's attention to Russia for over a decade, prominent observers were arguing in 2012 that 'little is known about Putin's past and fundamental nature',[72] and, as one experienced Russia-watcher noted, having for years been fixated on Putin 'the KGB thug', the West was still surprised when he acted like one in Ukraine in 2014.[73]

Historical analogies: into the hall of ever simplifying mirrors

Another feature of the mainstream Western discussion about Russia is the prominence of repetitive but superficial historical analogy. Parallels are drawn with a range of historical contexts and episodes. Post-Soviet Russia has been compared to Weimar Germany, and analogies have been drawn with the idea of the Russian 'Time of Troubles', in reference to different periods of Russian history that were particularly uncertain and marked by domestic unrest. More specific domestic examples include the analogy of the Pussy Riot court case with the nineteenth-century Dreyfus affair in France, and Boris Nemtsov's murder compared to the murder of Kirov in 1934.[74] Similarly, there were multiple analogies drawn between the protest demonstrations in 2011 and the so-called 'Arab Spring' in North Africa and the Middle East,[75] the 2004 'Orange Revolution' in Ukraine, and the collapse of the USSR.

Analogies are also used to explain Russian actions on the international stage. Since the mid 2000s, Russia's relations with the West have increasingly often been described as a 'new Cold War'. Some have suggested that Russia's recovery and international behaviour under Putin is similar to aggressive Soviet behaviour: Russian action during the Russo-Georgia War in 2008 was compared by some senior officials and observers to the Soviet invasion of Hungary in 1956 and Czechoslovakia in 1968.[76]

Others have asserted Nazi analogies, mostly obviously during the war in Ukraine when officials and observers alike invoked a series of analogies with the Anschluss and the Nazi annexation of Sudetenland, and Western actions of the Molotov–Ribbentrop Pact and the Munich accords.[77] During 2014, Putin himself, already often compared to numerous Russian and Soviet leaders, including Peter the Great, Nicholas I, Leonid Brezhnev, Nikita Khrushchev, Yuri Andropov and Mikhail Gorbachev, was increasingly compared to Joseph Stalin and Adolf Hitler.

Historical comparisons are drawn by Russians themselves. Putin himself has suggested that Pyotr Stolypin, prime minister from 1906 to 1911, is a model (though without taking the comparison too far, since Stolypin was assassinated), and Putin's press secretary Dmitri Peskov caused a stir by acknowledging the comparison of Putin with Brezhnev, suggesting that the Brezhnev era was 'a huge plus' for Russia.[78] During the 2011 protest demonstrations the imagery of the Orange Revolution was used by both the authorities and the protesters: pro-government demonstrators, for instance, waved flags with an orange snake gripped in a black fist, while protesters sought to recreate a 'maidan' atmosphere.

Yet analogies create much additional noise that distorts our understanding of current developments in Russia. They distract attention from developments rather than informing understanding of them: during Russia's invasion and annexation of Crimea, for instance, the Western discussion was dominated by Sudetenland comparisons rather than the Russian military operation or Russia's evolving military capabilities or security thinking.[79]

The problems of 'unreasoning by analogy' are well-known and do not need to be elaborated in depth here, nor is this the place to pick each analogy apart.[80] But three related points are worth making. First, analogies compare as yet unclear and poorly under-stood developments with an abridged, simplified and unambiguous idea of an event (or collection of events) that is itself poorly under-stood and of which the specifics and context have been forgotten or shaved off. Indeed, the analogy rests purely on the basis that it appears familiar, not its relevance, accuracy or detail.

Second, analogies blur the differences between the presumed and the known to create a narrative of 'irresistible force' – but one that is an artificial edifice.[81] Analogy renders history as myth, a shorthand, primitive explanation for the world that often reflects a sacred or emotive tale: it is invoked to justify certain policies by generating immediate associations that do not brook debate because of their moral appeal. The emotive appeal of the analogy is its elliptical quality that forestalls logical questioning of the parallel being drawn, and short-cutting the process of thinking to trigger agreement. The analogy therefore abridges complex developments into simple, unambiguous and politically charged symbols.

Third, analogies are often reflected back onto each other, creating the effect of a hall of ever simplifying mirrors, reflecting images that we want to see. The analogy of the Russian protest demonstrations in 2011 variously with the collapse of the USSR, 'Arab Spring' and Orange Revolution offers a good example, reflecting as they do the persistent desire to see progress towards (liberal Western) democracy.[82] Not only were these reflected back and forth onto each other, as the Orange Revolution and 'Arab Spring' were compared to each other and the collapse of the USSR, but the comparisons were misleading. The 'Arab Spring' protest movements had varied causes and different goals which could not be boiled down to an oversimplified narrative of democracy, freedom and human rights.[83] The 'Orange Revolution' was a much larger protest demonstration that occurred in the wake of an election in which victory had been snatched from one candidate by another in what was a close result – when in Russia, there was no such close result.

Reflecting on surprise: the unlearnt lessons of Soviet studies?

The state of surprise so prevalent in the West is the result of a complex of problems that have led to a series of miscalculations about Russia, miscalculations that are often guided by wishful thinking and an inability to distinguish fact from fancy. The post-Cold War turn to other priorities and reduction in attention to Russia – and the consequent decline of resources devoted to its study – has resulted in a shortage of expertise. Expertise which exists has become limited and dispersed, and often neither at the highest levels of politics, nor able effectively to transmit information to those levels. Many of the most senior people in the field are long-serving Soviet studies specialists or those who built their careers in the optimistic transition period of the early-to-mid 1990s. If it is true, therefore, that some subjects are well covered, such as human rights abuses and electoral failings, many important gaps have opened up: for instance there are very few with the requisite specialist knowledge of economics, or military and security affairs. Furthermore, only very few young Russia specialists have emerged to prominence in public policy, academia, think tanks or the media since then.

The consequences of this situation are that there is limited institutional memory about post-Cold War Russia in many Western governments, and a limited capacity to decipher the vast amount of information about Russia, distinguishing the signal from the noise. Attempts to address this by moving staff around have produced only limited benefit: individuals or small teams are temporarily switched from the Middle East or North Africa to look at Russia. Competent they may be, but they often lack knowledge of Russia, even of basic background context. What remains of non-governmental expertise is often drowned out by the more numerous and vocal non-subject matter experts in high-profile media.

The decrease in the capacity of Russia expertise, however, is just one of a series of problems that underlie the state of surprise about Russia in the West. It is exacerbated by other important failures, all of which have long been recognised in international affairs and forecasting studies, and many of which would be familiar to those who have analysed the flaws of Soviet studies. Indeed, despite the prolonged debate about the failure to forecast the end of the Soviet Union, many of the 'lessons' appear not to have not been digested.

The first point is the pronounced ethnocentrism and 'mirror-imaging' that has pervaded Western interpretations of post-Cold War Russia. 'End of history' optimism and the conviction that Russia was embarking on a transition to democracy and a return to the Western family of nations has proven remarkably persistent. On one hand, it has sustained a false belief that Russian decision-making has operated on much the same principles, understanding of history and international affairs, and thus strategic calculations, as its Western counterparts. The assumption that the Russians are not so different and see the world and react to events in the same way as Westerners has obstructed understanding Russian intentions, prejudices, hopes, fears and motivations. On the other hand, the notion that Russia can be understood by the imposition of the same categories that explain Western societies and politics has remained strong. These assumptions often miss small but important differences – and understanding of Russia becomes distorted.

Related to this, the second point is the increasing abstraction of Russia. Those who carried out post-mortems on Soviet studies would recognise, for instance, the hypnosis on a limited range of questions, the frequent use of historical analogies that masquerade as evidence and the reduction, indeed distortion, of a complex and evolving situation in Russia to a series of unambiguous symbols magnified by the often mythical or conspiratorial lenses through which they are looked at. Observers of the politicised debates between 'totalitarians' and 'revisionists' about developments in the USSR and the role of Mikhail Gorbachev would recognise similar debates about Russia from 2008, particularly the role of Dmitri Medvedev – whether he was really a more liberal reformer and, if so, whether he would succeed. But like Gorbachev then, in Western debates Medvedev (and his role as president) has increasingly became an abstraction and developments added as proof of views already held, rather than an opportunity for fresh thinking to improve understanding of Russia.[84] This is emphasised by a discussion that is increasingly partisan and emotional, one in which the harshness of criticism increasingly appears to replace cool analysis – again, much like the late 1980s.

The desire to see certain developments combined with the practical limits on and related inability to analyse Russia in breadth or depth has meant that the discussion about Russia has often been framed in formulaic judgments, and loose and imprecise terms, suffering language inflation and factual imprecision in the mainstream Western discussion that becomes 'laundered' into the historical record over time, whether it be over Russian foreign and military policy and the war in Ukraine, or the nature of Putin's regime and protest demonstrations in 2011. Furthermore, as the limits of 'transitionology' have become increasingly clear, the worst excesses of Kremlinology have crept back in as hearsay, gossip and unchecked rumour take on lives of their own.

The third point relates to forecasting failure and surprise. Nate Silver warns that whenever information growth outpaces our understanding of how to process it, danger looms: to deal with an overwhelming amount of information, many engage with it only selectively, 'picking out the parts we like and ignoring the remainder'. Thus the 'story the data tells us is often the one we'd like to hear and we usually make sure that it has a happy ending'. In many cases, prediction is tied to the notion of progress.[85] There is a strong tendency to focus on signals which fit orthodoxy and advance preferred theories: signals which do not match these orthodox patterns are often overlooked; the unfamiliar or undesirable is often confused with the improbable, which, since it is improbable, need not seriously be considered.

This is particularly relevant to post-Cold War Russia studies, in which the underlying theme has been about Russia's progress and transition to democracy. The Russia that is being predicted is often an abridged version, one of silhouettes and caricatures, and many predictions are based on repetitive, threadbare analogies or unchecked speculation masquerading as evidence, or simply reflect the triumph of wishful thinking.

This has been compounded by a lack of self-correction. As a result, much of the mainstream discussion about Russia has become based on exchanges of opinion (as opposed to research). Indeed, if anything, errors and mistaken predictions tend to be quickly forgotten rather than reconsidered, and certain mainstream narratives such as the strength of Putin's 'vertical of power', or the tension between Putin and Medvedev, have remained strong despite much visible evidence against them. Forecasters' hits are thus bought at a very high price in misses and false alarms, and bear all the hallmarks of 'broken clock' analysis. A notable aspect of Philip Tetlock's critical analysis of expert political judgement is the distinction between experts who stick to their assumptions regardless of the evidence, and those who adopt a more nuanced, flexible approach that bends with the evidence. Yet many of those debating Russia have not shown adaptability, despite the shaky nature of conventional wisdom.

Many of these problems will be difficult satisfactorily to address. Russia will always create surprises. Moreover, a reinvigoration of the scale of Russia studies will require time and sustained investment and it remains unclear that this will take place to the necessary levels, given the range of competing priorities and continuing austerity measures. Furthermore, even if some growth in Russia expertise were to be achieved, helping to address the problem of 'unknown unknowns', the more subtle and perhaps more important problem is the conversion of 'unknown knowns' and 'assumed knowns' into informed high-level decision-making – in other words, successfully overcoming political short-termism, mirror-imaging and ethnocentrism. This will be complex and difficult: reporting complexity and long-term trends to politicians is often an exercise in frustration, if not futility.

Nevertheless, if the state of surprise is to be meaningfully addressed, a return to core skills is necessary. This includes reviving the skills of area studies for the twenty-first century. Area studies is not 'Putinology', nor is it mausoleum-watching, nor the simplistic incorporation of plausible rumour and speculation. It is the careful observation of developments in Russia, shaping an understanding of who the Russians are, the interpretation of the political language and culture and a better grasp of how the state does and does not function and why. It means reversing the process of abstraction and deciphering Russia, and attempting to see the emergence of new figures not just in the opposition but within the system. Most of all, it means avoiding making the mistakes of 'mirror-imaging', a problem that is particularly dangerous during crisis situations.

Notes

1 A. Kuchins, 'Does Obama really understand Putin?', *CNN* (30 March 2014), http://edition.cnn.com/2014/03/28/opinion/kuchins-obama-putin/index.html?iref=allsearch.

2 *Towards the Next Defence and Security Review, Part II: NATO,* House of Commons Defence Committee 3rd Report (31 July 2014), p. 35, www.parliament.uk/business/committees/committees-a-z/commons-select/defence-committee/publications/; P. Breedlove, 'The meaning of Russia's campaign against Ukraine', *Wall Street Journal* (16 July 2014), http://online.wsj.com/articles/phil-breedlove-the-meaning-of-russias-military-campaign-against-ukraine-1405552018.

3 N. Granholm, J. Malminen and G. Persson (eds), *A Rude Awakening: Ramifications of Russian Aggression Towards Ukraine* (Stockholm: FOI, June 2014).

4 This failure inspired work beyond Soviet and Russian studies. A sobering example is P. Tetlock, *Expert Political Judgement: How Good is it? How Can we Know?* (Princeton: Princeton University Press, 2005).

5 'David Miliband tells Russia it must avoid starting a new Cold War', *Telegraph* (27 August 2008).

6 J. Ferguson and A. Henderson, *International Partnership in Russia: Conclusions from the Oil and Gas Industry* (London: Palgrave Macmillan, 2014), pp. 242–244.

7 Nate Silver, an American political scientist, describes it thus: 'the signal is the truth. The noise is what distracts us from the truth'. Noise consists of random patterns that might be mistaken for signals, and can consist of numerous competing signals. The presence of too many signals can make it more challenging to discern meaning, since they drown each other out. N. Silver, *The Signal and the Noise: The Art and Science of Prediction* (London: Allen Lane, 2012), p. 17.

8 C.J. Dick, 'Catching NATO unawares: Soviet army surprise and deception techniques', *International Defence Review*, 1 (1986), p. 26.

9 The names of these three groups are variations on Donald Rumsfeld's well-known quote about 'known knowns': though he did not use the terms 'unknown knowns' and 'assumed knowns'.

10 D. Lynch, 'OSCE early warning and the August conflict in Georgia', *Uluslararası İlişkiler*, 7:26 (Summer 2010), pp. 139–148, www.uidergisi.com/wp-content/uploads/2013/02/osce-early-warnings.pdf; C.W. Blandy, *Georgia and Russia: A Further Deterioration in Relations. ARAG Caucasus Series, 08/22* (Swindon: Defence Academy of the UK, 2008).

11 K. Yalowitz and M. Rojansky, 'The slow death of Russian and Eurasian studies', *The National Interest* (23 May 2014); A. Stent, 'Why America doesn't understand Putin', *Washington Post* (14 March 2014).

12 'Lack of Russia experts has some in US worried', *Washington Post* (30 December 2015), www.washingtonpost.com/news/powerpost/wp/2015/12/30/lack-of-russia-experts-has-the-u-s-playing-catch-up/?postshare=5091451735724607&tid=ss_mail.

13 S. Cohen, *Failed Crusade: America and the Tragedy of Post Communist Russia* (London: W.W. Norton and Co., 2000), p. 208. Cohen cites officials from the State Department and senior figures in the US intelligence community.

14 While there is still some fine journalism, news organisations closed or significantly reduced their foreign bureaus and capacity to cover international news developments, including in Russia.

15 A. Stent, *The Limits of Partnership: U.S.-Russian Relations in the Twenty-First Century* (Oxford: Princeton University Press, 2014), pp. 59–60.

16 'Key Russia programme axed amid US government cuts', *Moscow Times* (4 November 2013). Official cited in C. King, 'The decline of international studies: why flying blind is dangerous', *Foreign Affairs* (July/August 2015).

17 'Ukraine call up of Cold Warriors', *Sunday Telegraph* (7 June 2014).

18 W. Hague, 'The best diplomatic service in the world: strengthening the FCO as an institution' (8 September 2011), www.gov.uk/government/speeches/the-best-diplomatic-service-in-the-world-strengthening-the-foreign-and-commonwealth-office-as-an-institution.

19 'Rory Stewart interview: Britain's strategic gap', *Prospect Magazine* (18 September 2014).

20 Tefft, who speaks Russian, has long experience in the region. He served in the embassy in Moscow in the 1990s, and as Deputy Director of the Office of the USSR/Russia and CIS (1989–1992) and Deputy Assistant Secretary of State for European and Eurasian Affairs (2004–2005). He also served as ambassador to Ukraine, Georgia and Lithuania.

21 'Breedlove: Russia intel gaps "critical"', *Defence News* (30 April 2015), www.defensenews.com/story/defense/policy-budget/policy/2015/04/30/breedlove-russia-intel-gaps/26642107/.

22 *The European Union and Russia: Before and Beyond the Crisis in Ukraine*, European Union Committee, House of Lords, 6th Report of Session 2014–2015 (London: The Stationery Office, February 2015), pp. 24–26, 63.

23 P. Rutland, 'Getting Russia wrong', *The Moscow Times* (9 April 2014); M. Schrad, 'Endangered species: essay on the difficulty of finding a job for an expert on Russia', *Inside Higher Education* (30 April 2014).

24 Rutland, 'Getting Russia wrong'.

25 O. Seliktar, *Politics, Paradigms and Intelligence Failures: Why So Few Predicted the Collapse of the Soviet Union* (London: M.E. Sharpe, 2004); M. Cox (ed.), *Rethinking the Soviet Collapse: Sovietology, the Death of Communism and the New Russia* (London: Pinter, 1998).

26 D. Engerman, *Know Your Enemy: The Rise and Fall of America's Soviet Experts* (Oxford: Oxford University Press, 2011).

27 P. Cockburn, *Getting Russia Wrong: The End of Kremlinology* (London: Verso, 1989), pp. 25–26; L. Labedz, 'The use and abuse of Sovietology', *Survey* (March 1988), p. 86.

28 P. Rutland, 'Sovietology: who got it right and who got it wrong and why', in Cox, *Rethinking the Soviet Collapse*, p. 32; P. Rutland, 'Sovietology: notes for a post mortem', *National Interest*, 31 (spring 1993), p. 112.

29 C. Merridale, *Red Fortress: The Secret Heart of Russia's History* (London: Allen Lane, 2013), pp. 352–353.

30 R. Conquest, *Policy and Power in the USSR* (London: Macmillan and Co. Ltd., 1961), pp. 3–14. See also G. Breslauer, *Khrushchev and Brezhnev as Leaders: Building Authority in Soviet Politics* (London: George Allen and Unwin, 1982), pp. ix–xi.

31 S. Fortescue, 'T.H. Rigby on Soviet and post-Soviet Russian politics', in S. Fortescue (ed.), *Russian Politics from Lenin to Putin* (Oxford: Palgrave, 2010); Engerman, *Know Your Enemy*, especially chapter 12.

32 With this focus, the discipline of Russia studies was seen to have joined the political science mainstream, with Russia being studied as a 'normal country' by well-trained political scientists. Cox, *Rethinking the Soviet Collapse*, p. 3.

33 Stent, 'Why America doesn't understand Putin'.

34 T. Carothers, 'The end of the transition paradigm', *Journal of Democracy*, 13:1 (2002), p. 1, www.journalofdemocracy.org/articles/gratis/Carothers-13-1.pdf; Carothers is now vice president for studies at the Carnegie Endowment for International Peace and has built a career on international support for democracy, human rights and governance. Cohen, *Failed Crusade*, p. 23.

35 Carothers, 'The end of the transition paradigm', p. 2.

36 The 'Rose' Revolution in Georgia in 2003, the 'Orange' Revolution in Ukraine in 2004 and the 'Tulip' or 'Pink' Revolution in Kyrgyzstan in

2005. According to some, the Orange Revolution 'represented a second wave of democratisation or democratic breakthrough in Ukraine', A. Aslund and M. McFaul (eds), *Revolution in Orange: The Origins of Ukraine's Democratic Breakthrough* (Washington, DC: Carnegie Endowment, 2006), p. 193.

37 The overthrow of President Yanukovich in Ukraine led to discussion about whether such a revolution was also possible in Russia. For discussion of how the democratisation in waves study returned to the forefront of political science in the aftermath of the Colour Revolutions and 'Arab Spring', see S. Greene, *Moscow in Movement: Power and Opposition in Putin's Russia* (Stanford: Stanford University Press, 2014).

38 Another important feature was the comparison of Putin's autocracy with Boris Yeltsin's democracy. Two prominent Russia watchers suggested that without democratic change, Russia faced the 'Angola model'. M. McFaul and K. Stoner-Weiss, 'The myth of the authoritarian model: how Vladimir Putin's crackdown holds Russia back', *Foreign Affairs*, 87:1 (January–February 2008); *Russia's Wrong Direction: What the United States Can and Should Do*, Council on Foreign Relations Report No. 57 (2006), www.cfr.org/iran/russias-wrong-direction/p9997.

39 For an overview of the literature, B. Harasymiw, 'In search of post communism: stalking Russia's political trajectory', *Canadian Slavonic Studies*, LIII:2–4 (June–October 2011). Kotkin called it the '*myth* of Russia's overturned democracy'. S. Kotkin, 'The myth of the New Cold War', *Prospect* (27 April 2008), www.prospectmagazine.co.uk/features/mythofthenewcoldwar; R. Sakwa, '"New Cold War" or twenty years' crisis? Russia and international affairs', *International Affairs*, 84:2 (2008), pp. 241–267.

40 This view was still being reiterated in 2014. M. McFaul, 'Confronting Putin's Russia', *New York Times* (23 March 2014).

41 M. Bennetts, *Kicking the Kremlin* (London: OneWorld Publications, 2014), p. xvi. He (correctly) diagnosed this as a 'knee-jerk approval'.

42 'Russia risks Soviet-style collapse as Rouble defence fails', *Telegraph* (16 December 2014).

43 'Interview with foreign media' (19 January 2014), http://eng.news.kremlin.ru/news6545; 'Has Russia abandoned the path to democracy?', Roundtable discussion at National Endowment for Democracy (30 October 2014), http://imrussia.org/en/news/2076-has-russia-abandoned-the-path-to-democracy.

44 Z. Brzezinski, 'Russia, like Ukraine, will become a real democracy', *Financial Times* (11 December 2013); McFaul, 'Confronting Putin's Russia'; D. Remnick, 'Watching the eclipse', *New Yorker* (11 August 2014).

45 Cohen, *Failed Crusade*, p. 31.

46 For much of the 2000s, it was a regular point of discussion that 'we should see Russia as it is, rather than as we would like to see it'.

47 This is emphasised by the common assumption that all information is available on the Internet and is in English. This is part of the problem of distinguishing between the large amounts of information and knowledge about complex subjects.

48 T. Remington, *Presidential Decrees in Russia: A Comparative Perspective* (Cambridge: Cambridge University Press, 2014).

49 Bennetts, *Kicking the Kremlin*, p. 117.

50 It is noteworthy that many of the assessments of Navalniy also tend to draw on Navalniy's own work: either his blog or other statements, or the hagiographical series of interviews with him edited by a political ally. K. Voronkov, *Alexei Navalniy: Groza zhulikov i vorov* [Alexei Navalniy: Buster of Crooks and Thieves] (Moscow: Eksmo, 2012).

51 M. van Herpen, *Putin's Wars: The Rise of Russia's New Imperialism* (London: Rowman & Littlefield, 2014); 'Vladimir Putin: our despot of the year', *Bloomberg* (29 December 2014), www.bloomberg.com/politics/videos/2014-12-29/vladimir-putin-our-despot-of-the-year.

52 Greene, *Moscow in Movement*, p. 3. One reporter, for instance, estimates the protest on 6 May 2012 as being 50,000–100,000 in size. A. Arutunyan, *The Putin Mystique: Inside Russia's Power Cult* (Newbold: Skyscraper Publications, 2014), p. 238. Drawing on Western media sources, which themselves had drawn on protest organiser's estimates, one UK parliamentary report thus suggested that the protest in Moscow on 24 December 2011 numbered 120,000 and 'large demonstrations in other centres'. B. Smith, *The Russia Crisis and Putin's Third Term* (London: House of Commons, SNIA/6289, 12 April 2012), p. 5.

53 This is a shorthand but inaccurate reference to Cardinal Richelieu as a means of characterising the roles of senior figures in the Presidential Administration. There are several alleged 'grey cardinals', including Alexander Voloshin, Igor Sechin, Vladislav Surkov and Vyacheslav Volodin. This offers a telling image but has little value beyond imparting a vague and misleading sense of non-transparent power. At best it is a silhouette, more often it is an alibi covering up the lack of more detailed attempts to understand these individuals and the roles they play.

54 This very important point has been emphasised by a senior Kremlin official. 'Many facts were simply wrong and actors' motivations were misrepresented', the official suggested. A. Ledeneva, *Can Russia Modernise? Sistema, Power Networks and Informal Governance* (Cambridge: Cambridge University Press, 2013), p. 115.

55 Putin's mental and physical health is often the subject of debate, as is that of others, such as Igor Sechin. When photos indicated that he had lost weight, there was much gossip about Sechin having cancer.

56 L. Harding, *Mafia State: How One Reporter Became an Enemy of the Brutal New Russia* (London: Guardian Books, 2011). This is not to

suggest that there is not crime, even at senior levels of the state and in law enforcement in Russia, as illustrated by the 'Three Whales' and Kushchevskaya cases. Rather it is to suggest that criminality is often asserted or *insinuated*.

57 In his novel *S*N*U*F*F**, he described a futuristic society in which professional reporters engage in a daily process of generating superficial discourse and slogans about artificially created events. Since everything was staged, nothing could be confirmed or denied.

58 R. Brope, 'Russia', in R. Dover, M. Goodman and C. Hillebrand (eds), *Routledge Companion to Intelligence Studies* (London: Routledge, 2013), p. 227.

59 A. Soldatov and I. Borogan, *The New Nobility: The Restoration of Russia's Security State and the Enduring Legacy of the KGB* (New York: Public Affairs, 2010), p. 110. For more discussion, see Brope, 'Russia'.

60 D. Satter, 'Why journalists frighten Putin', *Wall Street Journal* (14 January 2014).

61 See A. Monaghan, *The Russian Vertikal: The Tandem, Power and the Elections*, Chatham House Programme Paper (June 2011), on which the following passage draws.

62 For an early example of Medvedev's liberalism, F. Kempe, 'Russia's Medvedev deserves handshake, nosehold', *Bloomberg* (29 February 2008), www.bloomberg.com/apps/news?pid=newsarchive&refer=colu mnist_kempe&sid=aunbnki00EWU; Obama cited in 'Obama: Putin is keeping one foot in the old ways', *Guardian* (2 July 2009), www.the guardian.com/world/2009/jul/02/barack-obama-vladimir-putin-russia.

63 Yu. Latynina, 'Tvitter-prezident i vostorzheniye liberali', *Yezhenedel'ni Zhurnal* (4 April 2010).

64 S. Kotkin, 'Sticking power', *Times Literary Supplement* (2 March 2012).

65 'Pentagon think tank claims Putin has Asperger's – has Putinology gone too far?', *Guardian* (5 February 2015).

66 See editorial comment, *Johnson's Russia List* (14 March 2014).

67 Stephen Cohen notes that no Soviet leader since Stalin has been so personally villainised. S. Cohen, 'Distorting Russia: How the American media misrepresent Putin, Sochi and Ukraine', *The Nation* (11 February 2014), www.thenation.com/article/178344/distorting-russia#; H. Kissinger, 'To settle the Ukraine crisis, start at the end', *Washington Post* (5 March 2014), www.washingtonpost.com/opinions/henry-kissinger-to-settle-the-ukraine-crisis-start-at-the-end/2014/03/05/46dad868-a496-11e3-8466-d34c451760b9_story.html?hpid=z2. A version of this is the portrayal of Putin as a pariah, a theme that regularly re-emerges in which Putin himself is directly held responsible for an atrocity, whether it be Alexander Litvinkeno's murder or the shooting down of flight MH17 in July 2014.

68 For a collection of these views, all given by prominent Russia watchers, S. Glasser, 'Putin on the couch', *Politico* (13 March 2014). Glasser

reminds us that in the early 2000s, Putin was seen by Bush's National Security Council members as a 'liberal economic moderniser'.

69 Reports were prepared in 2008 and 2011, but emerged in early February 2015 thanks to a freedom of information request. 'Putin suffers from Asperger's Syndrome, Pentagon report claims', *Telegraph* (5 February 2015). The report was prepared having watched film of Putin dating back to 2000, but none of the authors had met him, nor had they seen brain scans. Jane Harris, of the UK's national Autism Society, suggested that 'this kind of speculative diagnosis is fraught with risks and is unhelpful', and that the study was 'driven by the wilder reaches of military intelligence'. 'Putin has "some form of Autism" Pentagon experts conclude after watching films of him', *Independent* (5 February 2015). Harris's comments were not carried by the *Telegraph*. Another reporter wondered whether this was 'taking Putinology too far'. 'Pentagon think tank claims Putin has Asperger's – has Putinology gone too far?', *Guardian* (5 February 2015).

70 As discussed in Chapter 4, Patrushev, Ivanov and Medvedev have all long been part of Putin's inner team.

71 'Henry Kissinger: to settle the Ukraine crisis, start at the end', *Washington Post* (5 March 2014), www.washingtonpost.com/opinions/henry-kissinger-to-settle-the-ukraine-crisis-start-at-the-end/2014/03/0 5/46dad868-a496-11e3-8466-d34c451760b9_story.html.

72 J. Yaffa, 'Reading Putin: the mind and state of Russia's president', *Foreign Affairs* (July–August 2012).

73 Author's correspondence with Henry Plater-Zyberk, December 2014. Journalist Thomas Friedman is one who has called Putin a thug, also indulging in comparing Putin with Nazi officials. 'Czar Putin's next moves', *New York Times* (28 January 2015).

74 'Weimar Russia? Why post-Soviet authoritarianism did not turn Fascist', Wilson Centre discussion (15 November 2011), www.wilsoncenter. org/event/weimar-russia-why-post-soviet-authoritarianism-did-not-turn-fascist; N. Ferguson, 'Look back at Weimar – and start to worry about Russia', *Telegraph* (1 January 2005). 'Times of Troubles' include during the reigns of Peter the Great and Catherine the Great, Alexander I, Alexander II and Nicholas II. It was an analogy often drawn with Russia during the 1990s, but was also in evidence during the protest demonstrations in 2011 and 2012 and emerged again in 2014. 'Vladimir Putin's unhappy new year', *Wall Street Journal* (30 December 2014); 'Pussy Riot's stunning victory over Putin's bureaucrats', *Telegraph* (14 August 2012); 'Nemtsov: Kremlin watchers find an eerie parallel in an 80-year-old murder', *RFE/RL* (1 March 2015), www.rferl.org/content/russia-nemtsov-kirov-eerie-parallel/26876076.html.

75 The events in North Africa and the Middle East also generated many analogies. Many commentators sought to describe complex and diverse Eastern events as a march towards democracy, and the term 'Arab Spring' was coined: a term that evokes Western developments

such as the European Spring of 1848 and the Prague Spring of 1968. F. Gaub, 'The Arab Spring for dummies', *Security Times* (February 2013).

76 Condoleeza Rice, then Secretary of State, compared Russian actions to the Soviet invasion of Czechoslovakia. Cited in 'Georgia conflict: key statements', BBC (19 August 2008), http://news.bbc.co.uk/1/hi/world/europe/7556857.stm.

77 Western officials who have made such comparisons include David Cameron, Hillary Clinton, Stephen Harper and Wolfgang Shauble. '12 prominent people who compared Putin to Hitler', *Business Insider* (22 May 2014), www.businessinsider.com/people-who-compared-putin-to-hitler-2014-5?IR=T. This is not new. 'Poland compares German-Russian pipeline to Nazi-Soviet pact', *EU Observer* (2 May 2006), http://euobserver.com/foreign/21486.

78 Peskov cited in I. Gorst, 'Putin spokesman: Brezhnev rules OK', *Financial Times* (5 October 2011); F. Hill and C. Gaddy, 'Putin and the uses of history', *The National Interest* (January–February 2012).

79 B. Lo, 'Crimea's Sudenten crisis', *Project Syndicate* (18 March 2014).

80 Historians have done this elsewhere. For instance, M. Brown, 'Ukraine crisis is nothing like the invasion of Czechoslovakia', *The Conversation* (4 April 2014).

81 R. Neustadt and E. May, *Thinking in Time: The Uses of History for Decision-Makers* (London: Collier Macmillan, 1986), chapter 3, pp. 35–39; D.B.G. Heuser and C. Buffet, *Haunted by History: Myths in International Relations* (Oxford: Berghahn Books, 1998).

82 Though compared to these other popular protests, the demonstrations in late 2011 and early 2012 were often hailed as 'unprecedented'. As discussed in Chapter 3, few commentators appeared to recollect the 'pensioner's protests' of 2005, nor their almost identical discussion about Russia of that time, including comparisons with the Orange Revolution and Putin's imminent departure from power.

83 Gaub, 'Arab Spring for dummies'.

84 Engerman, *Know Your Enemy*, pp. 319–322.

85 Silver, *The Signal and the Noise*, pp. 4–5, 7.

2

Towards strategic dissonance: Russia as 'a Europe apart'

Moving on together? The West and Russia after the Cold War

After the collapse of the Soviet Union, many Western officials and observers believed that Russia would return to the 'Western family of nations' after decades of Soviet era isolation. Fuelled by an optimistic sense that the end of the Cold War represented the triumph of the Western way and the 'end of history' through the failure and defeat of the major systemic alternative, there was widespread hope not just of bringing an end to East–West confrontation, but of forging a 'strategic partnership' with Russia, and integrating it into the West on the basis on one hand of shared common interests and challenges, and, on the other, common values.[1] Indeed, there has been a prolonged sense of inevitability about Russia rejoining the West, even during the periodic crises and disputes that were often seen as temporary, transient hitches along the route to eventual partnership.[2] Indeed, as one experienced Western observer has noted, Western discussions of globalisation never began to reflect on how Russia might fit into an Asian-driven twenty-first century, instead only focusing on Russia, an old and declining power that needed Western assistance to mitigate its decline, and thus as either being part of Europe or being isolated.[3]

Over time, however, this mood has evolved. First, it has gone from optimism about Russia's *voluntary* return and desire to establish meaningful cooperation and 'strategic partnership', to increased frustration with, and criticism of, perceived Russian intransigent opposition to Western policies and Moscow's increasingly obvious departure not just from shared values but from a shared view of international developments. As a result, the optimism has evolved more towards hope that Russia had been sufficiently weakened by developments such as the 2008 financial crisis that it would *be obliged* to drop its objections to Western policies and come over to the West and seek partnership. These assumptions have lain at the heart of the ongoing belief, even expectation, that Moscow would simply drop its opposition to the West over high-profile issues such as Russian recognition of South Ossetia and Abkhazia, the US-led ballistic missile defence programme and how to handle the conflict in Syria, and intensified the sense of frustration at Moscow's intransigence when it did not.

Even from the early 1990s, however, there have been cracks in the foundations of the relationship that mean that many of these Western assumptions are based on misapprehension. For much of the post-Soviet era, and increasingly obviously since the mid 2000s, the Russian leadership has interpreted both Russia's own position and international developments in another, rather different light. Senior Russian officials argued that Russia had emerged as one of the victors from the Cold War, peacefully delivering Russia and Eastern and Central Europe from totalitarianism – and thus deserved an equal voice in European decision-making as its due reward. As the Russian state began to recover after the collapse of the USSR, Moscow became more assertive in its attempts both to emphasise this point and promote Russia not only as a ubiquitous power in regional systems across the world, but as an indispensable partner in international affairs, one whose interests and voice had to be taken into account, even if it disagreed with the West.

Dmitri Medvedev, then Russian president, illustrated this gap in 2008 when he stated that Russia had 'come in from the cold' from a century of (self) isolation, and actively returning to global politics and economics. But he also pointed to what Moscow saw as selective and politicised approaches to a common history, and added that 'it is highly symptomatic that the current differences with Russia are interpreted by many in the West as a need simply to bring Russia's policies closer in line with those of the West. But we do not want to be embraced in this way'.[4] If senior officials continue to stress the point that Russia shares much with Europe, this stance has only become more emphatic: despite the financial crisis and other events such as the major changes in the US energy situation which many see as weakening Russia, Vladimir Putin has repeatedly emphasised his commitment to Russia's independent, sovereign development with 'traditional Russian values'.[5]

One of the results of this discrepancy between 'common Europes' is that the West's relationship with Russia has been beset by tension, misinterpretation and a dissonance in relations. Moving on from the Cold War has proved difficult, with officials on both sides accusing the other of adhering to the thinking and practice of the Cold War era, even suggesting that relations are worse than during the Cold War. Russian Foreign Minister Sergei Lavrov, for instance, suggested that the West was more tolerant towards the USSR than it is to today's much freer Russia, and that 'at the heart of the crisis in confidence in our relations with the US and the West in general lay a "conflict of expectations". There was a lack of common understanding about what the end of the Cold War meant.'[6] In his first major speech as NATO Secretary General, for instance, Anders Fogh Rasmussen stated that, of all NATO's partnerships, the NATO–Russia relationship was the most 'burdened by misperceptions, mistrust and diverging political agendas'.[7] Despite the effort that went into 'resets' or 'reloads' of Russia's relations with the West, this has remained the case.

Both sides have numerous complaints about the other. Western observers criticise Moscow for being an unreliable partner – whether regarding energy supplies or Moscow's failure to fulfil treaty obligations to which it has subscribed.

The Russian authorities accuse the West of being unreliable and pursuing ambiguous policies – the most obvious example being the assertion by senior Russian officials, including Vladimir Putin, that NATO consistently says one thing yet does another. As discussed in the introduction, this accusation goes right back to the belief in Moscow that senior Western officials had given Soviet leaders a promise that NATO would not enlarge beyond reunified Germany. Such accusations have since been compounded by other examples of 'saying one thing and doing another': Moscow presents NATO's air campaign in Libya as bending the truth. Putin raised the two issues together in April 2014, stating that 'we were promised … that after Germany's unification, NATO would not spread eastward'. He continued by noting that the reset did not fail because of Crimea, but much earlier, in Libya: Medvedev upheld the (UN) resolution about a ban of flights of the Libyan government air force as an act of humanitarian assistance. But in Moscow's view, the actual result was an air campaign, the overthrow of Gaddafi and his murder, and the murder of the US ambassador and the collapse of Libya – in effect mission creep towards regime change without appropriate international mandate. 'This is where distrust comes from', he stated.[8] He again raised the issue in a long interview with *Bild* newspaper in January 2016.[9]

These problems have created a complex sense of strategic dissonance between the West and Russia,[10] as the relationship is stuck between a series of longer-term Cold War era problems and new, post-Cold War problems, with each compounding the other. Although cooperative projects have been established, therefore, talk of 'strategic partnership' faded in the mid 2000s and an increasing sense of dissonance, even competition, has emerged, as illustrated and emphasised by the war in Ukraine. This is reflected in the official documents of both sides, and by the gaps between the official rhetoric and reality. Adding to this are divergences in what appears to be common language, creating confusion about the intentions and actions of the other, and limiting the possibility for developing practical cooperation.

This chapter first sketches out an overview of the relationship, the creation of official partnership and practical cooperation, and the emergence of political tension. Important cooperation has taken place, and many new mechanisms for dialogue have been created, and met with increasing frequency, but this did not result in the improvement in relations that optimists hoped for. This background is important because the public policy and media discussion about Russia suffers from short-termism and a lack of a sense of context and history: many of the problems in the West's relationship with Russia are presented as 'new', though they have long and deep roots.

The second part of the chapter explores conceptual differences that lie at the core of the dissonance. Although there are numerous questions and interests that appear to be 'common', they are not 'shared' in terms of how they are defined or in how the sides seek to respond to them. This distinction has served to undermine attempts to develop cooperative relations, and increased friction between the two sides. This, too, warrants exploration given the perennial hope in the West that Russia will simply drop its opposition to Western policies – whether over missile defence or Syria – and 'join the West'.

Moving on from the Cold War?

For much of the period since the end of the Cold War and the fall of the USSR, Russia's place in the changing landscape of the Euro-Atlantic area has been the main question of Russia's overall relationship with the West. It might be summed up as whether Russia would have a 'seat at the table' of Euro-Atlantic politics, in a position to be an active actor in international developments, or be 'on its menu', a passive object of decisions taken by others.

The debate was well captured by the Russian observer Vladimir Baranovsky, who framed the question as whether Russia was 'a part of Europe', or 'apart from Europe'. He pointed to the ongoing existential ambivalence of both Russia and Europe towards each other and the difficulties of establishing a relationship that would meet the hopes and requirements of the other: while Moscow expected the West to welcome the new Russia as an equal partner in the European theatre and elsewhere, since there were clearly common interests, the West's Cold War logic had been replaced by a policy of preventing Russia from becoming disengaged without letting it in.[11]

The institutional frameworks of Russia's relationship with the Euro-Atlantic community have evolved significantly since 1992, and numerous formal arrangements have been established. Russia, a member of the OSCE, joined the Council of Europe in 1996 and then became a member of the G8 in 1997. Formal relationships have also developed with the two main international organisations in the Euro-Atlantic area, the European Union and NATO.

Russia's relations with the EU have developed from the signing of the Partnership and Cooperation Agreement in 1994 to the shaping of the Four Common Spaces at the EU–Russia St Petersburg summit in 2003 to address a wide range of common interests on the basis of common values,[12] and the establishment of biannual summits and numerous mechanisms for cooperation such as the Permanent Partnership Councils (PPCs). These PPCs meet as often as deemed necessary at the ministerial level, and are the main mechanism for the functioning of the relationship across numerous areas of cooperation, including foreign policy, justice and home affairs, energy, transport, agriculture and culture. In 2005, the EU and Russia agreed Road Maps, which laid out specific objectives and sought to put the Common Spaces into effect.[13]

Perhaps most surprising, however, is the structural transformation in Russia's relationship with NATO. In 1997, the NATO–Russia Founding Act on Mutual Relations, Cooperation and Security was signed, establishing the Permanent Joint Council (PJC). This created a formal bilateral relationship and prepared a road map for cooperation to establish lasting and inclusive peace in the Euro-Atlantic area. At the 2002 Rome summit, the NATO–Russia Council (NRC) was established to replace the PJC – an important development, since it included Russia as an *equal partner* with the NATO members, as opposed to the 'NATO+1' format of the PJC. The purpose of the NRC is to

> promote continuous political dialogue on security issues with a view to the early identification of emerging problems, the determination of common approaches, the development of practical cooperation and the conduct of joint operations where necessary. Work under the [NRC] focuses on all areas of mutual interest identified in the Founding Act. … since its establishment, the NRC has evolved into a productive mechanism for consultation, consensus building, cooperation and joint decision and joint action.[14]

This brief sketch of the basic structural elements of the relationship is important for two reasons. First, it reminds us of the considerable extent of the evolution of the relationship since the end of the Cold War. This is too often forgotten. These numerous mechanisms, such as the PPCs and NRC, which include Russian officials, provide for exchanges and meetings from the working level all the way up to summit levels, and mean that Russia has numerous seats at the Euro-Atlantic table, as well as its relationships with individual states.

On this basis, second, important cooperation has taken place. Again, it is worth emphasising what are perhaps the most surprising elements of this cooperation between the former adversaries – those in the political and security domain – because these are too often forgotten. Russian military forces, for instance, cooperated with those of the West in peacekeeping as part of the NATO-led Implementation Force (IFOR) peace enforcement force in Bosnia-Herzegovina for one year from December 1995, for instance, and joined NATO's Operation Active Endeavour in the Mediterranean.

Indeed, NATO and Russia drew up a lengthy list of cooperative projects. This included a counter-terrorism plan in 2004, and a range of cooperative exercises in civil defence and emergency management, theatre missile defence, nuclear materials management and submarine search and rescue. Thanks to the experience of the latter, Russian lives were saved when a UK-led NATO team raised the Russian submersible AS28 off the coast of Kamchatka in 2005.[15]

All told, therefore, a basis for relations was established in the decade after the end of the Cold War. Indeed, neither the format such as the PPC and NRC, which include Russian officials, nor the agenda and practical cooperation achieved, bilaterally or with the EU and NATO, could have been expected, even by optimists, in the 1990s, and would have still seemed unlikely in the early 2000s.

Cooperation, albeit in specific areas and at a more technical level, has tended to survive the periodic political crises that beset the relationship, even in politically contentious areas. It has provided the foundations on which, despite the crisis occasioned in Russia's relations with the West, and particularly with NATO, by the Russo-Georgia War in 2008, relations could be resumed, the agenda honed and cooperation continued. NATO and Russia completed, for instance, a joint review of twenty-first-century common security challenges, which comprised cooperation in Afghanistan (including counter-narcotics), non-proliferation of weapons of mass destruction and their means of delivery, counter-piracy, counter-terrorism and disaster response. Official statements suggest that 'important progress has been made since then',[16] and exercises such as the (submarine rescue) exercise Bold Monarch in 2012, and in other areas such as counter-piracy operations and military medical projects, continued.

Cooperation stands out in two notable areas of common concern. The first is in relation to Afghanistan, where NATO (and the USA) and Russia agreed to cooperate on the transit of NATO equipment to and from Afghanistan via Russia, counter-narcotics operations and helicopter maintenance. Even during the Ukraine crisis and after the USA imposed sanctions on Russia, elements of this cooperation endured, for instance, the contract signed in 2011 between Rosoboronexport and the US Department of Defence for Russian Mi17V5 helicopters for Afghanistan.

The second relates to counter-terrorism cooperation. This led to the development of the Stand-off Detection of Explosives and Suicide Bombers (STANDEX) project, launched in 2009, and the Cooperative Airspace Initiative (CAI) that provides for the airspace monitoring and the sharing of information to allow for the early detection of suspicious activities in the air. These projects have resulted in exercises, such as Vigilant Skies in September 2013, and the development of a device for bomb detection in crowds as part of a transport infrastructure protection scheme.[17]

Such cooperation stands alongside wider efforts to repair the relationship between Russia and the West, particularly the attempts to 'reset' Russia's relations with European capitals (such as the Poland–Russia relationship), and the US–Russia 'reset' of 2009. This latter effort led to the signature and ratification of a new START treaty in 2011 and support for Russian entry into the World Trade Organization (WTO) in 2012.

From frustration to bitterness: a chronology of compounding dissonance

If an increase in mechanisms for interaction and the frequency with which meetings take place has altered the relationship's structural nature since the early 1990s and resulted in some cooperation, it has not translated into a closer, warmer relationship, let alone the 'strategic partnership' for which many had hoped. Indeed, frustration and bitterness has increased on both sides. This is partly because of the early optimistic mood on both sides, and the resulting lengthy agenda for possible cooperation stretched well ahead of what was realistically feasible. Furthermore, if the senior leadership on both sides attempted to forge a relationship, not all on both sides were convinced of the desirability of such a partnership.

A sense of stagnation pervades the EU–Russia relationship. Although Road Maps were developed for the EU–Russia relationship, important technical roadblocks were not satisfactorily dealt with, hindering progress, and many, if not the majority, of the points of projected cooperation anticipated as a result of the Rome declaration between NATO and Russia remained unfulfilled. Of course, there were many reasons for the lack of progress in fulfilling the set agenda – both sides, for instance, had other international and domestic priorities to which to attend. Nevertheless, the inability to establish substantial cooperation served to generate frustration on both sides.

More important, though, was the emergence of increased political tension between the West, particularly the EU and NATO and some of their member states, and Russia. Indeed, with hindsight, the period from 2002 to 2004 represents a watershed in Russia's relations with the West. If the NRC and PPCs were established in these years, setting out an agenda for cooperation to achieve 'strategic partnership', at the same time an increasingly systematic dissonance between Russia and the West became more obvious.

Of course, there had been friction during the 1990s, particularly regarding NATO enlargement, and disagreements over the Kosovo War of 1998–1999. But at the same time, there were efforts to establish a cooperative relationship as described above, and these were underpinned by assertions of common values. Yet from 2002 and 2003 a chronology of dissonance became increasingly intense, as mutual recriminations became harsher and interpretations of events more visibly incongruous. The list of disagreements over both international issues and Russia's internal development warrants brief elucidation to pick out some of the main features and the recurring problems. It became increasingly clear both that values were not shared as Moscow sought to develop 'sovereign democracy', and that understandings of international affairs differed.[18]

In some ways, the two-year period at the end of Putin's first term as president set the benchmark for themes that would dominate the relationship between Russia and the West for the following decade, as dissonance emerged over issues old and new. Old themes included NATO enlargement, since prospective new members included the Baltic states. Reflecting the ambiguity of relations between NATO and Russia, if the Prague summit in 2002 had set in place the NRC, it also set in motion the second round of NATO enlargement. Although senior leaders on both sides sought to emphasise continuing cooperation between NATO and Russia, there was strong opposition to this wave of enlargement from within the Russian parliament and in Russian military circles, as the Alliance moved closer to Russia's borders and former Soviet states became members.

If the main Russian response remained 'calmly negative', it also revealed the emergence of differing interpretations of the international situation. As Sergei Ivanov, then Minister of Defence (now head of the presidential administration) said in 2004, 'we cannot see any connection between creating new military structures on the territories of new NATO member states and the problems of combating international terrorism and the proliferation of weapons of mass destruction, recognised by NATO and Russia as the highest priorities'.[19]

At the same time, a series of newer disagreements emerged that have subsequently resonated throughout relations. In 2002, the USA withdrew from the Anti-Ballistic Missile Treaty. Russian opposition to the withdrawal was initially muted, but this opened the way for Russia's unilateral suspension of the CFE treaty and subsequent and ongoing disagreements over the USA's ballistic missile defence programme. Russia also opposed the US-led invasion of Iraq in 2003, with Putin calling it a 'great political error'. The invasion also served to underline Russian concerns about Western interventionism that had been first stimulated by the Kosovo campaign, and has since featured prominently in Russian concerns about Western-led regime change operations and the USA generating regional instability.

If there had previously been unease in the West about Russia's internal development, most obviously about human rights and the ongoing war in Chechnya, these grew as concern about a roll-back of democracy under Putin intensified for three reasons. The first was the increasing state control over media outlets. The second was the loud Western criticism of the arrest of Mikhail Khodorkovsky and the start of the Yukos case. And the third was the electoral defeat and departure from the Russian parliament in 2003 of all the representatives of the parties recognised in the West as more liberal or democratic.

In 2004, these disagreements were intensified by the 'Colour Revolutions', particularly the Orange Revolution in Ukraine, and the complex negative impact of the terrorist attack in Beslan. The Russian authorities vigorously rejected Western criticism of how they had handled the attack, and suggested Western support for those who sought to attack Russia, including terrorists. President Putin's subsequent introduction of legislation for the direct presidential appointment of regional governors in late 2004 only increased Western criticism of a 'roll-back' of democracy.

If the period 2002–2004 had set the dissonant tone, the following years compounded it, as criticism, disagreements and problems multiplied. 2006 was a particularly difficult year. It was the year of the high-profile murders in London of the former Russian security services member Alexander Litvinenko, who had just become a British citizen, and, in Moscow, the well-known journalist Anna Politkovskaya. Both murders have echoed through Russia's relations with the West ever since: Politkovskaya's murder has served as the beacon for criticism of the plight of journalists in Russia, and the UK–Russia relationship is still hampered by the dispute over the responsibility for Litvinenko's murder and how justice should be achieved.

Three other important developments came to light in 2006 that soured the relationship further. First, in April, the Russian authorities introduced legislation that added an extra documentary burden on both Russian and foreign non-governmental organisations (NGOs) to register and provide detailed personal information. Many NGOs were denied registration for failing to meet these requirements. Other elements of the legislation included the requirement to supply annual reports registering the sources of all foreign donations and how these funds were used, and the prevention of foreign nationals from establishing NGOs in Russia. The legislation elicited much protest from Russian NGOs, and loud criticism of Russia by the USA, EU and Council of Europe, and, of course, international NGOs that the Russian authorities were asserting state control over NGOs and restricting and obstructing their activities.[20]

The other two disagreements came over international developments. The first of these was the ongoing divergence in views of Iran. Washington and Moscow had approached the matters of Iran's nuclear capacity and arms trade from different perspectives. Concerned about the dangers of nuclear proliferation, Washington had urged Moscow to abandon its nuclear assistance to Iran with the construction of the Bushehr nuclear facility. Moscow did not see the question in the same light, however, contending that there was little proliferation threat.[21] In mid 2006, US concerns about Russian military cooperation with Iran led to Washington imposing sanctions on Rosoboronexport and Sukhoi.[22]

The second related to European energy security and the first year of major Western political concern about the reliability of Russian energy supplies to Europe, as a dispute between Gazprom and the Ukrainian company Naftogaz Ukraini led to a short disruption of gas supplies to parts of Europe. This episode, which had long roots in the post-Soviet era, resulted in significant tension between the EU and Russia as the EU began to seek alternative energy suppliers.

By the time Russia took over the G8 presidency in mid 2006, therefore, relations were tense. It was increasingly clear that 'strategic partnership' was failing, and that Russia was neither 'coming home' nor meeting Western hopes. In remarks that reflected the Bush administration's position, Dick Cheney accused the Russian leadership of both improperly restricting the rights of the Russian population and using its hydrocarbon resources as 'tools of intimidation and blackmail'.[23] Although the Russian authorities made some moves to seek to assuage the criticisms, Moscow increasingly firmly re-stated its positions and rebutted Western criticism either as inappropriate or hypocritical (or both).

Indeed, as one Russian observer phrased it, Russia appeared to have spun out of the Western orbit and onto a trajectory of its own, determined to find its own system. Western critics could express their dismay all they wanted, Dmitri Trenin argued, but there would be no change in Russian policies, since Moscow had given up on becoming part of the West.[24] There were loud mutual recriminations, and much talk of a 'new Cold War', talk that was only emphasised by what was interpreted in the West as a harsh speech by Putin himself at the Munich security conference in February 2007. The sense of tension increased that summer when Putin announced both that Russia would suspend its application of the CFE treaty and resume long-range patrols by Russian strategic bombers.

A year later this tension reached a crescendo, most obviously in terms of the strain in the relationship between Georgia (that had sought NATO membership)[25] and Russia, culminating in a short war in August 2008. The suspension of NATO–Russia relations over the Russo-Georgia War illustrated the wider scale of the crisis, but it was followed almost immediately in late 2008 and early 2009 by a second gas dispute between Gazprom and Naftogaz Ukraini, which both lasted longer than the 2006 dispute and had a more substantial effect on gas supplies to members of the EU.

Altogether, as one Western writer suggested, a 'sense of crisis' pervaded wider European security. This drew on both 'concrete realities and from differing perceptions'. The concrete developments included the uncertainty over the Euro-Atlantic arms control regime that led to increasing opacity in military developments at regional and sub-regional levels, and unresolved conflicts in Moldova, Georgia and Nagorno-Karabakh. The perceptions included political double standards, the stalling of the democratic transformation in Europe and the emergence of new dividing lines, and the absence of effective instruments to resolve problems.[26] Not only were NATO–Russia relations beset by ambiguities and problems, but so was the EU–Russia debate, as each side sought something different from the relationship. The EU–Russia Partnership for modernisation, for instance, reflected divergent priorities – for the EU, the focus was the development of civil society, but for Russia it was technological development.

Although the immediate crisis passed and relations were resumed in a series of 'resets' and 'reloads' in 2009, tensions remained. High-profile espionage scandals, including the Russian spy ring broken by the Federal Bureau of Investigation in 2010, and the arrest of Ekaterina Zatuliveter, a Russian who worked for British MP Michael Hancock,[27] ensured continuing discussion of a 'new Cold War' and a lack of trust between the two sides. Disagreements dominated the public agenda, whether over Russia's recognition of the independence of South Ossetia and Abkhazia, over the US ballistic missile defence programme, over the NATO action in Libya, over possible Western-led intervention in Syria, and over other matters such as Western criticism of Russia's human rights record and the protest demonstrations in Russia in late 2011 and early 2012. These built up collectively, and although there was no direct crisis in the relationship of the type that took place in 2008, most observers acknowledged the end of the US–Russia reset and few spoke of strategic partnership.

Towards a dual history: same evidence, different conclusions

The deepening intensity of this dissonance reflects two inter-locking problems. First, as noted above, the disagreements were self-compounding, in that each new episode formed part of a repeti-tively negative official and public narrative that usually ignored the successes in the relationship. The (albeit few) positives such as IFOR cooperation and the raising of the AS28 submersible were quickly forgotten, but the long-running disagreements kept resurfacing and were compounded by new developments, and inflamed by other, new disagreements. This process has contributed to the sense of a repeating cycle in relations as they deteriorate towards crisis, the scale of which leads to the top leadership giving an impulse to restore relations.

There is an ambiguity here, too. In one sense, each time the relationship has been 'reset', it has become *more developed*: the establishment of the NRC after the Kosovo crisis, and the practi-cal successes of the US–Russia 'reset' and the NATO–Russia reload after the Russo-Georgia War. At the same time, this improvement has been fashioned from a *reduction in the scale and scope* of possi-ble partnership and as the West and Russia move in different politi-cal directions.

The second problem that it highlights is that both sides drew substantially different conclusions from the same body of evi-dence – not only on almost every point in this chronology of dis-sonance, but on many other issues. Two examples illustrate the widening gap. First, the global financial crisis in 2008, for instance, seriously affected the Russian economy. Many observers in the West assumed that, as a result, it would undermine the increasingly confident, even strident tone in Russian foreign policy and lead to Moscow adopting a more cooperative approach to relations with a West that it now needed in order to modernise. Russian officials, however, saw it as another blow to Anglo-Saxon influ-ence, weakening the influence of the USA and EU, and showed the post-Second World War international financial architecture to be dysfunctional and outmoded.

The 'Arab Spring' provided the second illustration, as the West and Russia drew very different conclusions about its nature and underlying forces, and particularly the revolution in Egypt, and civil wars in Libya and Syria. While many in the West tended to see the events more enthusiastically as democratic movements which could and should be supported, including with arms, if necessary, to lead to a more liberal post-Spring order, Moscow was more sceptical about both providing support to the revolutionary elements and the likelihood of a benign outcome. Russian officials saw the unfolding developments more in terms of security and stability and questioned the nature and aims of the rebels and opposition movements themselves, and the desire and capacity of the West to help them. Moscow strongly opposed the idea of Western-led intervention in Syria, arguing that the civil war is not substantially about democracy, nor even a responsibility to protect.

In every instance in the chronology of dissonance noted above, although the evidence is largely the same, the context, causes, guilty parties and consequences are differently interpreted and understood. Moscow's suspension of the CFE treaty and resumption of strategic flights, for instance, aroused criticism in the West for taking threatening and unilateral steps that undermined Euro-Atlantic security; yet more signs of a more assertive and aggressive foreign policy. Moscow instead laid the blame on the West, arguing instead that the suspension of the CFE treaty was in the context of the US missile defence programme and the ongoing failure of some NATO members to ratify the revised treaty agreed in 1999.[28] As for the strategic flights, Putin stated that Russia unilaterally stopped these flights in 1992, but others had not followed suit. The persistence of strategic flights by other states created certain problems for Russian security, he argued.[29] These different conclusions have evolved to take a complex multifaceted form with the result that these dissonant episodes have acted as a wedge being driven into the wood of Europe's post-Cold War history, splitting it into two separating and increasingly divergent histories.

The Russo-Georgia War is the best illustration of this problem, as not only have the conclusions differed dramatically at several levels, but they have had a clear and direct impact on policy. Most observers and officials in Western capitals placed the blame for the war squarely at Moscow's door, blaming Russia either for starting the war or for provoking Tbilisi into launching the attack. Russian officials, however, laid the blame with Tbilisi for launching the attack on South Ossetia and killing Russian peacekeepers, and with the West for providing specific support to Georgia and creating the wider conditions in which the crisis took place. If the war was seen in the West as a result of Russian pressure on Georgia, therefore, it was seen by Moscow in the context of NATO's enlargement and Georgia's potential membership of the Alliance.

These different conclusions were compounded by further divergences over the results of the war. Some in the West, for instance, saw the war as a reflection of Russian weakness because the Russian armed forces did not win 'efficiently', instead using disproportionate force against Georgia, and the results either as ambiguous or as a loss for Russia: Russia may have won on the battlefield, some argued, but the result of the war was that the financial, foreign policy and moral costs were much higher for Russia. Andrei Illarionov, a former advisor to Putin who had emigrated to the West and become a prominent and influential critic, argued that Moscow failed to achieve its main goal (regime change in Georgia), and that the international community saw Russia as the aggressor and Georgia as the victim – and as a result, Russia was isolated.[30] Stephen Blank, a US observer, argued that although Moscow won the war in tactical terms, it was becoming clear that Russia's strategic losses were mounting and with time would eclipse the gains through the use of force.[31]

Although many Russian observers subsequently questioned the performance of the armed forces and Moscow's failure in the information war, the Russian authorities saw the war in a different light, which included conflict and instability on Russia's southern border and NATO enlargement. For Moscow, the result of the war met these concerns. The war to all intents and purposes resolved the unresolved conflicts of South Ossetia and Abkhazia. It also, as then Russian Ambassador to NATO Dmitri Rogozin pointed out, seriously prejudiced Georgia's accession to NATO (there has been little advance on Georgian membership in the subsequent six years).[32]

These differing interpretations and the effect of this 'dual history' began to be felt in policy, which reflected a disagreement over existing mechanisms, for example the role of the NRC. The alliance suspended the formal workings of the NRC in response to what it saw as the disproportionate use of force by Russia (another source of disagreement between Russia and the West, since Moscow did not view the force used as disproportionate), while Moscow complained that the NRC should be exactly for discussing and resolving such differences – and suspended much of the military dimension of the relationship in protest.

The war also served to multiply differences over Moscow's proposals to rethink the European security architecture. Many members of NATO saw the war as yet more evidence for the existence of the alliance, another reason to emphasise collective defence and to reflect on Russia's obviously aggressive behaviour – and thus were less inclined to look favourably on the proposals. There was even a sense that Moscow would surely drop them after the war. The Russian authorities, however, saw the war as yet further proof of the failings of the current European security architecture – and the increased necessity of the proposals, which were subsequently pursued in the Corfu Process.

If the above has focused on the NATO–Russia relationship, similar problems course through the EU–Russia and US–Russia relationships. Both have been burdened by similar mistrust and crises.[33] In sum, together with the increasingly obvious divergence over common values that underpinned the Rome and St Petersburg summits in 2002 and 2003, these compounding disagreements, diverging agendas and dual histories emphasise the difference in how the world is seen in Moscow on one hand, and Western capitals and Brussels on the other, and how each sees the world differently and as a result misunderstands the other.

From Vladivostok to Vancouver: an agenda 'common' but not 'shared'

If compounding disagreements caused by differing histories are an important cause of tension, they do not by themselves explain the failure to develop strategic partnership. Returning to the question of Russia's involvement in Euro-Atlantic security, and peeling away further layers, other conceptual problems come to light and gaps in the interpretation of wider Euro-Atlantic developments become ever more obvious. The problem of definition of terminology goes to the heart of the strategic dissonance, and apparently similar terms are understood in a different way. This has meant that even when a cooperative agenda has been set on apparently common interests, its foundations have been weak and realistic prospects inherently limited, and problems have been exacerbated.

Diverging definitions, dividing security

A joint statement published following the NRC meeting in Lisbon in 2010 states that all nations represented 'recognise that the security of all the states in the Euro-Atlantic community is indivisible', and that they share common important interests and face common challenges.[34] This apparently innocuous and inclusive statement, however, was an optimistic assessment. Instead, a series of distinctions and divergences in understandings have hindered the development of an agenda for practical cooperation and its implementation.

Western officials have often hailed the major transformations that have taken place in Europe since 1991, saluting the vision and emergence of a Europe that is whole, free and at peace – a development that is in significant part the result of the enlargement of the EU and NATO. NATO's Strategic Concept emphasises the goal of a Europe 'whole, free and at peace' (and that NATO enlargement contributes to that goal), and the EU's security strategy stated in 2003 that Europe had 'never before been so prosperous, so secure, nor so free. The violence of the first half of the 20th Century has given way to a period of peace and stability unprecedented in European history.'[35] The Russian authorities have a very different view that asserts not just a lack of major transformation, but a Europe that is fragmented, insecure and bound by bloc mentalities inherited from the Cold War. This gap has had far reaching implications.

The first and best known implication, of course, is that many Russian observers and officials not only distrust NATO, but argue that it should have been disbanded at the end of the Cold War, since, following the dissolution of the Warsaw Pact, there was no need for it to exist.[36] Indeed, for many in Russia the alliance represents a hostile entity with designs not only on Russia's international influence, but even on Russia itself. These concerns include NATO's agenda, and its development of a wider international area of activity and partnership, particularly out of area operations under its own mandate.

The most significant concern, however, is that NATO's eastern enlargement is understood as bringing hostile forces closer to Russian borders, weakening of Russian influence in its own neighbourhood, and, in the context of NATO's out of area operations such as Afghanistan and wider partnership activities, part of a process of encirclement of Russia. Thus for Moscow the enlargement of NATO (particularly in tandem with the EU's enlargement) is seen in a negative light as a danger to Russia, with the potential to become a multiple political and military threat.

Russian concerns about and objections to NATO have been hard to grasp for Western leaders. Javier Solana stated in 2009 that 'for us the idea of Russia feeling threatened is absurd', and from the perspective of officials in NATO and the EU, 'Russia's Western borders have never looked so peaceful and unlikely to produce an attack as they do today. If anything, Western officials suggest NATO and EU enlargements have produced a strategic stability there that is probably unmatched in history.'[37] That view is not shared in Russia for a number of reasons, in large part because of the role of Western interventions both in Europe (Kosovo) and elsewhere in the world, whether in Iraq, Afghanistan or the Middle East, and the resultant chaos, have generated a high degree of concern in Moscow about US and NATO activities and intentions. Enlargement is therefore seen not in the light of spreading peace and stability, but in terms of possible intervention.

This basic but significant gap in understanding leads to the second and deeper implication, the different conceptualisation in Moscow of the nature of security threats and the wider Euro-Atlantic institutional architecture. Not only were there long-term unresolved conflicts in European security,[38] but the Euro-Atlantic space was fragmented into blocs that offer different levels of security and that coexist with friction. This reveals a further divergence about the core definitions of wider Euro-Atlantic security, particularly Rasmussen's point about the indivisibility.

In the West, the term 'indivisibility of security' is understood to relate to, first, the comprehensive nature of security in its three dimensions (human, economic and political-military); second, the indivisibility of security among states, including the right of all states to choose alliances and no state to have a sphere of privileged interests; and third, the recognition that European and Eurasian security are embedded in wider global security and that security within states is as much a part of security as security among states.[39]

In Moscow, however, the concept of indivisibility of security is understood to mean a whole and balanced pan-European common security space. This entails resolving what is seen as a two-tier European security architecture in which the pan-European structure, the OSCE, is seen to offer only political commitments, while regional organisations such as the EU and NATO offer legally binding political commitments. This division serves to expel states that are not members of these regional organisations and thus fragment European security. Thus Sergei Lavrov told the OSCE in June 2009 that, after the end of the Cold War, 'it did not in the event prove possible to put into place a stable and effective system that would bring together the countries of the West and East'. 'We have been unable to devise guarantees', he continued, 'to ensure the observance of the principle of the indivisibility of security', and it was possible today to violate the 'obligation to refrain from strengthening one's own security at the expense of the security of others'.[40] Without these legal commitments, Moscow

sees European security as divided, and fragmented by the enlargement of NATO and the EU.

This difference illustrates the divergence between the Western version of a Europe whole, free and at peace, and the Russian version
of a Europe bound by bloc mentality, fragmented and insecure, and
for NATO specifically, it again places the question of trust squarely
at the heart of the matter. Of course, the demand for legally binding guarantees appears as an echo of the broken promise to not
enlarge, discussed above. But it also has important ramifications
for the future of the relationship. Russian officials have stated, for
instance, that Moscow wants to see the proclaimed principles of
indivisibility of security translated into practice, and expects that
the principle will be confirmed by all, not only in words, but in
achieving a practical embodiment of how business is done.

But this divergence goes further, not just representing the gaps in
priorities between Russia and the West, and has an important bear-
ing on both the EU–Russia and NATO–Russia relationships, strik-
ing at the heart of a 'common' agenda and suggesting that rather
than pursuing the more comprehensive understanding of security
adopted by the EU and NATO, Russia was focused on specifically
political-military matters. The difference in understanding of the
indivisibility of security is the conceptual centrepiece of Moscow's
proposals for a new European security architecture. As Dmitri
Rogozin, then Russia's Permanent Representative to NATO, suggested, while the current arrangements may suit the West, they do
not suit Russia – 'we don't like it'.[41]

There are numerous examples of apparently common vocabulary reflecting different concepts and understandings of European
security, including on post-Cold War questions. These discrepancies
mean that interests and threats may be 'common', but they are not
'shared': in other words a list may be drawn up of issues that both
the West and Russia see as important, but in which each side defines
differently the nature of the problem, where it lies in its hierarchy of
priorities, and how best to approach it.

International terrorism

Terrorism is a prominent common challenge for the West
and Russia, illustrated by attacks on London, Madrid, New
York, Paris and Moscow and the attempts to develop counter-
terrorism cooperation. But while some technical cooperation has
taken place, as noted above, and while the longer-term effects on

relations of the Boston bombings in April 2013 and the subsequent trial, conviction and sentencing of Dzhokhar Tsarnaev remain to be seen, it depicts well the gap between 'common' and 'shared'. Indeed, it illustrates the complex knot of disagreements, dissonant definitions and divergent priorities that hamper Russia's relations with the West.[42]

The overarching problem has been the considerable difficulty in establishing a common definition of who terrorists are and how to deal with them, largely because this was entwined with wider disagreements between the West and Russia, particularly the lengthy war in Chechnya. Many in the West saw the war in terms of Chechen independence from Russia, and referred to the Chechens as freedom fighters or rebels – whereas the Russian authorities defined them as terrorists, as noted in the introduction by the problems caused in interpretation and use of the word 'povstanets'.

This difference took on practical ramifications when Chechens who had fled Russia, such as Akhmed Zakayev, were granted asylum in the EU. As a result, the disagreement evolved, since it widened the debate into contentious and politicised areas of the relationship – the West placed emphasis on Russian oppression and flawed legal processes, and the Russian authorities accused the West of double standards, harbouring terrorists and thus undermining the common anti-terrorist front.

At the same time, this has drawn attention to different approaches to countering terrorism. While the Russian authorities have attempted to increase economic and social measures to counter terrorism in the North Caucasus, the approach has retained a very robust security element. This could be defined as 'catch and destroy', which is at strong variance with the West's more idealistic approach, particularly EU members, which could be described more in terms of attempts to 'find and try'.

Although much of the focus in the West has been on Putin's harsh approach to terrorists, Dmitri Medvedev was equally robust while he was president, asserting the need to 'stamp out the scum with unflinching resolve', and, when they were caught they were to be killed without hesitation or emotion. As president, he also introduced new legislation that meant that terrorists should not be tried by jury but by selected judges and that penalties for those associated with terrorists, 'even those who cooked and cleaned for them', should be toughened. This forceful approach has led both to widespread criticism from many quarters in the West about Russia's human rights record (criticism rejected by Moscow) and meant that

Western states have had to be careful in advancing cooperation with Moscow, concerned that it might smack of endorsing these policies and methods.

A further complication is that if the Russian authorities accuse the West of double standards, there are also senior figures who accuse the West of not only of harbouring terrorists, but actively supporting them and even being terrorists themselves. Accusations focus on two levels. First, numerous senior Russian security personnel, including Putin himself, have asserted that the West has provided direct support for Chechen terrorists. Second, senior political and security service personnel suggest that this is part of a wider policy, and that the West's war on terror is a tool for advancing US interests and keeping Russia focused on the North Caucasus rather than playing a wider international role. For Moscow, there is ambiguity in the position of the West. Although it pursues a war on terror, at the same time it has supplied weapons to rebel groups in Libya and Syria.[43] Therefore, Moscow argues that the West is supporting its own enemy, since these rebel groups have links to Al Qaeda, and giving these groups such assistance destabilises international security and may facilitate the migration of the terrorist threat to Russia.

Finally, for Moscow, counter-terrorism is predominantly a Russian *domestic* question, focused on the terrorist activities emanating from the North Caucasus. This complicates and abbreviates cooperation because it links it to questions of Russian sovereignty: real cooperation might entail Western security services working with the Russian security services on Russian territory to resolve a Russian problem. As we have just seen, however, many of the senior Russian authorities involved believe that Western security forces aid and abet terrorism in Russia.

Cyber security

Cyber security is another example of diverging definitions and conceptions of apparently common challenges. In 2012, although the USA and the UK again sought cooperation with Russia and China on cyber security issues, a series of conceptual and linguistic problems have hampered cooperation. Although the language suggests superficial similarity, there are numerous differences in emphasis and approach, and they suggest that these gaps apply at several levels. At the highest conceptual level, there is no commonly agreed view of what constitutes cyber security – Russian and Chinese doctrines and writing do not subscribe to the Euro-Atlantic consensus on the nature and future of cyberspace, and emphasise a very different set of security challenges. Moscow, for instance, has long adopted a wider approach to information security rather than the narrower Western focus on cyber issues.

Beneath this conceptual level, there are further differences. Keir Giles and William Hagestad point to fundamental incompatibilities in terminology, noting that in some cases, terms have no direct translation, and in others there are important discrepancies. In English, cyber warfare consists of cyber attacks that are authorised by state actors against the cyber infrastructure in conjunction with a government campaign. In Russian, combat actions in cyberspace are cyber actions carried out by states, or groups of states or organised political groups against cyber infrastructure that form part of a military campaign.[44] As with the Cold War era understandings of 'peace' discussed above, the differences may appear slight, but the ramifications are significant. Consequences are two-fold – not only is progress in building cooperation hampered, but it contributes to the sense of dual history and divergent conclusions from the same evidence described above, illustrated by the cyber attack on Estonia in 2007.

'Soft power'

One final example of divergence over apparently common vocabulary that has emerged recently is the distinction in understanding of 'soft power'. This returns us to a higher level of how the West and Russia see international affairs more broadly – and, in a sense, although it may appear subtle, it represents the culmination of the three points outlined through this chapter: dual histories, differing conclusions from the same evidence and divergent definitions of apparently common language.

In the West, soft power is understood to mean the ability to affect others to get the outcomes one wants through attraction, rather than coercion or payment. Doing so, according to Joseph Nye, means 'economising on carrots and sticks'.[45] Soft power relies primarily on culture, political values and attractive foreign policies to persuade others to want what you want. For much of the post-Cold War era, most Western observers have focused on Russia's use of the traditional tools of hard power and coercion and payment.[46]

In 2013, however, Moscow published a new Foreign Policy Concept that stated the need for Russian diplomacy to increase its use of soft power assets. But this evolution has taken place in the context of the so-called 'Arab Spring', which has lent a very specific colour to the Russian understanding of what soft power is and how it is used. For Moscow, soft power represents Western interventionism as a destabilising force, part of a regime change or 'Colour Revolution' agenda: the Russian concept asserted the illegal use of Western soft power and human rights concepts to pressure sovereign states and intervene in their internal affairs to destabilise them by manipulating public opinion. Similarly, Moscow accused the USA of encouraging support for opposition parties in Russia at the time of the protest demonstrations in December 2011 and early 2012. Putin suggested that hundreds of millions of dollars of foreign money had been spent on influencing Russian domestic politics, and accused Hillary Clinton of giving the signal for activists to begin the demonstrations with the support of the USA.[47]

In short, if for the West soft power is a stabilising feature of international relations, since it minimises the need for force, for Moscow, soft power is different, and is about the need to engage in an information campaign, and provide state support both to promote Russian culture and language and to counter 'soft attacks' on Russia. For Moscow, soft power is a tool that can only be guided by the state (an interpretation not shared in the West) and is perhaps better defined, therefore, as 'soft strength'.

The Crimea crisis and the war in Ukraine: compounding strategic dissonance

The war in Ukraine compounded and intensified the strong sense of dissonance between the West and Russia, weaving together these threads of mutual distrust, the divergent histories and different conclusions from the same evidence, the conflicting views of the Euro-Atlantic security architecture and the role of NATO (and EU) enlargement, and the use of soft power, information and propaganda. Many of the old themes returned to the fore: the question of NATO's non-enlargement promise, for instance, and, as discussed in Chapter 1, the debate about a 'new Cold War', with many comparing Putin not just to Stalin, suggesting that he sought to rebuild the USSR, but to Hitler and late 1930s Nazi Germany.

Often referred to as the Ukraine 'crisis', a turning point or sudden change, and a decisive moment, it was more accurately a 'paroxysm' – an episode of increased acuteness or severity, a sudden worsening of the symptoms. Indeed, the compounded intensity of the paroxysm reflected the most serious deterioration in the West's relations with Russia for many years, much deeper and more prolonged than even the effects of the Russo-Georgia War.

There is much to be said about the war, but three important points stand out for mention here. First is the difference in how the events in Ukraine were understood in Western capitals and in Moscow – and who was to blame for them. It is perhaps the most pronounced example of the drawing of different conclusions from the same body of evidence. As one experienced Western observer remarked, even the start date of the war is disputed: for the West, the war began with the Russian occupation of Crimea in February. In Moscow, however, those who followed military affairs would argue that because the Ukrainian troops in Crimea did not fire back, it was not a war – and that the war began with Kyiv's 'anti-terrorist operation' against the separatists in Donetsk and Lugansk.[48]

But, importantly, it also showed an increasing divergence, as the two sides began to draw different conclusions from *different* bodies of evidence about the same developments. The situation might be said, therefore, to have evolved from 'dual histories' to 'duelling histories'.

Differences emerged on almost every issue, including over the nature of the end of the Yanukovich regime – with Western emphasis on a democratic upheaval against corrupt leadership, and Moscow asserting a US-backed, unconstitutional coup, about the role of and number of fascists in Ukrainian politics, about the referendum in Crimea and about the shooting down of flight MH17, and about the roles of Ukrainian forces. The differences reflected the point that Western capitals and Moscow were drawing on separate narratives – the West seeing it as an extension of the post-Cold War democratic transition and Moscow seeing it as a new wrinkle in the Western-generated 'Colour Revolutions' and instability. This is related to the confusion caused by the term 'hybrid' warfare: many in the West suggested that Moscow's actions in Ukraine reflected a new form of Russian warfare, one largely invented by Chief of General Staff Valeriy Gerasimov. This caused some confusion in Moscow, where 'hybrid' warfare was seen as a response to new Western forms of conflict understood as 'war by humanitarian intervention' or 'war by Colour Revolution', as illustrated by the so-called 'Arab Spring' and now being deployed in Ukraine by the USA.

These differences were also evident in regular mutual accusations of lying, exchanges of 'fact sheets',[49] and assertions of each side living in different realities. Angela Merkel, for instance, was cited in the German newspaper as having wondered whether Putin was 'no longer in touch with reality', for instance, and Vitaliy Churkin, Russian Ambassador to the UN, suggested that Western powers 'distorted reality'.[50]

Second, and building on this, the war has had a significant practical impact on relations. Important aspects of the institutional framework have been suspended: Russia's participation in the G8, for instance, as has the work of the NRC. The negotiations for Russia's accession to the Organisation for Economic Cooperation and Development (OECD), begun in 2007, were suspended in March 2014, and the Council of Europe voted to have the Russian delegation suspended from the Parliamentary Assembly – after which there has been prolonged discussion about whether Russia would remain in the Council.[51]

Moreover, the two sides have begun to accuse the other of undermining the post-Cold War international order. NATO (and some of its member states) have asserted that in annexing Crimea and intervening in eastern Ukraine, Russia is undermining the post-Cold War European security order. Russia, for its part, has asserted that the USA and NATO have been a destabilising force in international affairs, citing interventions in Kosovo, Afghanistan, Iraq, Libya and now Ukraine.

This has led to a range of practical responses by each side. The reciprocal imposition of sanctions has significantly affected the scale of business and economic cooperation. And the build-up of NATO has emphasised that Russia poses a challenge to some of its members and implemented measures designed to provide reassurance – including the Readiness Action Plan and a significantly increased schedule of exercises.

Third, the combination of these effects has accelerated mutual concerns about the 'soft power' interference of the other. Some in the West have suggested that Russian military actions in Ukraine were a response to Putin's declining popularity – that the protest demonstrations in Russia in 2011 reflected this decline, and that, combined with the economic slowdown, the Russian president had become vulnerable. The annexation of Crimea reversed this, as Putin's popularity rose to over 80 per cent: thus some suggested that Russia might repeat such operations in response to any future waning of support for Putin or in response to internal trouble within

Russia.[52] The protest demonstrations and the extent of decline of popular support for Putin will be addressed in the next chapter, but it is important to note that there is considerable concern in the West about possible Russian interference in the Baltic states, about Moscow inciting ethnic Russian minorities there to destabilise the states and challenge NATO's defence commitments. At the same time, Moscow's interpretation of events in Ukraine and the imposition by the USA and EU of sanctions accelerated concerns in the Russian leadership about an attempt by the USA to use public organisations, NGOs and other politicised organisations to 'destabilise the internal situation' in Russia and 'planning actions' for the electoral 2016–2018 cycle.[53]

The war in Ukraine provoked a serious deterioration in relations between the West (particularly the USA, NATO and the EU) and Russia, therefore, and is a serious problem in its own right. But it is a symptom of the wider strategic dissonance: fundamental differences in understandings of, and interests in Euro-Atlantic security have become ever more evident, relating to the post-Cold War European architecture and the question of the indivisibility of Euro-Atlantic security, and the nature of Russia's representation in it. This is a deep division in how European security and the roles of NATO, the EU, the OSCE and Russia are understood by the various actors, and is at the heart of most of the current and likely future problems in European security, from the war in Ukraine to arms control, unresolved conflicts and ballistic missile defence.

Although the war has dominated attention, the problem of missile defence has long simmered, and compounds the problems still further. Again, important misinterpretations abound on both sides: the USA has long insisted that the programme poses no threat to Russia, and Moscow has long rejected this. Underlying this is the gap in messaging: what looks from the US side like flexibility for the programme to develop in accordance with an evolving threat, to Russia seems inconsistent, unpredictable and destabilising.[54]

The effects of the war in Ukraine are more profound not only because of the suspension of cooperation, but because the room for manoeuvre for resuscitating relations is more limited than on previous occasions. If, as discussed above, in the past crises have led to greater development in the relationship, it is difficult to see how a new 'reset' could be implemented and to what end. Mutual trust has reached a very low ebb, and the agenda for practical cooperation appears limited, while the scope for further differences, whether over missile defence or over elections in Russia in 2016 and 2018, is considerable. Equally, there are increasingly obvious and important differences in values. The attempts to create a 'strategic partnership' ground to a halt in the mid 2000s, and a 'values gap' became increasingly pronounced between the West and Russia over the nature of democracy, particularly in terms of human rights and the role of the state in society.

The idea of a values gap, however, no longer illustrates what is an increasing tangible sense of friction between the more liberal values of what might be termed 'EU Europe', and the more conservative values that Russia appears to advocate. Putin stated in 2013 that Euro-Atlantic countries are 'rejecting their roots, including the Christian values that constitute the roots of Western civilisation', and 'denying moral principles and all traditional entities', and are 'aggressively trying to export this model all over the world', 'taking a direct path to degradation and primitivism resulting in a profound demographic and moral crisis'.[55] This increasing friction, illustrated by the wars in Ukraine and Syria, has given rise to a sense of competition between the West and Russia. In many ways, therefore, Russia has moved from being 'a part of Europe to a Europe apart'.

Notes

1 H. Kissinger, *World Order: Reflections on the Character of Nations and the Course of History* (London: Allen Lane, 2014), pp. 312–316.
2 M. McFaul, 'Confronting Putin's Russia', *New York Times* (23 March 2014).
3 Correspondence with Jacob Kipp, May 2015.
4 'Speech at meeting with German political, parliamentary and civic leaders' (5 June 2008), http://archive.kremlin.ru/eng/speeches/2008/06/05/2203_type82912type82914type84779_202153.shtml.
5 'Meeting of the Valdai international discussion club' (19 September 2013), http://eng.kremlin.ru/news/6007.
6 S. Lavrov, 'Remarks at MGIMO University' (1 September 2009), www.mid.ru/brp_4.nsf/0/A91BB143AE7FD9CCC325762600393FE0.
7 Anders Fogh Rasmussen, 'NATO and Russia: a new beginning', speech at Carnegie Endowment (18 September 2009), www.nato.int/cps/en/natolive/opinions_57640.htm?selectedLocale=en.
8 'Direct line with Vladimir Putin' (17 April 2014), http://eng.kremlin.ru/news/7034.
9 'Interview nemetskomy izdaniyu Bild' [Interview to German newspaper *Bild*], Kremlin (11 January 2016), http://kremlin.ru/events/president/news/51154.

10 The author is grateful to Dov Lynch for a series of exchanges about 'dissonance' between Russia and the West.

11 V. Baranovsky, 'Russia: a part of Europe or apart from Europe?', *International Affairs*, 76:3 (2000), pp. 443–458; T. Casier and K. Malfliet (eds), *Is Russia a European Power? The Position of Russia in a New Europe* (Leuven: Leuven University Press, 1998), and the debate between Jonathan Haslam and William Odom about Russia's reintegration into the West, whether it was a place delayed, a place denied, or too many places at the table. J. Haslam, 'Russia's seat at the table: a place delayed or a place denied?', *International Affairs*, 74:1 (1998); W. Odom, 'Russia's several seats at the table', *International Affairs*, 74:4 (1998).

12 The Four Common Spaces are: the Common Economic Space, the Common Space for Freedom, Security and Justice, the Common Space of External Security, and the Common Space of Research and Education, including cultural issues. www.eeas.europa.eu/russia/common_spaces/.

13 The Road Maps are available at: www.eeas.europa.eu/russia/docs/roadmap_economic_en.pdf.

14 The NATO–Russia Council, www.nato.int/cps/en/natolive/topics_50091.htm. 14 December 2013.

15 On this important but forgotten episode and the positive impact it had on UK–Russia relations, see I. Riches, 'Saving the AS-28', in A. Monaghan (ed.), *The UK and Russia – a Troubled Relationship. Part I*, Russian Series 7/17 (Swindon: Defence Academy of the UK, 2007).

16 NATO's relations with Russia, NATO (3 December 2013), www.nato.int/cps/en/natolive/topics_50090.htm.

17 For details of each, see www.nato-russia-council.info/en/articles/2012 1123-nrc-10-years-standex/; www.nato-russia-council.info/en/articles/20130513-nrc-cai-update-april/.

18 Readers will have their preferred crises or disagreements, but may note the absence from the discussion here of wider issues such as Russian activity in the former Soviet space often described by Western observers and officials as 'neo-imperial' or attempts to 'recreate the USSR', or more specific ones such as the 'spy rock' scandal that affected UK–Russia relations in 2006 and the cyber attack on Estonia in 2007. Each of these episodes represents a complex and contentious knot of issues, many of which have long roots. The list sketched out here seeks only to illustrate that numerous problems old and new came to roost in a comparatively short period to generate dissonance.

19 Estonia, Lithuania, Latvia, Slovenia, Slovakia, Bulgaria and Romania were invited to join NATO at the Prague summit in 2002, becoming members in 2004. Ivanov cited in D. Alexeev, *NATO Enlargement: A Russian Outlook*, CSRC Russia Series, 04/33 (Swindon: Defence Academy of the UK, 2004).

20 D. Schmidt, 'Russia's NGO legislation: new (and old) developments', *Russian Analytical Digest*, 03/06, www.css.ethz.ch/publications/pdfs/RAD-3-2-6.pdf; A. Kamhi, 'The Russian NGO law: potential conflicts

with international, national and foreign legislation', *The International Journal of Not-for-Profit Law*, 9:1 (December 2006), www.icnl.org/research/journal/vol9iss1/art_6.htm.

21 P. Kerr, 'Russia, Iran sign deal to fuel Bushehr reactor', *Arms Control Today* (November 2006), www.armscontrol.org/act/2006_11/RussiaIran.

22 A. Kassianova, 'Russian weapons sales to Iran: why they are unlikely to stop', PONARS Policy Memo, 427 (December 2006), http://csis.org/files/media/csis/pubs/pm_0427.pdf.

23 'Cheney rebukes Russia on rights', *New York Times* (5 May 2006), www.nytimes.com/2006/05/05/world/europe/04cnd-cheney.html?_r=0.

24 D. Trenin, 'Russia leaves the West', *Foreign Affairs* (July/August 2006), www.foreignaffairs.com/articles/61735/dmitri-trenin/russia-leaves-the-west.

25 At its summit in Bucharest in 2008, NATO declared that both Georgia and Ukraine would join the Alliance, albeit at an unspecified later date.

26 D. Lynch, 'The Corfu process', in A. Monaghan (ed.), *The Indivisibility of Security: Russia and Euro-Atlantic Security* (Rome: NATO Defence College, 2010).

27 Zatuliveter was exonerated by the Special Immigration Appeals Commission in November 2011.

28 B. Akçapar, 'Arms control: the canary in the coal mine', in Monaghan, *The Indivisibility of Security*.

29 'Russia restarts Cold War patrols', *BBC News* (17 August 2007), http://news.bbc.co.uk/1/hi/world/europe/6950986.stm. Putin did not mention, however, that one of the reasons for Moscow's unilateral decision to stop flying in 1992 was a lack of fuel.

30 'Illarionov: Russia lost the Georgia War', *The Other Russia* (13 August 2008), www.theotherrussia.org/2008/08/13/illarionov-russia-lost-the-georgian-war/.

31 S. Blank, 'Georgia: the war Russia lost', *Military Review*, 88:6 (November–December 2008), www.questia.com/library/journal/1G1-189653704/georgia-the-war-russia-lost#articleDetails.

32 A. Monaghan, 'Conflict in the South Caucasus', *Immediate Report*, NATO Defence College (August 2008); K. Giles, 'Understanding the Georgia conflict two years on', Parts 1 and 2, *Reviews*, NATO Defence College (September 2010).

33 For an overview of US–Russia relations, see A. Stent, *The Limits of Partnership: U.S.-Russia Relations in the Twenty First Century* (Oxford: Princeton University Press, 2014).

34 NATO–Russia Council Joint Statement (20 November 2010), www.nato.int/cps/en/natolive/news_68871.htm.

35 *Active Engagement, Modern Defence. Strategic Concept for the Defence and Security of the Members of the North Atlantic Treaty Organisation* (19–20 November 2010), www.nato.int/cps/en/natolive/official_texts_68580.htm. *A Secure Europe in a Better World: European*

Security Strategy, Brussels (12 December 2003), www.consilium. europa.eu/uedocs/cmsUpload/78367.pdf.

36 In one lecture, for instance, Lavrov stated that 'the existence of NATO has become a problem for all'. 'Remarks at MGIMO University'.

37 B. Fagerberg, 'The EU and the debate on Euro-Atlantic security', in Monaghan, *The Indivisibility of Security*, pp. 48–51.

38 D. Lynch, *Engaging Eurasia's Separatist States: Unresolved Conflicts and de facto States* (Washington, DC: USIPP, 2004).

39 Remarks at the OSCE Council Plenary by James Steinberg, US Deputy Secretary of State (1 December 2009), www.state.gov/s/d/former/ steinberg/remarks/2009/169327.htm.

40 S. Lavrov, 'Statement at the opening session of the OSCE Annual Security Review Conference', Vienna (23 June 2009), www.mid.ru/ brp_4.nsf/0/ADED9C34EE795D2BC32575DE003DECD1.

41 'Roundtable Summary: Dmitri Rogozin: Russia, NATO and the future of European security', Chatham House Roundtable (20 February 2009), www.chathamhouse.org/sites/files/chathamhouse/public/Research/ Russia%20and%20Eurasia/200209rogozin.pdf.

42 This section draws on A. Monaghan, *The Moscow Metro Bombings and Terrorism in Russia*, NDC Research Paper No. 59 (June 2010), www.ndc.nato.int/research/series.php?icode=1.

43 Another ambiguity lies in how Moscow sees NATO's role in Afghanistan: while NATO's presence is in some respects positive since it saves Russia having to fight terrorism there, Moscow has opposed a more permanent NATO presence in Central Asia.

44 K. Giles and W. Hagestad II, 'Divided by a common language: cyber definitions in Russian, Chinese and English', paper for 5th International Conference on Cyber Conflict, 2013, www.ccdcoe.org/ publications/2013proceedings/d3r1s1_giles.pdf.

45 J. Nye, 'What China and Russia don't get about soft power', *Foreign Policy* (29 April 2013), www.foreignpolicy.com/articles/2013/04/29/ what_china_and_russia_don_t_get_about_soft_power.

46 J. Sherr, *Hard Diplomacy and Soft Coercion: Russia's Influence Abroad* (London: Chatham House, 2013).

47 Cited in 'Putin blames Moscow protests on US', *Financial Times* (8 December 2011).

48 Correspondence with Jacob Kipp, May 2015.

49 'President Putin's fiction: 10 false claims about Ukraine', Office of the Spokesperson, State Department (5 March 2014), www.state. gov/r/pa/prs/ps/2014/03/222988.html; 'Russian fiction the sequel: 10 more false claims about Ukraine', Office of the Spokesperson, State Department (13 April 2014); 'Address by the President of the Russian Federation' (18 March 2014), http://eng.kremlin.ru/news/6889; 'Direct line with Vladimir Putin' (17 April 2014), http://eng.kremlin.ru/ news/7034.

50 Churkin cited in 'Ukraine crisis: Russian convoy prompts Western anger', *BBC News* (23 August 2014), www.bbc.co.uk/news/world-europe-28903829.
51 'Russia delegation suspended from Council of Europe over Crimea', *Guardian* (10 April 2014).
52 *Towards the Next Defence and Security Review: Part II – NATO.* House of Commons Defence Committee. Third Report of Session 2014–2015. HC 358 (London: The Stationery Office, 31 July 2014), p. 19.
53 'Zasedanie kollegii FSB' [Federal Security Service board meeting] (26 March 2015), http://kremlin.ru/events/president/news/49006.
54 This point is owed to Keir Giles. Correspondence with the author, September 2013.
55 'Meeting of the Valdai international discussion club' (19 September 2013), http://en.kremlin.ru/events/president/news/19243.

3

'Reflexive transitionology' and the 'end of Putin'

The inevitability of Russia's change?

The protest demonstrations in December 2011 and early 2012 have become a watershed event in the Western discussion of Russia, and the backdrop for much subsequent comment and analysis – including, as noted above, as part of the undercurrent of the war in Ukraine. At the time, they were seen by many in the West to reflect the emergence (finally) of the urban middle class as a revitalising force in Russian political life after the 'de-democratisation' of Vladimir Putin's second term as president and the disappointments of Dmitri Medvedev's term. The almost unanimous enthusiasm the protests generated in the mainstream Western discussion led to the emergence of an expert orthodoxy that they represented the beginning of the end of the Putin era, that Russia was, at last, moving on.

Observers suggested that the 'amazing' mass protest gatherings were a 'new phenomena', and emphasised that they 'rattled' the Russian authorities – even that the regime was insecure, 'on the defensive' and had 'lost its nerve' and was in 'inexorable decline', and then, if making mention of some electoral 'concessions', focused on the more 'ruthless' repressive measures implemented by the Putin leadership in response. Thus, the 'democracy embattled' narrative was emphasised, illustrated through the metaphor used by some of progressive democratic spring to regressive authoritarian winter. Subsequently, the events have been roughly hewn down to an abridged story of public frustration with corruption and (especially) the cynical power swap in September 2011 between Medvedev and Putin, the fraudulent parliamentary elections in December 2011, reflecting the (surprise) decline of the United Russia (UR) party, the party of power associated with and led by Vladimir Putin (and, since May 2012, Dmitri Medvedev),[1] followed by the eruption of liberal 'white ribbon' middle class protest, pressure on Putin and, instead of adjusting to the new realities, his revival of authoritarian repression in response – not a sign of strength but an indication of weakness, a futile attempt to dam inevitable societal and political change.[2] As with all such frameworks, there are elements of truth to each of these parts of the story: there is considerable public frustration with corruption and the leadership, both in terms of UR and the Putin–Medvedev power swap. The elections were flawed, and the opposition has been put under pressure since Putin's return to the Kremlin: both 'non-systemic'[3] opposition leaders and protesters have been jailed.

But it is also a major abridgment, shaving off much of what makes these events important for understanding the evolution of Russian politics: the broad-brush strokes glossing over Russian history, blotting out political complexities and important nuances, and rendering a simplistic picture of Putin against the dissidents. As one Western journalist correctly suggested, the response to the demonstrations was a 'knee-jerk approval of the opposition, an instinctive keenness for my enemy's enemy', but without a real understanding of the nature of the protest groups,[4] and, he might have added, ignoring many salient features of the political landscape that did not fit the abridged story. Indeed, in many ways, this mainstream orthodoxy was an automatic response to the stimulus of seeing protests as precipitating democratic upheaval and the end of Putin, a reflexive return to 'transitionology' and the hope for democratic change in Russia.

In the excitement, the protest demonstrations, often hailed as 'unprecedented', were removed from their Russian context, both in terms of previous post-Soviet era Russian protests, but also that election year which lasted not from the announcement of the power swap in September, and then from the parliamentary elections in December 2011 to the presidential ones in March 2012, but from the regional elections held in March 2011 through to spring 2012. The protests were also exaggerated both in their scale and in their liberalism. Many were seduced by the claims of the leaders of the opposition, particularly those who appeared to be new, such as Alexei Navalniy, who were seen to be 'democracy campaigners', even 'Western', in the way they conducted their campaign using social media.[5] As discussed in Chapter 1, commentators often simply reiterated the estimates of the protest organisers, the scale of the protests ballooning accordingly. At the same time, the emphasis was placed on the pro-democracy and liberal nature of the protesters – the university educated, creative elements of society, the urban middle class represented by the white ribbon. Removed from their Russian context, they were placed instead in the contexts of the Arab Spring and the collapse of the USSR, in effect a second round of the 'end of history'.

The mainstream Western discussion about the protests and the actions of the authorities thus became saturated with the repetition of old themes. This was both explicit – repetition of simplified images of Kremlin 'puppet masters' and 'crackdowns' on the opposition, which had been the main theme of debate since 2004; and apparently unconscious, in that they repeated almost verbatim the debate that had taken place about the possibility of a Colour Revolution in Russia and Putin being forced from power in 2005.[6]

Taken together, therefore, the mainstream debate about Russian domestic politics has often complemented the view about Russia being a member of the Western family of nations discussed in Chapter 2: initial optimism about Russia voluntarily joining the West was replaced by hope that external factors such as the economic crisis in 2008 would undermine resistance, even *oblige* it to join the West. Domestically, hopes that first Putin, then Medvedev would lead liberal change that would underpin partnership with the West gave way to hope of internal change in which a new, post-Soviet and more Western-oriented generation would emerge to replace them and lead change. This has remained strong, re-emerging in 2014 as observers hoped to see the sanctions leading to the Russian population exerting pressure on Putin to change his policies towards Ukraine, and even pointing to the possibility of protest-led regime change in Russia.

This chapter attempts to see if there is more to wring out of this year of elections and protests in terms of understanding Russian politics. This may provide not just a more rounded and nuanced picture of these important developments, but also perhaps some material for learning lessons from the episode in the run up to the parliamentary elections scheduled for 2016 and presidential elections scheduled for 2018.

It explores the year in three related parts. The first explores the results of the December elections, contextualising the decline of UR. The second part turns to reflect on the protest demonstrations, comparing them to previous protests, then exploring their size, make-up and sustainability, before turning to the presidential elections and Putin's victory. The third part changes focus to look at the political 'reset' that the leadership has attempted to implement.

United Russia's third election blues and the rise of the political left

UR has been the dominant political party in Russia for much of the Putin era. Formed in 2001 with the merging of the Unity and Fatherland-All Russia parties, the party won 37 per cent and 225 seats in parliament in 2003. In 2007, in a climate of strong economic growth, it won a landslide 64.3 per cent, and 315 seats – full control of parliament and a 'super-majority' that meant that enabled it to change the constitution, and also command of the parliamentary committees. In 2011, support fell to an official tally of 49 per cent, retaining 238 seats in parliament.

For many in the West, this apparently precipitous decline in the party's fortunes (as one prominent Western observer suggested, 'in summer 2011, it had been widely believed that come December 2011, UR would obtain the super-majority it had achieved in 2007'), combined with the flaws in the election process were the main points.[7] Flaws in the process included the context of blurred lines between the government and UR, and the use of government/administrative resources slanting the campaign in the party's favour, a 'cleansed' electoral field on which there were no credible alternatives, and the denial of registration to several political parties narrowing competition. At election time, numerous criticisms emerged, particularly regarding large-scale falsifications of the results, with attention focusing on procedural violations such as ballot-box stuffing and an attempt to limit the role of Golos, an independent election monitoring and civil society organisation, as well as cyber attacks on a number of politically more liberal organisations. The newspaper *Vedomosti* ran a front-page article trying to work out how a party that appeared to have won 25 per cent ended up with 45 per cent.[8] Even despite these flaws in the election process, therefore, UR registered a loss of 15 per cent and 77 seats, a (surprise) result deemed by many to be a disaster for the party, particularly its loss of the super-majority. And it certainly reflected a decline in wider public support for the party, known to many in liberal Russian and Western circles – as a result of Alexei Navalniy's anti-corruption campaign – as the 'Party of Crooks and Thieves'.

Some context helps to parse this decline. If the job switch between Putin and Medvedev in September was a cause for protest, this built on a longer-term dissatisfaction born out of pervasive corruption and the prolonged and deep impact of the 2008 economic crisis. Together, this combined to emphasise a sense of 'third election/fourth term' syndrome of frustration, widespread voter fatigue and increasing opposition to UR. Indeed, support for UR had already been in decline since 2009.[9] This was reflected in the March 2011 regional elections and then pre-election polls that autumn. Although UR had won the March elections, in seven of the 12 regions in which elections were held it gained 45 per cent or less of the vote.[10] In October 2011, polls held across Russia published by Russian media suggested that UR would win some 41 per cent of the vote. The polling organisation VtsIOM thought it likely that the party would go on to win some 50 per cent in December, though noted that it would struggle in Moscow (where it had polled 29 per cent in October), and St Petersburg (where it had polled 31 per cent in October).

UR's results in December were not, therefore, so much the precipitous collapse of support but the illustration of longer-term decline: as one Russian commentator suggested, the March regional elections had shown the relative weakening of UR and the rise in the protest mood.[11] Others suggested that it was a 'serious warning for the party, illustrating an increasing mood to protest in the regions', and that it reflected the decreasing effectiveness of UR's 'time-honed electioneering strategies' – 'administrative resources, pressure on state employees to go to the polls to "vote the right way", and most important, capitalising on the popularity of party leader and Prime Minister Vladimir Putin'.[12] Officials too, noted the decline: in November 2010 Vladislav Surkov, then first deputy head of the presidential administration and responsible for domestic politics, had already suggested that the party would find it much more complicated to achieve the same results as it had in 2007 and that important (constitutional) decisions would have to be taken in coalition.[13]

If the spotlight lit up UR's losses, though, it is important to note the other side of this coin – all of the parliamentary opposition parties, known as the 'systemic opposition', gained.[14] Although there was no substantial shift in power, there was a shift in balance in the parliament as the other parties gained representation not just in seats but in parliamentary committees: UR lost control of nearly half of the parliamentary committees. UR deputies now chair 15 of the 29 committees. While opposition parties mainly lead second-tier committees, it is noteworthy that Vladimir Komoedov, a Communist Party deputy, chairs the Defence Committee, and Leonid Slutsky, an Liberal Democratic Party of Russia (LDPR) deputy, chairs the Committee for the Commonwealth of Independent States.

A shift to the left?

Of particular note was the success of the political left. The Communist Party (KPRF) gained most, winning 19 per cent of the vote and 92 seats, an increase of 35 seats. The KPRF has long been the main systemic party of opposition in Russian politics across the country, a point again illustrated in the March 2011 regional elections, in which it had come second in nine of the 12 regions. December's results exceeded expectations, however, and enabled the KPRF to bargain for leadership of six parliamentary committees. Despite such gains, the KPRF was not close to winning power, nor is it widely popular beyond a core vote. But support for the party remained stable in 2011: in the regional elections in March, the party polled 18–25 per cent, similar to its results in both the parliamentary and presidential elections, and two interesting points emerged.

First, the KPRF led some opposition in parliament: it generated a petition to dismiss Medvedev's government – and gained over 100,000 signatures. As one Russian journalist noted, the government would not fall because the KPRF wanted it to, but the scale of the petition meant that it had to be heard in parliament and would cause concern in the government. Putin himself observed that he gave 'credit to the legal opposition, and the [KPRF] one of its strongest components, for reacting to what the authorities do. This is the opposition's constitutional right ... it's knowing there's a pike in the river that keeps the carp alert. I therefore give credit to the KPRF for its persistence ... but if you're asking me, would I vote for the government's resignation, my answer would be "no"'.[15]

Second, what was perhaps more surprising in the December elections was the level of support for the KPRF in Moscow. With St Petersburg, Moscow is usually considered to be the best ground for the liberal opposition parties. Instead, in December 2011, it was the KPRF that offered the main opposition in the capital. An initial report by *Vedomosti* on 6 December based on exit polls suggested that UR had won 27.5 per cent of the vote, while the KPRF had won many areas in Moscow and 25.5 per cent of the overall vote in the city, with the liberal Yabloko party in only fourth place with 15.7 per cent. The paper reported that in the Gagarin region, for instance, UR won 23.7 per cent, while the KPRF won 26.35 per cent.

Outside Moscow, the KPRF won in numerous regions including Vladivostok, Ryazan, Orel, Voronezh, Irkutsk, Bratsk, Angarsk,

Ekaterinburg, Omsk and Novosibirsk.[16] The close-run result in Moscow was deemed illegitimate and challenged by Communist Party activists who argued that victory had been stolen from them, and some of those demonstrating at Bolotnaya Square on 10 December were communists calling to be 'given back their city'. This re-emerged in 2013, with a study that suggested that the KPRF had even defeated UR in December 2011.[17]

The other aspect of this shift to the political left were the results of the centre-left Just Russia (JR) party. Created in 2006 as a coalition of three parties, some suggest that it was created by the Kremlin authorities as a means of drawing off support from the KPRF. The party was largely written off before the election, but won 13 per cent and 64 seats – a gain of 26 seats, nearly doubling its representation in parliament.

The protest demonstrations: context, size and make-up

If the increase in support for the systemic opposition parties suggested wider frustration and protest, the most visible indications of public frustration and stagnation in the country, were, of course, the large public protests that began in the wake of the parliamentary elections in December. Although initially small, the demonstrations grew appreciably in size, and, as noted above, were hailed by many in the West to be an 'unprecedented' sign of both disaffection being directed against Putin and his system, and an energised 'real' opposition movement. Yet the protests made for a complex canvas that requires careful consideration about their historical and political context, size and make-up.

A brief history of Russian protest

The protest demonstrations in 2011–2012 were unusual in Russian political and social life. They do, however, fit into a longer context of Russian protest that has included other mass events.[18] As one Western observer noted, they were 'neither a radical break with the past, nor a flicker of unrest, but a continuation of longer-term trends on the Russian protest scene'. 'Rather than the Russian people suddenly waking up, the protests are the result of a longer, slow stirring that is evident in thousands of protest events over recent years', he continued.[19] There have been other sizeable post-Soviet protest demonstrations, including against shock therapy in 1992–1993 and the collapse of industry in the late 1990s. In 1997, more than 250,000 demonstrators took part in marches in Vladivostok, Nakhodka, Arsenev and other cities in the Russian Far East to protest wage arrears, and an end to economic reforms that they claimed forced 80 per cent of the region's population below the poverty line. These protests continued and grew in 1998 and 1999.[20]

While such protests undoubtedly decreased in scale and purpose during the Putin era, they have continued. In some cities, particularly in Moscow and St Petersburg, in December 2006 and March 2007, there was a series of protests (the so-called 'Dissenters' Marches'), which called for Putin to go, dismissals of other officials, and criticised corruption and falsification of elections.[21] In Vladivostok in late 2008, several hundred protesters demonstrated against the government's plans to raise tariffs on imported cars. The size of that demonstration of course does not compare to those that took place in Moscow in December 2011 – but it was larger than the December 2011 protests in Vladivostok.

In Kaliningrad in January 2010, demonstrators gathered to protest a 25–30 per cent tax increase in housing, electricity, water and transport costs and demand the resignation of the regional governor, Georgy Boos.[22] The demonstrations involved KPRF, LDPR and other parties, and resulted both in a partial reduction of transport taxes and the dismissal of Boos later in the year. Again, it is worth noting that these protests were larger than the subsequent demonstrations in Kaliningrad in December 2011.

Internet protest was also growing. In March 2010, 44,387 citizens signed an online 'Putin must go manifesto', criticising the leadership for being a kleptocracy, corruption, and the lack of freedom, a 'vivid demonstration', according to one observer, that nowadays quite a few Russians are prepared openly to oppose a government that prioritised growth over democracy.[23] And in July and August that year protests began against the building of a motorway between Moscow and St Petersburg which would have incurred significant deforestation in the Khimki region near Moscow.

Nevertheless, the large and sustained demonstrations that took place in 2005 protesting the attempt by Putin's government to introduce a series of social reforms, including the monetarisation of pensions, remain the most substantial protests against Putin's leadership. Their scale is not easy to verify. Some left-wing sources suggest 300,000 protesters took part across Russia, which would dwarf the 2011 protests. Others, perhaps more realistically, suggest some 100,000 across Russia in 2005, roughly comparable in size to those of 2011.

These 'pensioner protests' were the first, and remain the most important, socio-political challenge to Putin, not least since they came in the context of the 'Colour Revolutions', particularly the 'Orange Revolution' in Ukraine. Indeed, what was especially important about these protests was not only their size but also their outcome: the sustained protests in 2005 both forced the government into a policy reversal and seemed to make Putin more cautious in his approach to subsequent reforms. Often forgotten in the West, they have not been forgotten by the leadership: even eight years later, Putin reminded Alexei Kudrin about his role in the reforms that led to the protests. It is worth quoting Putin at length, since it is also perhaps an indication of why Putin has not yet appointed Kudrin prime minister. During an exchange in Putin's annual 'Direct Line' conversation in 2013, Putin stated that Kudrin was recognised as the 'best finance minister, but not the best minister of social protection'. He continued:

> some time ago, Mr Kudrin and other officials who are now sitting on huge money in banks, were the initiators of introducing cash payments instead of benefits. We debated it for a long time, and I told him, 'Mr Kudrin, you will not be able to do it right, it won't work'. He said, 'yes, we will'. We all know what happened in the end. We had to pour money to cover up the problems at a great social and political cost. Frankly, I thought that was how it would end up from the start … why am I telling you this? Because tough economic measures without regard for the consequences in the social sphere are not always justified, especially in our country where incomes are still very modest.[24]

The rise and decline of the December protest movement

The scale of the protests has proven to be a source of considerable debate. As noted in Chapter 1, understandably disinclined to accept official estimates, which tended to be low, commentators have instead often tended towards adopting the much higher estimates given by opposition leaders and protest organisers, which led to considerable inflation. Over time, this has often settled into rather vague assertions – 'tens of thousands' or, occasionally, 'tens, and then hundreds of thousands'.[25] It is worth attempting greater precision.

The first protests began in the wake of the results, and on 5 and 6 December some 5,000–7,000 took to the streets in Moscow. The demonstrations grew significantly, however, on 10 December, particularly in Moscow but also in many other cities across Russia. Police reports estimate some 25,000 protesters – unsurprisingly since the officially sanctioned scale of the demonstrations was 30,000. The estimates of organisers grew during the day, first to 80,000–85,000 at 4 p.m. and then at 4:40 p.m. to 100,000–150,000. Russian media sources at the time were much more conservative, from lenta.ru's estimate of 30,000, through gazeta.ru's 40,000 to *Kommersant's* 50,000.[26] This 30,000–50,000 range is the most accurate for 10 December: still a notably large protest, and rare for Moscow, but some distance from the figures proposed by some Western commentators, let alone the organisers' estimates. Russian media reports suggested that in St Petersburg, some 7,000 turned out, in Novosibirsk 8,000, in Tomsk 3,000 and in Ufa 1,000. In Vladivostok, there were up to 500, in Kaliningrad, 200–300.

Mass protests took place again on 24 December in Moscow and in some 90 other cities across Russia. Those in Moscow were approximately twice the size of the demonstrations on 10 December: if the police estimated 30,000, and the organisers some 120,000, independent witnesses suggested 60,000–90,000.[27] The next largest demonstrations were in St Petersburg and Krasnoyarsk. All told, perhaps up to some 100,000 people across Russia turned out to protest that day. At the same time, if in some cities, including Rostov-on-Don, Tambov and Krasnodar, the scale of the demonstrations was larger on 24 December than on 10 December, in many others, including St Petersburg (3,000), Novosibirsk (2,000), Tomsk (1,500), Ufa (200), Vladivostock (150) and Kaliningrad (100), the demonstrations were substantially smaller.

Although more protests took place in Moscow in the run up to the elections in early February and March 2012, and again for Putin's inauguration in May, that of 24 December reflected the peak size across Russia. They began to evolve in approach – into 'controlled strolls', 'the people's walks', and what some of the organisers named as 'Marches of Millions'. But if the organisers themselves continued considerably to inflate the numbers,[28] the size of the demonstrations was clearly in decline. Protests in other cities across Russia were otherwise measured in hundreds, rather than thousands. Apart from a small surge in numbers at the time of the inauguration, the protests became limited to core activists and appeared more as reflections of public frustration than a swelling opposition movement, a shaking of the fist at the regime rather than a serious political alternative.

A wide range of people turned out to protest. To a degree, the major protests in December and early February were enhanced by those who might be called the more liberal urban middle class. But at the core of all the events were the activists of groups of unregistered, small political parties and coalitions, such as the Pirates Party of Russia and the Left Front, as well as the liberal ones such as Yabloko and Solidarity parties and PARNAS coalition.[29] As with the scale of the protests, precision in terms of the mix and balance of protest demonstrations from December 2011 is difficult, not least because it evolved as the protests themselves did. Nevertheless, the diversity of the protesters deserves attention since the protests were not uniformly 'liberal', and contained significant portions of nationalists and particularly leftists from various communist factions such as the Left Front.[30] Although united in their decrying of the elections, therefore, they were often at odds beyond that basic foundation. As one Russian observer put it, therefore, there was 'no unifying idea beyond that of being against the enemy'.[31] Indeed, given the diversity of the group, it is not surprising that the protesters were divided over political and economic issues: the incompatibility of the liberal 'white ribbon' agenda with that of the communist hammer and sickle meant that few, if any, of the speakers at the rallies were roundly cheered.

The protest leaders themselves illustrated these problems. Few of the leaders or organisers of the protests were 'new' political figures – all of the leaders of the liberal movement, for instance, have been in politics for years. As a result, one observer noted the 'wide gulf' between the protest leaders, 'with their lined faces and oft-heard views', and the 'younger, more vital' elements of the crowd, quoting the frustrations of restless demonstrators with speakers who were 'just old farts'.[32] Even Alexei Navalniy and Sergei Udaltsov, though certainly of a younger generation and less well known, had been building political careers during the previous decade. These leaders were unable to offer a unified front and often appeared at odds with each other, even within factions – as revealed by the publication of private phone conversations between leading liberal figures. Not only were the disagreements over policies – there were also differences over the approach the opposition movement should take, as some proposed more proactive and combative demonstrations, while others refused such an approach.

Although the leadership formed the Coordination Council (CC) after the elections to address these fractures and try to sustain the movement, these splits over agenda and approach became more obvious.[33] A year later the CC, already riven by internal factions,[34] ceased to exist, as insufficient numbers gathered to create a quorum and Alexei Navalniy, among others, stated that he would not participate in a new CC. The splits in the opposition continued. In 2012 PARNAS was dissolved and re-named RPR-PARNAS, and then in February 2014 split amid mutual recriminations: Vladimir Ryzhkov, leader of the RPR, withdrew, accusing Nemtsov and Kasyanov of being 'banal raiders' and seeking to take complete control of the party themselves, and Nemtsov and Kasyanov accused Ryzhkov of conspiring with the Kremlin to wreck the party.[35]

Nor did the protests manage to stimulate wider public support, and the 'million man marches' summoned by Navalniy and Ryzhkov failed to materialise. This reflected the inability of the opposition leadership to generate wider public support. Polls conducted by the respected Levada Centre indicated that Kasyanov, Nemtsov, Ryzhkov and Navalniy did not find favour with the population: in January 2012 just 15 per cent sympathised with the non-systemic opposition, while 66 per cent did not.[36]

Other polls in December 2011 suggested that although 45 per cent of respondents thought the elections were not very honest or completely dishonest, only 25 per cent of respondents expressed a willingness to support the demand for the invalidation of the results, and 55 per cent disagreed with the demand. Although a quarter of respondents agreed that Vladimir Churov, Chairman of the Central Election Committee, should resign, 47 per cent did not want him removed. Although two-thirds thought that violations were committed, only 14 per cent said that such falsifications were so sizeable that they changed the election results significantly, and 40 per cent said that the falsifications corresponded to their actual preferences. In the end, 51 per cent were satisfied with the result to some extent (15 per cent completely, 36 per cent partly), and 20 per cent believed that violations would be reduced for the presidential election. Thus gazeta.ru reporters suggested at the end of December 2011 that the parliamentary elections may have been dishonest, but that was irrelevant. By March 2012, Levada polls suggested that just 8 per cent were willing to march in a demonstration, only 32 per cent supported them and 52 per cent opposed them.[37] Mickiewicz thus points out that, although the youth may cheer Navalniy for exposing corruption, they would still vote for UR, and placed a higher value on their careers than on joining the mass protests that they did not consider a means of affecting policy.[38]

The protests did, however, spur much discussion about whether Putin could win in the first round of the elections, or whether he would be forced into a second round run off, or even whether he could win legitimately at all. But a combination of the limited wider public support for the protests and Putin's own campaign meant that in the run up to the presidential election in March, the polls began to show that Putin would win comfortably. Polls by the Levada Centre suggested both that Putin would win 66 per cent and that the number of those who thought the December elections to have been fair or more fair than not rose from 35 per cent in December to 43 per cent in January.

In the end, official figures gave Putin 64 per cent of a 65 per cent turnout. Even opposition or independent sources accepted that he had won the election with some 54 per cent. The closest challenger was Gennadiy Zyuganov, with 17 per cent. Some 110,000 Putin supporters gathered to celebrate victory, and on 5 March Putin met three of the other candidates (Mikhail Prokhorov, Vladimir Zhirinovsky and Sergei Mironov attended, while Zyuganov refused to recognise the legitimacy of the result and declined to attend), and stated that combat operations were now over – and the atmosphere was of the victor meeting the defeated at the signing of a peace treaty.

'Resetting' Russian domestic politics?

If the elections and protest demonstrations naturally were the focus of mainstream Western attention, an often overlooked but nevertheless important aspect was how the leadership team understood and responded to the political situation in Russia during that cycle. First, it is important to acknowledge that the authorities introduced a series of more punitive measures which provide the basis for the accusations for a more repressive response to the protest demonstration.[39]

These measures included the trials (on charges of rioting and violence) and subsequent imprisonment of protesters and some of the more prominent protest organisers, including Sergei Udaltsov, the leader of the Left Front, and Alexei Navalniy. They also include legislation to restrict freedom of public assembly, curb the freedom of media outlets such as lenta.ru, Dozhd television, and affecting NGOs, such as the foreign agent law, which requires NGOs to register as foreign agents with the Ministry of Justice if they received foreign funding and engaged in political activity. Thus Swedish analysts have described such measures as having created an atmosphere where 'freedom of speech is at peril, and reflecting an increasingly authoritarian system'.[40]

In part, this reflected the often stated concerns that the Russian authorities have about foreign (particularly US) interference in Russia's domestic politics, and their view of mass public movements as sources of instability. In the wake of the election and protests, and in the context of the Orange Revolution and 'Arab Spring', senior Russian figures have accused the USA of interference and financial support for the opposition.

But the authorities' responses were more complex, and can be framed in two interconnected groups. In the wake of the elections and as the protest demonstrations emerged, the leadership adopted a further series of responses. First, within the system, the authorities responded by dismissing some officials and indicating that there would be a more serious 'rotation' of personnel after the presidential election. After the December elections, and during the winter, a number of regional governors and city mayors resigned or were fired following poor results for UR in their regions,[41] and others, including senior figures such as Boris Gromov, governor of Moscow region, indicated that they would retire.

Boris Gryzlov, a long-term Putin ally, the highest ranking member of UR (except Putin) and Speaker of Russian Parliament, resigned in the wake of the elections. Sergei Naryshkin, head of the presidential administration, replaced Gryzlov, and, in turn, was replaced as head of the presidential administration by Sergei Ivanov. Other important changes included the appointment in December of Vyacheslav Volodin, deputy chairman of United Russia, a senior figure in the All-Russian Popular Front (ONF), and chief of staff of the government, as first deputy chief of staff of the presidential administration, replacing Vladislav Surkov. This rotation of personnel was continued after the election, culminating in the confirmation of a new cabinet in May 2012. These personnel moves, however, were not a 'reshuffle' – they were tantamount to an adjustment of the system to broaden and strengthen it, rather than sweeping change.

At the same time, the authorities responded more specifically to the electoral aspects of the protest demonstrations. The major response was Putin's own campaign. In the past, Putin had stated both that he does not like campaigning and yet that the leadership is always campaigning. In fact, Putin's 2011–2012 campaign – in which Putin himself, public campaign manager

Stanislav Govorukhin and political manager Vyacheslav Volodin, all participated – was unusual for Putin, who had not previously campaigned in that way, and centred on advocating his own 'stability' agenda, of steady development without upheavals. The campaign consisted of holding meetings with senior figures in the media, campaign visits around Russia's regions, and launching a website (www.putin2012.ru).

The platform was built around a series of articles written by Putin and published in leading newspapers. The first article asserted the stability that his team had brought to Russia, and the subsequent ones sketched out a manifesto for taking this forward, echoing his speeches as prime minister and elaborating on the six programmatic lines set out on the website. If steady development without upheaval was the message, the campaign emphasised the attempt to give Russia a form of social and political immunity from upheaval, in the process underscoring social guarantees. It thus could be considered a form of conservative modernisation – a slogan of UR during the economic crisis and the 2009–2010 debates about modernisation. The articles received mixed reviews from other political figures and in the media – Dmitri Rogozin was effusively supportive of Putin's article on defence, while Gennadiy Zyuganov dismissed the article on the economy as 'the same old liberal mush'. *Novaya Gazeta*, an opposition newspaper, pointed out that the articles were little more than repetitions of promises Putin had repeatedly made in the past.

Though Putin played a central part, of course, the role of his campaign team was important: members of his team, for instance, stood in for Putin in the presidential debates. Members of the campaign team were drawn not from UR, which hardly featured in the campaign, but more specifically from a group called the ONF, which Putin had established in May 2011 in the expectation that UR's electoral fortunes could decline. Putin himself ran as a non-partisan candidate rather than UR's nominee.

The campaign also evolved to mirror the opposition to absorb or negate elements of it. Although the opposition leadership argued that it represented the 'creative' elements of society, Putin sought to echo this by referring to classics of Russian literature in his speeches and incorporating numerous big names from the arts, film and music industries into the team. While scandals emerged about some of these personalities being pressured into joining the team,[42] many cultural figures are genuine subscribers to Putin's campaign: an obvious example being Govorukhin, the prominent and popular film director.

Similarly, the Putin team sought to echo the opposition protest demonstrations, mounting their own, which were cast specifically as 'anti-Orange', rather than 'pro-Putin' events – one campaign symbol was an orange snake gripped in a black fist. These grew in scale in February, and although scandals emerged about participants being paid or pressured to participate, the result was that the campaign was able to mobilise support, and the largest of the anti-Orange demonstrations exceeded the size of the largest opposition protests. The anti-Orange demonstrations became the largest public demonstrations since the collapse of the USSR.

Putin's campaign also co-opted some of the main features of the opposition's agenda and addressed explicit problems. The campaign team sought to emphasise the need for fair and monitored elections: the campaign highlighted, for instance, that it was Putin's idea to have polling booths monitored by closed-circuit television (CCTV) cameras. The idea to place CCTV in over 90,000 polling booths was popular with the public (though it was less popular with those who had to implement it, who noted the difficulty of finding sufficient numbers of cameras and the cost of over half a million dollars). Putin's team also said that it would cooperate with the League of Voters, a movement established in mid-January by prominent cultural figures of more liberal persuasion to monitor the presidential elections. Putin additionally offered a monitoring role to observers from the Yabloko part – an unusual move since parties unregistered to participate in the election ordinarily do not play such a role.

But the authorities' political activity did not begin purely as a response the demonstrations in December 2011. Indeed, we must now turn back to well before the December elections to understand the range of measures the leadership had begun to introduce to attempt to address UR's decline and soak up opposition, beginning in spring in response to the party's poor results in the March regional elections, and becoming what the leadership called a 'reset of the political system'.[43]

This 'reset' consisted of three parts. The first part related to the attempt to reinvigorate UR in preparation for the December elections. In spring and during the summer of 2011, the leadership dispatched 'federal locomotives' to head the party lists in the most troubled regions and to address local problems, positioning them as replacements for those regional governors who were unpopular or difficult for the Kremlin.[44] These were some of the most senior, experienced and influential figures in the Russian political system, including Sergei Shoigu, Dmitri Kozak, Sergei Naryshkin, Igor Shuvalov, Yuri Trutnev, Viktor Zubkov and Igor Sechin, and some of those who might best be described as 'up-and-coming', such as Vyacheslav Volodin, Andrei Vorobyov and Andrei Bocharov. Some of these figures were already well established in the public eye: Shoigu has long been a party figure and one of the most popular ministers, likewise Trutnev was an elected mayor and governor in Perm the 1990s and Volodin an elected representative in Saratov, but others, particularly Sechin, who led the party list in Stavropol, had not previously taken such prominent public political roles in the past.

The results, however, were not universally successful. In the majority of regions in which the vice premiers headed the lists, UR won less than 40 per cent.[45] In Perm and Krasnoyarsk, where Trutnev and Shoigu headed the lists, the party's results were 36 and 37 per cent respectively, a significant drop from the party's results in 2007 and less than the overall result across the country. Similarly in Leningradskaya oblast, led by Naryshkin, and Volgogradskaya oblast, led by Zubkov, the party won just 24 and 36 per cent. Indeed, of this list of 'federal locomotives', only in Stavropol and Saratov regions, led by Sechin and Volodin respectively, were the party's results notably better, with an increase respectively to 49 and 64 per cent.[46] This was better than expected in Stavropol, which had posed problems for the party, not least because of the unpopularity of the regional governor, Valeri Gaevsky.[47]

The second feature of this contextual shift was the attempt to adjust the wider political context. One element of this, though somewhat confused and enshrouded in rumour, was the search for a leader for the systemic opposition and an attempt to build the Pravoe Delo party into a more substantial organisation that could soak up more liberal voters.[48] This episode became more prominent later in the summer, but appears to have begun in March after the regional elections: in late March, the party's political council suggested that the party sought a federal level political figure to lead it into the December elections, and sought to attract active sectors of society, particularly in business and youth, and so increase its share of the vote from 1 to 15 per cent in the Duma elections to become the second party in a more multi-party parliament.[49] Alexei Kudrin and Arkadi Dvorkovich were rumoured to be possible candidates, and Igor Shuvalov was reported to have been given preliminary agreement to head the party and the presidential administration and government had given their consent. These plans failed to materialise, however, apparently because to have accepted the party leadership would have meant Shuvalov resigning his position in the government.[50] Only in mid May was a leader confirmed: businessman Mikhail Prokhorov, who promised to develop a party that represented the middle class, with a reformist, pro-business and more liberal socio-economic agenda. Reports suggested that his candidacy had the support of both Putin and Medvedev, though Prokhorov himself denied this.[51]

This attempt to build up a more liberal party as part of the systemic opposition failed. Prokhorov's tenure was short-lived: elected by the party on 25 June at the party's congress, he was dismissed that September amid mutual recriminations at the party congress. Prokhorov himself claimed that the presidential administration, particularly Vladislav Surkov, had conspired to control Pravoe Delo and have him dismissed. But this was not the whole story: Prokhorov had alienated many of the party's senior figures by parachuting his own people into the party ahead of those who had formed it, and advocating a political line that departed from the party's more traditional liberal agenda. If Surkov had sought his dismissal, therefore, he found many willing executors in the party – the vote was 75–0 against Prokhorov, with two abstentions. The result, as one Western observer phrased it, represented a 'debacle of the first order' for the Kremlin's effort to build a more liberal systemic opposition.[52] The party won less than 1 per cent in the December elections.

The other part of this adjustment of the political environment included the establishment of a number of 'para-institutional' organisations, two of which, the Agency for Strategic Initiatives (ASI) and the ONF, have come to play increasingly important roles in Russian politics, attempting to provide a direct link between the leadership and business (ASI) and the leadership and society (ONF). These organisations offer young professionals a way into the political world, a form of social and political mobility that co-opts them into the system in an effort to consolidate society and the elite.

Putin proposed setting up the ASI at a regional meeting of UR in May 2011 to involve young specialists in the regions. Its tasks were to include support for new business, the organisation of start-ups and overseeing the adaptation of promising companies to the market and the better coordination of businesses and bureaucracy. This latter task included monitoring the implementation of projects and addressing obstacles, such as resistance from the bureaucracy or legal problems. The ASI was also intended as a springboard for young and energetic people to move up the career ladder.[53] In the wake of the elections and protest demonstrations, its task evolved to play a role in ensuring that business did not become part of the opposition, providing a channel between business and the leadership.[54]

Similarly, as noted above, the ONF was formed in May 2011 to attempt to consolidate social consensus beyond UR.[55] With the decline in support for UR, the ONF, open to both individuals and organisations, provided a platform for Putin during the presidential elections and served as a means of co-opting different elements of the political landscape under a broader, more inclusive umbrella than UR could provide. The agenda is indeed a broad one: love of the Fatherland, strengthening the state, and enhancing social welfare and justice.[56] As a result, it has drawn members from UR and the KPRF, the Patriots of Russia party, and also from business. These have included figures such as Alexander Shokhin, head of the Russian Industrialists Association and a critic of the government, and Igor Yurgens, a critic of Putin's economic policies, who was invited to join the ONF in June 2013, apparently to 'diversify the debate within the movement and show expanding support for the president, including on the part of liberals'.[57]

The ONF's tasks have evolved since it was established in 2011, and it has become a more active, 'supra-party' movement with the intention of uniting people with different views around the president. As one Russian observer phrased it, Putin's popularity is some 80 per cent, while UR's is approximately 50 per cent – and the ONF's task is to absorb that 30 per cent difference. Following a founding congress in June 2013, it established its own bureaucracy with offices across Russia, and took on roles such as an anti-corruption campaign ('for fair procurement'), absorbing other political parties and opposition factions,[58] monitoring regional governors and searching for new cadres.

The 'reset' of the Russian political system continued after Putin's election, given what Volodin called the 'necessity for further corrections' to the system.[59] These included legislation banning senior officials and politicians from having foreign bank accounts,[60] and another counter-corruption campaign: on 6 March 2012 Igor Sechin submitted the first results of an investigation into state companies to Putin, providing more than 200 instances where top managers faced conflicts of interest, for whom Putin promised criminal proceedings.[61]

This 'reset' also included a series of political reforms, which Putin and other senior officials suggested amounted to a 'liberalisation' of political activity.[62] This included a return to the mixed electoral system, and direct election of regional governors. This represented a reversal of the policy introduced in 2004 of presidential appointment of governors – and the leadership team had not long previously indicated that it would not seek to alter the system in this way. The move gained a majority of popular support in polling, but, though it was subsequently implemented, it was diluted, and the president retains considerable influence over appointments.

Another reform (re-)introduced the easing of regulations for registering political parties. On 23 March the parliament unanimously passed legislation announcing that political parties need only 500 signatures to register (a reduction from 45,000), and that reduces the level of electoral support for a party to enter parliament from 7 to 5 per cent. Interestingly, this reform did not initially gain popular support: polls suggested that a majority thought that there were too many parties already, and only a minority supported the move. There was also concern among small opposition parties, especially non-systemic ones, that the new legislation would facilitate the further fragmentation of the opposition, particularly the more liberal ones. This concern had some justification: by 2013, 54 parties had been established, and by 2014 there were 69. Nevertheless, it is intended to reflect a transition to limited competition in regional and local elections, and opposition candidates have been elected – Yevgeniy Roizman, for instance, was elected mayor of Yekaterinburg, defeating UR's representative Iakov Silin.[63]

It is important to note, however, that this 'opening up' of the system means evolutionary change *within* the system, the drawing in and co-option of opposition elements into the system to attempt to strengthen itself, rather than fundamentally reforming it or creating any alternative to it: according to one senior official, opposition candidates would have to start at the municipal level and work their way up the electoral ladder, rather than attempt to set out posing as an immediate alternative at the highest level.[64] Putin has also made reference to the 'legal opposition' – making a clear delineation between those who are in the system and those who are not. Furthermore, opportunities for opposition figures remain limited to positions that are not influential, and despite the lowered barriers for registering parties, small parties across the political spectrum find that administrative obstacles remain. Problems are emerging with respect to registering – many parties have not nominated candidates, and most elections for regional governors have simply confirmed the power of incumbent governors, who, with only two exceptions, are UR members.

Moreover, this 'reset' is not without problems: as some Russian observers have pointed out, although the authorities have sought to emphasise the legitimacy of wins in the yearly election days, it has remained hard to generate popular enthusiasm for voting. Despite the 'reset', widespread disillusionment remains strong and voter turnout is in decline. Although the authorities suggested that a 32.3 per cent turnout for the Moscow mayoral elections was standard for such elections,[65] the turnout for the Moscow city council a year later declined further to approximately 20 per cent.[66] As one Russian observer suggested, therefore, for the leadership it has become less a question of stuffing ballots to ensure victory for the party of power, and more of a question of stuffing ballots for all parties to inflate turnout in the attempt to raise the legitimacy of the elections.[67]

Towards a consolidation of power?

The premature 'end of Putin' orthodoxy that emerged in late 2011 was a reflexive assessment based on wishful thinking. Putin has remained the most popular political figure in the country – in other words, the politician with the greatest capacity to mobilise support. His popularity rose substantially after the election in 2012, reaching highs of some 85 per cent during the war in Ukraine in 2014 and into 2015. Indeed, despite the protests, there was little direct or sustained political challenge to Putin in the electoral period 2011–2012, partly because few substantive figures have been able to forge careers in opposition to Putin's leadership team, partly because the opposition itself, particularly the 'non-systemic' liberal elements of it, has long been both divided among themselves and unpopular, and partly because of the responsive measures that the authorities have implemented that have limited it.

Two important points emerge from this discussion about the leadership and the opposition. The first returns us to the question of 'surprise', discussed in Chapter 1, and the question of timing in understanding Russia. The fall in support for UR in December and its election results were roughly in line with the results of earlier regional elections and polling: the weakening of its near monopoly on power gained in 2007 had begun even in 2009, and was clear by the March 2011 elections. That the leadership had noted the decline in support was visible from their responses.

The elections, protests and responses by the authorities are best understood, therefore, not in terms of a 'September, then December to May' timeline, but a 'March 2011 to May 2012' timeline – in other words as part of a year-long election season, from the regional elections in March 2011 to Putin's inauguration in May 2012. Doing so throws into better relief the decline of popular support for UR, as well as the range of responses by the leadership and how the system evolved. These went beyond the purely punitive post-demonstration responses, and included the use of 'federal locomotives' to attempt to reinvigorate UR and the attempt to develop a party (Pravoe Delo) that could soak up the more liberal vote in the election. These did not work as planned. Prokhorov's subsequent political efforts have also not worked – in March 2015, he resigned from his Civil Platform party citing a schism in the party. Like other political parties, it had been split by the war in Ukraine, and some party members, including Rifat Shaikhutdinov, a senior figure in the party, had attended the 'anti-Maidan' demonstration.

But the slow 'reset' of Russian politics that the leadership began to implement in 2011 is important. While there has been a longer-term migration of support away from UR, it has retained its dominance of the systemic political landscape in the yearly regional elections – but winning majorities from low turnouts. Nevertheless, Russian observers suggest that the shift to a mixed electoral system may help UR, noting that if the December 2011 elections had been held on a mixed system, UR would probably have won another overwhelming majority.[68] Perhaps more important is the emergence and growing roles of 'para-institutional' organisations such as the ASI and ONF. The ONF may well support candidates in regions and districts where UR is likely to do badly. The result is a small but important shift in the landscape of Russian 'systemic' politics, one that will lead to the likely shift in the structure of parliamentary politics and the emergence of new figures in regional and municipal positions. Over time, these younger figures will be tried and tested and emerge onto the political scene for 2018 and 2024.

Putin undoubtedly faces opposition. If there is limited opposition in terms of popular leadership or coherent agenda, social protest remains a visible feature of the Russian political landscape, whether in the form of anti-war protests in 2014, or against healthcare reform: in November 2014, there were demonstrations in cities across Russia protesting potential cuts in medical staff numbers and hospital closures. Though the latter were not of a scale comparable to the December 2011/2012 demonstrations, the anti-war demonstration was sizeable. More recently, in late 2015 long-haul lorry drivers began a protest against new road taxes, creating disruption on federal highways, threatening blockades and using social media to avoid countermeasures. Increasing economic hardship as a result of the prolonged the economic slowdown since late 2011 may increase the likelihood of social protest in the regions.

There is also the passive opposition of the bureaucratic system: despite the Putin team's dominance of Russia's political heights, the leadership faces numerous practical difficulties in having its agenda implemented because the vertical of power does not work. Orders remain unfulfilled, projects incompletely implemented and responses to crises slow and inefficient. Even so, Putin remained the dominant candidate: in one telling pre-election poll, when presented with all candidates and questioned about who could deal with the problems Russia faces, Putin was the only candidate to enter double digits. He received 14 per cent, defeated only by 'nobody can' with 32 per cent.[69]

But echoing the problems that the authorities face in generating support despite the resources at their disposal, the opposition faces difficulties in motivating support despite the evident wider popular socio-economic frustration and fatigue with the current establishment. Although the KPRF came second in the parliamentary elections, and its leader Gennadiy Zyuganov came second in the presidential elections, this does not mean that the communists posed a serious challenge to power, or offered a serious, competitive alternative to Putin. Although the KPRF led some nominal opposition to UR and to the Medvedev government, and even drew closer to some of the left-wing 'non-systemic' opposition such as the Left Front, it does not offer a substantial challenge. Furthermore, it suffers from internal dissent – fractions from within the communist party have formed the Communists of Russia party, and other left-wing parties including the Left Front and United Communist Party are attempting to register.[70] Nevertheless, the KPRF remains the largest systemic opposition party across Russia, and it, not the more liberal opposition, has been the main beneficiary of the protest vote, and its gains in the December elections reflected an important surge in support for the political left in Russia: Levada Center polls suggest that 40 per cent of Russians support socialist principles, and 20 per cent support communist principles.[71]

While there may have been a migration of public support away from UR, one that may lead towards a two-party system or even a more 'multi-party' parliament over time, as some of the leadership team have indicated, the opposition, both 'systemic' and 'non-systemic', was heavily defeated in 2012. Despite their gains in the parliamentary elections in 2011, all the 'systemic' opposition party leaders were well beaten in the subsequent presidential elections. Nor did the parties fare well in the subsequent regional elections in 2013 and 2014: Ivan Melnikov, the KPRF candidate in the Moscow mayoral election, won just 10.7 per cent. And, partly because of the incarceration of its leaders, partly because it is at odds with itself – as illustrated by the failure of the CC and split in RPR-PARNAS – the 'non-systemic' opposition leadership has remained marginalised and unable to gain wider support. Indeed, they have become further marginalised as a result of the war in Ukraine. Though they have participated in elections, and won victories, such as Roizman's, or 'close calls' such as Navalniy winning 27 per cent of the vote in the Moscow mayoral election in 2013, they do not appear to be either a concern for the leadership, or unexpected: prior to the mayoral vote, Volodin pointed out, for instance, that even if Navalniy won up to 25 per cent it would 'not be a concern'.[72]

In March 2015 the non-systemic opposition was still unable to gain sympathy with the wider population, still with only 15 per cent – indeed, those who did not sympathise with them grew slightly in number to 68 per cent.[73] As one Russian commentator noted, only 50,000–60,000 turned out to demonstrate on 1 March 2015, despite the war in Ukraine, a deteriorating economy and a major political murder. If such a situation resulted in only 0.5 per cent of the capital's population turning out, the 'authorities could do as they pleased'.[74] With the exceptions of individual high points such as 24 December 2011, this figure of approximately 50,000 reflects the rough 'barometer' figure for street protest demonstrations since 2010 (though the online figure may be slightly higher). The evolution of the protest demonstrations suggests that, to date, they can be described in terms of layers: a hard core of 5,000–10,000 frequent protesters, surrounded by another 20,000–30,000 at more major demonstrations, with an outer layer of a further 60,000 of very occasional protesters. The maximum scale we have seen so far, therefore, is approximately 100,000 across Russia. Partly, this is because, as one Russian political figure noted, the authorities speak to the socio-economic concerns of the population, while the non-systemic opposition asserts the need for freedom of expression and the release of political prisoners – an agenda that, although it chimes with foreign observers, does not resound with the wider population.

Indeed, given these results, the 2011–2012 election season appears in retrospect to have been less the end of the Putin era, and more of a watershed for the opposition. The liberal opposition has been completely marginalised, the political opposition that remains is left-leaning and protest is mostly social rather than political. Looking ahead to the parliamentary elections in 2016 and the presidential elections in 2018, opposition leaders may face internal politicking as a younger generation attempts to replace them and lay the groundwork for the next presidential elections. This is not only the case for the main systemic parties, the KPRF and LDPR, whose leaders will be over 70 by the time of the next election and may be thinking of retirement,[75] but also for the more liberal parties, and well-established figures such as Grigory Yavlinsky, who will be 66, may be among those in the liberal camp who find themselves under pressure from within their own party groups for not offering an electable agenda – and may even be replaced.

Furthermore, the opposition parties, 'systemic' and 'non-systemic', face internal divisions. If Prokhorov's Civic Platform party has split, as noted above, the KPRF faces competition from the Communists of Russia party, while fractions also appear to be breaking away from JR. In March 2015, Oksana Dmitrieva, a vice-chair of JR and a potential presidential candidate for the party, resigned from it (taking several deputies with her), and subsequently established a business-oriented 'Professionals Party' to participate in the Duma elections in 2016.

Notes

1 Putin accepted the invitation to become leader of the party in 2008. Though they have both led the party, neither Putin nor Medvedev are party members.
2 F. Hill and C. Gaddy, *Mr Putin: Operative in the Kremlin* (Washington, DC: Brookings Institute Press, 2013); N. Granholm, J. Malminen and G. Persson (eds), *A Rude Awakening: Ramifications of Russian Aggression Towards Ukraine* (Stockholm: FOI, 2014), pp. 27–29; E. Mickiewicz, *No Illusions: The Voices of Russia's Future Leaders* (Oxford: Oxford University Press, 2014), p. 51; W. Zimmerman, *Ruling Russia: Authoritarianism From the Revolution to Putin* (Oxford: Princeton University Press, 2014), pp. 300–301; A. Weiss, 'Winter has come', *Democracy*, 30 (Fall 2013), www.democracyjournal. org/30/winter-has-come.php?page=all. Note the reference to 'winter' that reflects both the wider context of discussion of political spring – the 'Arab Spring' to which the 'Russian spring' was compared, and

the polar positioning of the exhausted Putin regime with the energetic
Navalniy-led opposition. Putin's response, Weiss (and many others)
suggested was a return to Soviet-style values, 'bringing an end to the
period of relative openness and social mobility under Medvedev'.

3 That is, coalitions, parties and individual politicians not represented in
the parliament.

4 M. Bennetts, *Kicking the Kremlin: Russia's New Dissidents and the
Battle to Topple Putin* (London: OneWorld Publications, 2014), p. xvi.

5 Navalniy was widely lionised in many hagiographical Western reports as
a 'blogger and anti-corruption crusader', a new leader figure and 'democracy campaigner', able to unite a fragmented opposition – and thus be a
'thorn in Putin's side'. A. Arutunyan, *The Putin Mystique: Inside Russia's
Power Cult* (Newbold: Skyscraper Publications, 2014), pp. 287, 289.

6 'Morgan Stanley preduprezhdaet: glava gosudarstva uidiot' [Morgan
Stanley warns: the head of state will go], *Nezavisimaya Gazeta* (12
January 2005), www.ng.ru/politics/2005-01-12/1_revolution.html

7 Zimmerman, *Ruling Russia*, p. 274.

8 'Nash durdom golosuet "za"' [Our madhouse votes 'for'], *Vedomosti*
(6 December 2011).

9 Polls reported 46.1 per cent support for UR in local government elections in October 2009 (compared to the 66.2 per cent of the vote
assigned to the party). S. Malle, 'The policy challenges of Russia's post
crisis economy', *Post-Soviet Affairs*, 28:1 (2012), pp. 68–69.

10 For a useful display of the results, 'Partia vlasti regionalnovo naznache-
nia' [Party of power of regional assignment], *Kommersant* (15 March
2012), http://kommersant.ru/Doc/1600854.

11 '"Edinaya Rossia" sduvaetsa' [United Russia deflates], *Svobodnaya
Pressa* (14 March 2011), www.svpressa.ru/politic/article/40412/.

12 'Faktor Putina bolshe ne rabotaet' [The Putin factor no longer works],
gazeta.ru (14 March 2011), www.gazeta.ru/politics/2011/03/14_a
_3554241.html; 'United Russia wins regional vote but unconvincingly',
Moscow Times (15 March 2011).

13 'Surkov obyasnil, za kakoi novyi mirovoi poryadok boretsa Rossia'
[Surkov explained what kind of world order Russia is fighting for],
Newsru.com (18 November 2010), www.newsru.com/russia/18nov
2010/surkov.html.

14 The Liberal Democratic Party of Russia (LDPR) – a nationalist party –
won 12 per cent and 56 seats.

15 'Zachem zapadu pokazali Sergeya Ivanova' [Why Sergei Ivanov
was shown to the West], *Nezavisimaya Gazeta* (9 September 2013);
'Transcript of the Seliger 2013 youth forum' (2 August 2013), http://
eng.kremlin.ru/news/5812.

16 'Rebrending sistemy' [Rebranding the system], *Vedomosti* (6 December
2011).

17 'Experty: na vuiborakh v gosdumu pobedila KPRF' [Experts: the KPRF
won at the parliamentary elections], *RBK Daily* (12 March 2013),

www.rbcdaily.ru/politics/562949986181345. The study was published by an organisation led by Vladimir Yakunin, considered to be a close confidant of Vladimir Putin, and suggested that the KPRF had won 25–30 per cent compared to UR's 20–25 per cent.

18 The focus here is on non-systemic protest – and does not include discussion of the parliamentary 'bunt', when the KPRF, LDPR and JR staged a walkout from parliament in 2009, the first time they had done so in a decade.

19 G. Robertson, 'Protesting Vladimir Putin: the election protests of 2011–2 in broader perpsective', *Problems of Post-Communism*, 60:2 (March–April 2013), pp. 11–12.

20 G. Robertson, *The Politics of Protest in Hybrid Regimes: Managing Dissent in Post-Communist Russia* (Cambridge: Cambridge University Press, 2011), offers an excellent overview of protest in Russia, albeit one that was largely overlooked in the mainstream discussion about the December protests.

21 A 'Dissenter's march' in March 2007 in St Petersburg was estimated to have been some 15,000 strong.

22 '10,000 protest against transport tax hike in Kaliningrad', *RIA Novosti/Sputnik* (31 January 2010), http://sputniknews.com/society/20100131/157728046.html.

23 S. Malle, 'The policy challenges of Russia's post-crisis economy', *Post-Soviet Affairs*, 28:1 (2012), p. 81.

24 'Direct line with Vladimir Putin' (25 April 2013), http://eng.kremlin.ru/news/5328.

25 S. Greene, *Moscow in Movement: Power and Opposition in Putin's Russia* (Stanford: Stanford University Press, 2014). Another observer suggested 120,000. B. Smith, *The Russia Crisis and Putin's Third Term* (4 April 2012), House of Commons, SNIA/6289, p. 5.

26 For an interesting timeline of the day, http://lenta.ru/chronicles/protest/; 'Govorit ne s kem' [Nobody to talk to], *Vedomosti* (12 December 2011).

27 'Protest bez partii' [Protest without a party], *Vedomosti* (26 December 2011).

28 Sergei Udaltsov estimated 100,000 and Ilya Ponomarev asserted that 200,000 turned out on 12 June 2012. See http://grani.ru/Politics/Russia/activism/m.198332.html. The police were, of course, much more conservative, estimating some 18,000.

29 PARNAS, or the People's Freedom Party 'for a Russia without Lawlessness and Corruption' was established in 2010 as a merger of the Democratic Choice, Solidarity, Republican Party of Russia and Russian People's Democratic Union parties, bringing together the leaders of these parties, respectively Vladimir Milov, Boris Nemtsov, Vladimir Ryzhkov and Mikhail Kasyanov.

30 In interview, a prominent figure in the opposition estimated that the balance was 50 per cent liberal, 35 per cent leftists and 15 per cent nationalists. Interview with the author, September 2013.

31 G. Nikiporets-Takigawa, 'Protests 2.0: through networked negative consolidation to participation: why Russian Manezhka cannot become Ukrainian Maidan', *Russian Journal of Communication*, 6:3 (October 2014), pp. 246–259.

32 E. Mickiewicz, *No Illusions: The Voices of Russia's Future Leaders* (Oxford: Oxford University Press, 2014), pp. 164–165.

33 The opposition Coordination Council was initiated in June 2012 and elections to the council were held in October. 82,000 voted in the election, just under half the number that had registered. None of the more established liberal figures polled successfully: Navalny won 43,723, writer Dmitry Bykov came second with 38,520, and Garry Kasparov third with 33,849.

34 One observer describes the internal factions of the CC as a 'manifestation of personal egos'. Mickiewicz, *No Illusions*, p. 203. The Other Russia, a previous opposition coalition established in 2006, had also fallen apart in 2010 as a result of the members' disparate views, and mutual criticism.

35 'Vladimir Ryzhkov: Nemtsov i Kasyanov – banalnye reidery' [Vladimir Ryzhkov: Nemtsov and Kasyanov are banal raiders], *Moskovsky Komsomolets* (10 February 2014), www.mk.ru/politics/russia/interview/2014/02/10/982747-vladimir-ryizhkov-nemtsov-i-kasyanov-banalnyie-reyderyi.html. In July 2015, Mikhail Kasyanov, the only candidate nominated for the position, was elected to lead the renamed PARNAS party.

36 15: 3 per cent 'definitely yes', 12 per cent 'probably yes'; 66: 33 per cent 'probably not', 33 per cent 'definitely not'. www.levada.ru/27-02-2015/neobkhodimost-politicheskoi-oppozitsii-i-podderzhka-oppozitsionnykh-trebovanii.

37 Mickiewicz, *No Illusions*, pp. 48, 147.

38 Mickiewicz, *No Illusions*, p. 147.

39 While this is true, the responses of the police to the demonstrations were more nuanced – and were not the more simplistically violent responses of some authoritarian, let alone totalitarian regimes. How the police responded and what lessons they learnt from the demonstrations is a subject that requires more work.

40 Granholm *et al.*, *A Rude Awakening*, pp. 28–29.

41 Governors were fired in Arkhangel, Vologda, Volgodgrad and Stavropol.

42 Some reports suggested, for instance, that actress Chulpan Khamatova was pressured into supporting the campaign with a video on why she would vote for Putin.

43 'Kreml' prodolzhit perezagruzku vnutrennei politiki' [Kremlin will continue the reset of internal politics], *Kommersant* (10 July 2013). Much of this 'reset' has escaped attention in the Western discussion of Russia. One exception is R. Sakwa, *Putin Redux: Power and Contradiction in Contemporary Russia* (London: Routledge, 2014).

44 'Bei svoikh, ili proigraesh' [Beat up your own, or lose], *Vedomosti* (1 December 2011).

45 'Rebrending sistemy' [Rebranding the system], *Vedomosti* (6 December 2011).

46 'Partiynyi "parovoz" Igor' Sechin vuityanul Stavropol'e' [Party 'loco-motive' Igor Sechin has saved Stavropol] (6 December 2011), www.stav ropolye.tv/state/view/40296.

47 N. Protsenko, 'The rise and fall of a Russian energy baron', *Transitions Online* (19 July 2012), www.tol.org/client/article/23 264-kaitov-energy-russia.html. Sechin relinquished his mandate as a deputy but retained an interest in the region, installing measures to ensure the implementation of instructions and regularly visiting the region. Sechin publicly berated Gaevsky for failing to fulfil projects in September 2011. Gaevsky was dismissed by Medvedev on 2 May 2012.

48 'V poiskakh statusnykh pravykh' [In search of reputable right-ists], *Nezavisimaya Gazeta* (24 March 2011), www.ng.ru/poli-tics/2011-03-24/1_liberals.html. Pravoe Delo had been formed in late 2008/early 2009 with the merger of the Union of Right Forces, the Democratic Power of Russia and Civilian Power parties, all of which were losing support as individual parties.

49 'V poiskakh statusnykh pravykh'; 'Pravoe Delo mozhet stat parlament-skoi partiei pod rukavodstvom Shuvalova' [Pravoe Delo can become a parliamentary party under Shuvalov's leadership], newsru.com (25 March 2011), www.newsru.com/russia/25mar2011/pravdelo.html.

50 www.vedomosti.ru/opinion/news/1239483/poluchitsya_li_iz_ pragovo_dela_liberalnaya_partiya. By addressing these parts of society, it was envisaged that Pravoe Delo would be approaching the voters that UR could not.

51 'Prokhorov lukavit: ego kandidatura odobrena tandemom' [Prokhorov dissembles: his candidacy is approved by the tandem], newsru.com (17 May 2011), www.newsru.com/russia/17may2011/prohorov.html.

52 R. Sakwa, 'Prologue: an oligarch falls', *OpenDemocracy* (27 September 2011), www.opendemocracy.net/od-russia/richard-sakwa/ prologue-oligarch-falls. Sakwa gives a good overview of the background of the parties involved and how the affair played out. See also Malle, 'Policy challenges', pp. 82–84.

53 'Putin proposes new agency to help young Russians get ahead', *RIA Novosti* (6 May 2011), http://sputniknews.com/russia/20110506/16389 7723.html.

54 For a detailed examination of the ASI, see L. Freinkman and A. Yakovlev, *Agentstvo strategicheskikh initsiativ kak novyi dlya Rossii 'institut razvitia': pervye resultaty deyatelnosti, faktori uspekha i voz-mozhnye riski v kontekste mezhdunarodnovo opuita* [The Agency of Strategic Initiatives as a New Development Institute for Russia: First

Results of Activity, Factors of Success and Possible Risks in the Context of International Experience] (Moscow: Higher School of Economics, 2014).

55　One Western observer has suggested that the idea was already circulating in early 2010 that a new structure would be needed. Malle, 'Policy challenges', p. 69. Malle, who is one of the few Western observers to have explored the ONF in depth, gives a fine overview of its establishment.

56　See http://onf.ru.

57　Shokhin also has a prominent place in the ASI. Malle, 'Policy challenges', p. 68; 'Igoru Yurgensu nashlos mesto vo "Fronte"' [Igor Yurgens has been found a place in the Front], *Kommersant* (10 June 2013).

58　Correspondence with the author, December 2014.

59　'Kreml' prodolzhit perezagruzku vnutrennei politiki' [The Kremlin will continue the reset of internal politics], *Kommersant* (10 July 2013).

60　The ban applies to a wide range of public servants at federal and regional levels, military and law enforcement personnel, and those running for elected public office. For more details, see http://rbth.co.uk/politics/2013/05/06/new_russian_law_bans_foreign_bank_accounts_for_officials_25745.html.

61　'S novym srokom! Zachistka: Pervoe delo budushchevo presidenta Rossii' [Happy new term! Clean up: the first business of the future Russian president], *Vedomosti* (6 March 2012). As discussed above, Sechin was a 'federal locomotive' to the Stavropol region during the summer, and one of his tasks appears to have been to address corruption in the energy sector there. Protsenko, 'The rise and fall of a Russian energy baron'.

62　'Meeting of the Valdai International Discussion Club' (19 September 2013), http://eng.kremlin.ru/news/6007. In the sense that more candidates will be able to compete – though this is in a wider context of opposition candidates being imprisoned, and restrictions on the activities of NGOs and some media.

63　Roizman won 33.3 per cent, Silin won 29.7 per cent.

64　Interview with the author, September 2013.

65　In 1991, 1996 and 1999, turnout for the Moscow mayoral election was over 60 per cent, in 2003 it was over 55 per cent.

66　In the elections, 28 UR candidates were elected, ten independents, five from the KPRF (including the grandson of KPRF Gennadiy Zyuganov, Leonid Andreevich Zyuganov [b.1988]) and one each from Rodina and LDPR. http://duma.mos.ru/ru/168/duma. Other regions enjoyed a slightly higher turnout, but the wider problem of low turnout was acknowledged by Medvedev himself after the elections. http://rt.com/politics/187752-russia-hold-record-elections/. In 2005, turnout in the Moscow City Parliament elections was 35 per cent, in 2009 36 per cent.

67　In conversation with the author, February 2015.

68 T. Stanovaya, 'How Putin elects the Duma', Institute of Modern Russia (17 January 2013), http://imrussia.org/en/analysis/politics/368-how-putin-elects-the-duma.

69 See Levada Polls carried out in late January and published on 1 February 2012, www.levada.ru/01-02-2012/78-naseleniya-ozhidayut-pobedy-v-putina-na-prezidentskikh-vyborakh. Of the other candidates, Zhirinovsky and Zyuganov both polled 5 per cent, Prokhorov and Mironov both polled 3 per cent, Yavlinsky polled 1 per cent. 37 per cent did not answer. At that time, 78 per cent thought that Putin would be elected, and 3 per cent thought that Zyuganov would be.

70 The Communists of Russia were established in 2009 as a result of the merger of the Communist Youth Union of Russia and the All-Russia Communist Party of the Future, and registered in 2012. The party makes a point of being the youthful face of Russian communism. http://komros.info.

71 Cited in A. Litoy, 'The Kremlin has nothing to fear from Left-wing opposition', *Open Democracy* (23 December 2014).

72 'Snimat zapreshcheno' [Can't be removed], *Vedomosti* (26 August 2013).

73 3 per cent 'definitely yes', 12 per cent 'probably yes', www.levada.ru/27-02-2015/neobkhodimost-politicheskoi-oppozitsii-i-podderzhka-oppozitsionnykh-trebovanii.

74 A. Minkin, 'Zabud pro Demoktratiu' [Forget about democracy], *Ekho Moskvui* (2 March 2015), http://echo.msk.ru/blog/minkin/1503686-echo/. Minkin also noted the 'microscopic' turnout in support of Yabloko and the even smaller turnout in the anti-Maidan march.

75 Zyuganov and Zhirinovsky will both be in their seventies at the time of the 2016 election.

4

Beyond Putin? Deciphering power in Russia

The end of Putin (again)?

Since Putin returned to the presidency in 2012, 'Putinology' has dominated the mainstream Western discussion about Russia. It has become the central pillar of what appears as a form of 'neo-Kremlinology', as observers seek to interpret subtle and often ambiguous indications of the relative influence of those who are close to Putin and thus on decision-making, and seek to parse rumours of firings and appointments to attempt to divine 'who is up and who is down', 'cracks in Kremlin unity', power struggles and the implications of 'clan feuding'. There was much speculation during the war in Ukraine, for instance, about the shrinking inner circle of advisors to Putin and the rising influence of 'hardliners'. Rumours also circulated for months about the firing of Minister of the Interior Vladimir Kolokoltsev, and his replacement by First Deputy Minister of the Interior Viktor Zolotov.[1]

Indeed, the focus on Putin has become ever more intense as officials and observers have attempted on one hand to divine what it is that Putin 'really wants' and 'really thinks', or on the other, increasingly painted him as isolated from the wider Russian political landscape, whether from the population or from the political elite, or both. This has evolved into a heightened focus on the personalised nature of Russian power, and it has provided a platform for much speculation about the increasing narrowness of Putin's advisory circle, the inherent instability of 'Putin's' system and consequently (again) about the Putin era coming to an end and a possible post-Putin era.[2] Illustrative of the wider discussion, one observer suggested that the murder of Boris Nemtsov in February 2015, followed by the president's disappearance from the public eye for a few days in March 2015, demonstrated that Putin, 'known for his steely-eyed resolve in previous crises is losing control, can't give his entourage clear orders as to how to respond and is having problems pacifying the Kremlin's warring clans'. The 'spell of his machismo and invincibility has been ended', she continued, and 'doubt about his fitness to rule whether he controls the levers of power or not, will continue to spread'.[3]

Rumours, many of which originated from previously unknown and somewhat dubious sources, quickly spread both about Putin himself, suggesting that he had disappeared from view because he had died, or been incapacitated by a stroke. And there was speculation about friction between power groups in the wake of the murder of Boris Nemtsov, about the possibility of a coup – led, some suggested, by Secretary of the Security Council and former director of the FSB Nikolai Patrushev, and about the death of Zolotov.

This 'neo-Kremlinology' is partly a response to the obscurity of decision-making in Russia and the resulting limit to what we can know about the inner-functioning of politics, and its central pillar, 'Putinology', reflects the undoubted centrality of Putin to the current Russian political landscape. But it increasingly distorts our understanding of Russian political life and, by relying on dubious sources, speculation and assertion, generates much additional noise that distracts and obstructs our understanding of how Russia works. As noted above, one example of this was a Pentagon-supported study from 2008 was published in early 2015 suggesting that Putin suffered a form of autism. It suggested that 'his movement patterns and micro-expressions analysed on open source video, so clearly reveals that the Russian president carries a neurological abnormality, a profound behavioural challenge identified by leading neurologists as Asperger's Syndrome, an autistic disorder which affects all of his decisions'.[4] Leaving aside such psychological 'diagnoses' that occasionally emerge, it facilitates, as one observer has suggested, a discussion that is both hysterical and imprecise. Not only has it narrowed attention to only very specific aspects of the wider Russian political landscape, but, confusing suggestion and insinuation with evidence, it often asserts changes in the leadership team around Putin, and a significant change in Russian politics away from a more team-based, consensual style politics – the 'Collective Putin' – towards a more autocratic political personalisation that depicts the regime as increasingly brittle.

'Putinology' is thus entrenching an analytical context in which various assumptions are made about how 'Putin's Russia' and how it approaches its international actions. The central thread is that it is Putin alone who drives the current Russian stance, with the implication that without him those Russian policies that run counter to Western interests can be reversed – and even that Russia itself will change. Putin is seen as the system, therefore, and the system as Putin, a point observers reinforce by quoting Vyacheslav Volodin who, in a speech at the Valdai International Discussion Group in 2014, suggested that 'there is no Russia without Putin'.[5]

Thus the possibility of regime change in Russia has long been a focus of Western analysis: in 2005, observers were warning that popular discontent about hardline policies, corruption and the 'Orange Revolution' in Ukraine would lead to a second Russian revolution and Putin being forced from office.[6] But it has increasingly emerged as a central theme in the Western discussion about Russia – whether a 'Maidan' could happen in Russia, because Western sanctions create conditions in which the Russian population goes to the streets to demand change,[7] or whether the sanctions would create the conditions for a 'palace coup' in which Putin would be removed by senior figures within the leadership. By late 2014 and early 2015 the theme of a coup had become a frequent, even monthly, feature of the Western discussion about Russia, providing scope for a host of spurious analogies with Russian and Soviet history, and sensational but vague speculation that Putin was under threat from various hardliners, be they the security services or the military.[8]

In this way, it might be said to have replaced the question 'when would the tandem arrangement break up?' as the central analytical focus for debate. At the same time, as one Western observer has suggested, such an approach is neither new nor confined to Russia – it has featured in discussions about Iraq, Syria, Libya, North Korea and even Ukraine, in which the leader's departure not only leads to a 'clean slate', but is part of a progressive revolution creating stability.[9]

This chapter first sketches out an overview of the various understandings of the Russian political landscape, framing the considerable long-term continuity in post-Cold War Russian politics. It then turns to assess the vertical of power, framing it as a cascade from the core leadership team at the top, to 'federal locomotives', to those tasked with management. Finally, it looks at some of those who appear to be emerging figures, as managers and as players in the 'reset'.

The 'Collective Putin': depictions of the Russian political landscape

Observers have used various models to describe the broader picture of Russian political life. Two of the most prominent are those that, first, portray the 'dual state', and, second, the balance between so-called 'siloviki' (those in the security and intelligence services, military and interior ministry) and 'liberals'. Both of these approaches relate the discussion to the evolution and limits of Russian democracy. The first suggests that a 'dual order' has emerged which combines formal structures of state and informal rules, a constitutional order buttressed by an administrative regime – the hybrid result being a combination of democratic institutions but authoritarian practices. The regime operates through informal networks that criss-cross both government positions and those in big business, and often subverts the constitutional order – but is also constrained by it.[10]

The relative balance of power between 'siloviki' and 'liberals' has been the subject of much elaboration and debate since Putin's first term. A particular theme has been the roles and influence of figures with a security/armed forces background, a 'militarisation' of society, as observers have debated their role and dominance of the system – and how that influence is balanced by those of a more liberal or technocratic background. Again, this has reflected a debate about whether this was a deliberate creation of a police state mechanism into a declarative democracy, and thus an expression of an increasingly authoritarian political approach under Putin's leadership, even a shift from an oligarchy to a 'KGB-' or 'mafia-state', in effect creating what some have called a 'militocracy paradigm' as the main framework for understanding Russian politics which underpins the de-democratisation thesis.[11]

Elaborating on this broad canvas of balances between formal structures and informal rules, and 'siloviki' and 'liberal-technocrats', depictions of the Russian political landscape have featured more detailed analysis of the groups and factions involved, and the way they interact. Some have suggested that the president works publicly with two teams of officials, the government and the permanent members of the Security Council, who meet to take strategic decisions, and a third, smaller and informal 'tea-drinking' group of personal friends.[12] This interaction is underpinned by informal associations or networks of clans.[13]

These 'clans', networks and groups are often depicted as in constant tension and rivalry for resources, arbitrated by Putin.

Observers have proposed numerous models for these networks. The 'Kremlin Towers' model, offered by Vladimir Pribylovsky, divides the leadership team into nine clans, mostly based on a St Petersburg affiliation, such as the 'St Petersburg lawyers', 'St Petersburg Chekists' (security services), 'St Petersburg economists', 'Orthodox Chekists', and so on. The clans are grouped on business, kinship and career relationships, are each led by the most influential and powerful figures, and are composed of a hierarchical structure of people at different levels of government and business.[14] The 'Solar system' or 'Planets' model depicts relationships as they relate to Putin, who is the 'sun' at the core of the system. He is surrounded by three circles of planets – the inner circle or partners, the intermediate circle, or junior partners, and the outer circle, or loyal servants. The framework is more flexible as the position of the various planets can evolve, moving closer to or further from the core.[15]

A third approach, advanced by Evgeniy Minchenko, a Russian political consultant, proposes a 'Politburo 2.0' model, which represents an informal collective leadership based on three tiers. At the core, there is a 'full membership' of some 10 to 12 individuals who are leading figures in the security services, government and business. This then ripples out on a scale of some 50 other 'candidate members', again drawn not only from the power/security services, politics, big business and the government/administration, but also party politics and regional authorities, and then, beyond that, a lower, larger level of 'central committee members'. This grouping also evolves. When Minchenko published his 'Politburo 2.0' in 2010, there were 11 full members. By 2012, it had shrunk to nine full members, as Alexei Kudrin and Sergei Naryshkin dropped down into the 'Candidate members' group. In the 'Post Crimea' Politburo report of 2014, the full member group had again grown to 11 as Sergei Chemezov and Arkady Rotenburg had been added.[16]

Despite their (slight) variations, these models offer a broad consensus about who are the key figures in the leadership team. They include Sergei Ivanov, Dmitri Medvedev, Nikolai Patrushev, Igor Sechin, Yuri Kovalchuk, Gennadiy Timchenko, Sergei Sobyanin, Vyacheslav Volodin, Sergei Shoigu, Arkadiy Rotenberg and Sergei Chemezov. Among the 50 or so at the next level are Alexei Kudrin, Vladislav Surkov, Sergei Naryshkin, Dmitri Kozak, German Gref, Igor Shuvalov, Elvira Nabiullina, Sergei Lavrov, Alexander Bastrykin, Viktor Zolotov, Mikhail Fradkov, Alexei Miller, Anatoliy Chubais, Oleg Deripaska, Mikhail Fridman, Yuri Trutnev, Alexander

Khloponin and the senior systemic opposition figures such as Sergei Mironov and Gennadiy Zyuganov.[17]

Against this background, several important related points stand out about Russian political life. The first is that, despite well-publicised (though sometimes exaggerated) tensions and rivalries between factions, the factions belong to one wider team with vested interests in the continuation of the current system. To be sure, there are those who are rivals for power and resources, and those who espouse different priorities or means of achieving goals. Nevertheless, despite labels such as 'siloviki' and 'liberals', the groups' wider political orientations do not differ over ultimate goals: as some observers have noted, there is 'very little opposition' in either group to 'a "strong" or even "authoritarian" state'; and some, while labeled 'liberal' were fulfilling a role – if they had been given a role that was more conservative, then they would have acted as conservatives.[18] The emphasis, therefore, is overall on a *collective* leadership team with Putin acting as the central figure as arbitrator between these groups, and this collective serves to co-opt and balance competing groups into a whole.[19] When Putin first came to power in 1999/2000, he was initially considered to have no team, though by 2001 Russian media awarded the title of politician of the year to the 'Collective Putin'.[20]

Since 2000, and particularly during the mid-to-late 2000s, Putin (and Medvedev) have overseen largely joint appointments to senior positions of personnel with whom they have long and strong connections and who have proved themselves. The leadership team is built on two main pillars. One pillar consists of those in the core group who in the main are the friends, classmates and colleagues of Vladimir Putin (and Dmitri Medvedev), and have worked together since the early-to-mid 1990s. As one observer put it, 'it is not even just St Petersburgers, but classmates and personal friends and acquaintances of the president and prime minister who occupy all the key positions in the country'.[21]

The other pillar consists of those professional bureaucrats and a regional elite who have risen through the ranks in the government bureaucracy and party politics and become part of the leadership team. Two examples are Sergei Lavrov, Russian ambassador to the UN 1994–2004 and since then Foreign Minister (and member of the Security Council), and Sergei Shoigu, Minister for Emergency Situations from 1991 to 2012, then regional governor of Moscow Region, before replacing Anatoliy Serdyukov as Minister of Defence in 2012, also with a position in the Security Council. Shoigu, for years the only minister who registered in popularity polls, has had a long career in politics, also: in 1999, he headed the Unity party list, and subsequently becoming the leader of UR until 2005. The leadership team is thus woven into the longer-term political land-scape of Russia, and woven together in formal structures such as the presidential administration, the Security Council, the govern-ment, presidential advisory councils and big business.

Second, leading on from this, there has been considerable long-term stability and continuity in this leadership team. Most of the senior figures from both pillars of the team have occupied senior positions since the late 1990s. Indeed, it is important to remember that although Putin has instigated a number of changes, he inher-ited much of the structure of the system that he now leads; and a number of prominent figures such as Alexander Voloshin, Anatoliy Chubais, 'systemic' opposition figures Gennadiy Zyuganov and Vladimir Zhirinovsky, as well as Dmitry Rogozin and Sergei Shoigu held senior positions in Russian political, administrative and busi-ness life before Putin even came to Moscow.

This reflects a number of important points about Russian poli-tics, including the emphasis placed on broader stability, teams and loyalty, and the unwillingness of the leadership to fire people or conduct major 'reshuffles'. Changes have been limited to 'rotations', which broadly constitute moving the same senior figures to differ-ent positions: despite even serious, high-profile scandals, senior figures are rarely scapegoated or fired. When he was prime minister, Putin published an article entitled 'why it is difficult to fire some-one', in which he stated that even those who make mistakes should not simply be punished by being fired, and that it is not always clear whether the accusations being made in favour of someone being fired are merely political intrigue – since a constant theme of politics is the clash of interests. He also notes that he is convinced that constant, rushed changes will not make things better, either for getting things done, or for the people involved, since those who replace them will be much the same (if not worse). The task, there-fore, is to create a working environment and motivate people to do their work – and let them get on with it, rather than indulge in firings. Interestingly, he suggests that the time when it *is* appropri-ate to fire someone is when they suggest that a task set for them is 'impossible'.[22]

This is not to say that the leadership team has not evolved over time, including, on very rare occasions, the eviction of senior figures from the inner circle, though these are very few in number. One is

Viktor Cherkesov, a graduate of the law department of Leningrad State University and subsequent head of the St Petersburg FSB, before becoming first deputy director of the FSB under Putin and Patrushev and subsequently Putin's presidential plenipotentiary to the North-West Federal District, who was evicted in 2010.[23] Another is Alexei Kudrin, who resigned from his formal position as Finance Minister because of his publicly stated opposition to the leadership's spending plans, particularly on defence, though he continues to occupy influential positions, including on the Presidential Economic Council.

If Putin (and Medvedev) find it difficult to fire people, they have nevertheless made it clear that there are certain rules that must be observed: in November 2013, Putin stated 'I will have to remind [my colleagues] that there are fixed practices for resolving questions before going out into the media'. 'It is well known', he continued, 'that if someone does not agree with something, as Mr Kudrin did', then they can go over into the expert community and work with the leadership from there.[24] Kudrin had voiced his opposition to defence expenditure publicly in the USA, and at the time, Medvedev suggested that if he disagreed with the course of the president, there was only one course of action – resignation.[25] Similarly, Cherkesov's departure is often attributed to his public statements about internal divisions in the leadership team.

Other senior figures to have been fired or resigned include Anatoliy Serdyukov, who was fired by Putin having been implicated in a multi-faceted scandal including a major corruption case in the MoD, and Vladislav Surkov, another long-term senior figure, who was first moved from the position of first deputy head of the presidential administration during the 'rotation' in December 2011 to the position of deputy prime minister – from which he resigned in May 2012. Putin's press spokesman Dmitry Peskov confirmed that Surkov tendered his resignation after a meeting with Putin at which Putin had criticised the government for the implementation of his May Decrees. Reportage of the meeting suggested a disagreement in the feasibility of implementation of the instructions: while Surkov had suggested that the government had made progress, Putin sought 100 per cent fulfillment – a 'mobilisation' speed that was not possible to maintain.[26]

As in the case of Kudrin's move, there was much speculation about Surkov's departure. The 'resignations' of both Kudrin and Surkov appear to have been the result of a complex of reasons. Kudrin, some suggested, was not prepared to serve under Prime

Minister Dmitri Medvedev, and Surkov faced an investigation by the Investigative Committee for embezzlement. Vladimir Markin, the Investigative Committee's spokesman, also questioned whether Surkov should keep his position in the cabinet having made critical comments about Russia during a speech in London. Peskov explicitly denied that the public dispute between Surkov and Markin or the embezzlement investigation lay behind Surkov's resignation. Also like Kudrin, Surkov's 'resignation' was 'limited' – in effect what might be termed a rotation down, in which he has retained considerable influence, rather than 'firing' and complete departure from policy. Surkov did not go far from power, and he was subsequently appointed as an aide to the president in 2013 and to lead the department of Commonwealth of Independent States, South Ossetia and Abkhazia in the presidential administration, and appears to have played an active role in Russia's Ukraine policy since 2014. This again illustrates the point that when senior figures are removed from ministerial or senior political positions, they often retain prominent positions within the system. Boris Gryzlov and Rashid Nurgaliev, for instance, when relieved of their duties as Speaker of the Lower House of Parliament (2011) and Minister of the Interior (2012), both retained positions as permanent members of the Security Council. Indeed Nurgaliev, whose Ministry endured numerous scandals under his leadership (2003–2012), was appointed deputy secretary of the Security Council.[27]

It also reflects the effects of the somewhat faster rotations and dismissals at lower levels, and it is noteworthy that during Putin's third presidential term not only have regional governors continued to be removed from office by the leadership,[28] but so have ministers. Indeed, the turnover of ministers since 2012 has been notably higher: Viktor Ishaev, a long-serving governor of Khabarovsk region, then presidential plenipotentiary to the Far East for three years before being appointed the first Minister of the Far East when the ministry was created in 2012, was fired having endured at least two previous rounds of public criticism by Putin for ineffectiveness. Others to have lost their positions, apparently because of Putin's unhappiness with their performance, include Oleg Govorun, a prominent member of UR who had served in the presidential administration before briefly being appointed first presidential plenipotentiary to the Central Federal District in September 2011 and then in May 2012 Minister for Regional Development. He was relieved of his ministerial duties in October that year (but has subsequently returned to lead a department in the presidential administration).

The evolution of the team has also involved bringing people in as individuals have proved themselves and been promoted to senior positions – though observers suggest that earning Putin's trust is a difficult and long-term process. As Anatoliy Rakhlin, Putin's judo trainer put it, Putin works with a close group not 'because of their pretty eyes, but because he trusts people who are tried and true'.[29] One of the most prominent is Vyacheslav Volodin. Volodin, of whom more below, has extensive political experience, and was deputy prime minister and chief of staff to Putin's cabinet in 2010. In 2011, he was involved in the establishment of the ONF and in December that year he was appointed first deputy head of the presidential administration, responsible for the 'reset' of Russian politics.

This form of broadly stable but evolving collective leadership in Russia is often described as 'krugovaya poruka'. There are various translations for this feature of Russian political life, but in effect, it means 'circle of shared responsibility', and indicates the ties that bind groups together. Such a collective arrangement thrives, as one analyst has suggested, in an environment in which administrative and legal institutions are 'insufficiently developed to oversee the enforcement of legal rights and responsibilities'. It is, in effect, a mechanism to ensure that things are done. It offers a form of circular control that both ensures conformity and solidarity, submerging individual interests into a collective unit and binding individuals together into a network: all members of a group are held jointly responsible for the actions of individuals, and it thus acts as a means of burden sharing, mutual obligation and protection. It also underpins conservative network evolution, both in terms of collegial rule and decision-making and recruitment to the group. Appointments to positions are carried out cautiously, a longer-term process of testing an individual's loyalty, work ethic, reliability and ability to fulfil tasks.[30]

Building a vertical of power?

Against this background of the evolution of a collective leadership team with Putin at its heart, the vertical of power is a central feature of the Russian political landscape. As with the factions and the balance between formal instructions and informal rules, the vertical of power existed before Putin's rise, and its origins can be traced to the early post-Cold War era.[31] In the mainstream Western discussion about Russia, however, it is usually associated with Vladimir Putin's attempt to establish a vertical chain of hierarchical authority, establishing strong government with leadership from the top, and instilling unconditional discipline and responsibility to fulfil tasks. One Russian observer suggested that the need for this was almost immediately illustrated when Putin first came to power in 2000, with the sinking of the Kursk submarine. The way the military authorities 'systematically misled' him convinced Putin, according to Alexander Goltz, that the structure of authority needed to be overhauled, leading to a restructuring of power including the replacement in 2004 of direct elections for regional governors with presidential appointments.[32] This remained a work in progress, however, and during his presidency, Medvedev also worked to complete the vertical of power, often appointing technocratic managers to attempt to improve the state's effectiveness.

As noted above, most attention has focused on the appointments of ex-KGB and security services personnel to positions across the bureaucracy and big business and the undemocratic ramifications. Most observers suggest that Putin's attempt to build an ever more vertical of power has been, if flawed, largely successful. At the same time, whether the vertical of power works has received less detailed attention. In fact, official Russian sources have long conceded that the vertical does not work, and presidential instructions often remain unfulfilled or are only tardily or partially fulfilled, and responses to crises slow and ineffective. The leadership is reduced to micro-management (known as 'manual control'), whether in terms of routine administrative tasks and the implementation of policy, or in responding to specific problems. This is caused by a number of problems, including corruption, blurred lines of responsibility between ministries and agencies, limitations in bureaucratic capacity and a degree of passive resistance in the bureaucracy.[33]

Since late 2011, Putin has instigated an ongoing rotation of senior figures to enhance the alignment of power and administrative effectiveness. Changes include an economic rotation in June 2013, the creation of new ministries and rotations of presidential plenipotentiaries in August and September 2013 and May 2014 (the latter presented by the authorities as an attempt to align minister, presidential plenipotentiary and regional governor in strategically important areas). Similarly, as noted above, ministers and governors are monitored by the presidential administration and the ONF for their effectiveness.

Another way of looking at the vertical of power, therefore, is this search for effectiveness. How might the political landscape outlined above be drawn upon the better to understand the vertical of power, attempts to improve it, and the 'reset'? The cascade of networks can be framed in three groups – the 'leadership team', the 'federal locomotives', who are dispatched to oversee the most important tasks, and 'managers'.

The leadership team

In interviews with Putin in 2000, he was asked whose proposals he listened to, who he trusted and who was on his team. The answers were illuminating: Putin named Sergei Ivanov, Nikolai Patrushev and Dmitri Medvedev as those with whom he had 'brotherly closeness', and that he 'trusted' Alexei Kudrin.[34] This is illuminating, not just because of their backgrounds and long-shared experiences working for Anatoliy Sobchak in St Petersburg or the KGB, but because of the subsequent trajectories of these individuals, who have worked closely with Putin throughout his rise to power and then occupied senior positions since. Nikolai Patrushev, for instance, was appointed to senior positions in the presidential administration in 1998, and then as Putin's deputy in the FSB in 1999, before replacing him as Director in 1999, where he remained until Putin appointed him Secretary of the Security Council in 2008. Similarly, Sergei Ivanov served as Putin's deputy in the presidential administration in 1998–1999, before Putin appointed him Minister of Defence in 2001. Subsequently, he occupied positions as deputy and first deputy prime minister, before being appointed head of the presidential administration in December 2011.

Dmitri Medvedev worked with Putin in St Petersburg, and his career, too, has largely echoed Putin's. In December 1999, Putin appointed him head of the presidential administration and he ran Putin's presidential election campaign in 2000. Since then, he has occupied positions in Gazprom as chairman of the board of directors (during which he oversaw pricing negotiations with Belarus and Ukraine), the presidential administration, the government as first deputy prime minister in 2005 (responsible for national priority projects, including public health, housing and education) before becoming president in 2008. In his election campaign in 2007, Medvedev often stated his readiness to continue the course set by Putin. While this is not a complete list of the inner circle, today, these 'brotherly' figures represent the core of Putin's command team, occupying the heights of formal (and informal) Russian politics: Patrushev is Secretary of the Security Council, Ivanov is head of the presidential administration and Medvedev is prime minister.

'Federal locomotives'

Closely associated with this core leadership team is a somewhat larger group of those who are trusted to carry out the strategic agenda. As two prominent observers have pointed out, the 'existence of such figures is the difference between a bureaucracy that does not and cannot get things done and a group of individuals who can get things done and profit in doing so'.[35] This small group, some, but not all of whom, are from St Petersburg, includes individuals from politics, the government apparatus and big business, and is directly and personally accountable to Vladimir Putin. They are tasked with leading the fulfilment of strategically important projects, and trusted to deliver results – and are rewarded (and protected) by Putin on the basis of their performance. In one interview, Arkady Rotenberg stated that such individuals had to perform well in big, difficult projects, completing them within tight deadlines – there are very few people in Russia who can achieve this and they are 'not entitled to make a mistake', nor would Putin protect them if they were to abuse the responsibility they had been given.[36] In this group are those, as noted in Chapter 3, who led the effort to reinvigorate UR in 2011, and those such as German Gref, minister of economics and trade from 2000 to 2007 and now president of Sberbank, and Dmitri Kozak, who worked with Putin in St Petersburg City Council, before leading Putin's election campaign in 2004 and becoming presidential plenipotentiary to the Southern Federal District until 2007 and then becoming deputy prime minister in 2008. Since then Kozak, with Arkadiy Rotenberg and others from big business, was tasked with organising the Sochi Winter Olympics in 2014. Another is Yuri Trutnev: Trutnev was elected mayor of Perm in 1996. He was elected governor of Perm region 2000–2004, when he was appointed minister for natural resources and the environment, before becoming an advisor to Putin from 2012–2013. In 2013, he was appointed deputy prime minister and presidential plenipotentiary to the Far Eastern federal district.

Perhaps the most important 'federal locomotive' since Putin came to power, however, is Igor Sechin, who first worked for Putin in St Petersburg. Like those in the core leadership team,[37] his career has been closely tied to Putin's. Numerous Russian observers have suggested that Sechin quickly became Putin's trusted assistant, an 'inseparable colleague', even the only colleague that Putin took with him on all assignments. They emphasise Sechin's loyalty to Putin, and note that even from the early 1990s Sechin ran Putin's apparatus, coordinating departments before moving with Putin to Moscow and being appointed to different positions in the presidential administration.[38]

Indeed, subsequently, Sechin appears to have accompanied Putin every step of the way, running his timetable, and being put in charge of dealing with business conflicts. In 2004, Sechin became chairman of the board of directors of Rosneft, becoming, as another Russian observer put it, 'Putin's right hand in the energy sector'.[39] In 2008, he left the presidential administration, being appointed deputy prime minister for industry, energy and environment, leading numerous government commissions with authority well beyond the hydrocarbon sector, becoming chairman of the board of directors of the United Shipbuilding Company and Inter-RAO UES, and playing an important role in Russian foreign policy in China, Latin America and Eurasia. In 2011, Sechin was included on the list of candidates as a deputy for United Russia in the parliamentary elections, and early 2012, he became president of Rosneft and executive secretary of Putin's energy commission. Speaking in March 2012, Putin stated that he valued Sechin's 'professionalism and tenacity' – 'he can see things through to the end: if he takes something on, then you can be certain that the business will be done.'[40]

Managers

A third category, the largest and most diverse, consists of proven managers. The need for better management is one of the primary concerns of the Russian leadership, a point regularly made by Putin himself who critiques or praises individuals for their success or failure in this. These are individuals (and their networks) who have a proven track record in resolving problems, including well established figures such as Sergey Sobyanin, mayor of Moscow, Sergey Kirienko, head of Rosatom, and Anatoliy Chubais, head of Rusnano. Alexander Khloponin also fits into this category, having extensive experience in business and administration. Formerly chairman of Norilsk Nikel, Khloponin, a member of United Russia, has served as governor of Taymyr Autonomous Okrug and then Krasnoyarsk Krai, where he reversed economic decline. In 2010, he was appointed deputy prime minister and presidential plenipotentiary to the North Caucasus Federal District.[41]

Others who might fall into this category include those in the main bodies of the presidential administration, security council and government – those with long experience in these organisations, such as Larisa Brychova, longtime head of the presidential state-legal directorate in the presidential administration, and Alexei Gromov, who has served in the presidential administration since 1996, and since May 2012 as first deputy chief of staff. This also includes those such as Yuri Averyanov and Evgeniy Lukyanov, long-serving members of the Security Council apparatus, and now respectively first deputy and deputy of the Security Council.

Konstantin Chuichenko is another. A fellow student of Dmitri Medvedev's, he was appointed chief of Gazprom's legal department in 2001, rising to become the chairman of the board of directors of Gazprom media holding in 2003, and, in July 2004, executive director of RosUkrEnergo representing Gazprombank. In 2008, he was appointed head of the main control directorate of the presidential administration. Similarly, Anton Vaino began his career in the Ministry of Foreign Affairs, before joining the presidential protocol department in 2002. In October 2007, he was appointed the government's deputy chief of staff, becoming head of the prime minister's protocol. He was briefly chief of government staff before being appointed to the position of deputy head of the presidential administration in May 2012.

Towards the future: refreshing the system?

If networks, and testing for loyalty and effectiveness are at the heart of the evolution of the system as new managers are promoted, how has this been evident in the tightening of the vertical of power and the ongoing political 'reset'? The first point to note is the increasing prominence of organisations such as the ONF and ASI in both the tightening of the vertical and the reset,[42] and political youth organisations in the latter. The second is that these organisations appear to be playing the role envisaged for them: a springboard for the emergence of a new generation who reached state-level politics since 2007.

This newer generation includes those recently appointed to ministerial positions – Alexander Galushka, for instance, was appointed Minister for the Development of the Far East in September 2013. Born in 1975, he has risen quickly and holds a number of senior managerial positions across the presidential and governmental apparatus, including on the central committee of the ONF, the advisory council of the ASI, and the President's Economic Council. Others include Andrey Nikitin, born in 1979, who is chief executive officer of the ASI, and Alexander Brechalov – who holds a range of positions including as a member of the supervisory board of the ASI, the co-chair of the ONF's central committee, and president of the Russian organisation of small and medium enterprises (OPORA). Another is Andrey Bocharov, formerly a member of UR, who took up a position as head of the executive committee of the ONF, before Putin appointed him acting governor of Volgograd in summer 2014. Others who appear to be earning reputations as effective managers include the governor of Leningrad region, Alexander Drozdenko,[43] and Dmitri Kobylkin, governor of Yamalo-Nenetski autonomous region and member of United Russia's higher council.[44] As one well-placed Russian suggested, such individuals, along with important deputy ministers, are mainly of a similar (comparatively youthful) age, and there is a 'feeling of teamwork being developed' among them.[45]

The 'reset' also illustrates how the leadership team is evolving. Since 2011, Vyacheslav Volodin has led the political reset, including the development of the ONF. Volodin himself has long experience in regional politics, starting in the Saratov regional legislature, before being elected to the State Duma in 1999 as a member of the Fatherland-All Russia party faction – of which he became head in September 2001. In 2003, he was elected to the Duma again as a member of United Russia, and the following year became deputy duma speaker and first deputy head of UR. In 2007, he was elected deputy chairman of UR, before being appointed deputy prime minister and chief of staff of the government's executive office.

Others who are emerging in the context of the reset include Alexei Anisimov, who was involved in the establishment of the ONF, overseeing the formation of the organisation's regional offices, and acting as deputy chief of staff in Putin's presidential election campaign. In 2012, he was appointed head of regional policy in the domestic policy department of the presidential administration before becoming head of the ONF's executive committee in May 2014. Tatiana Voronova, born in 1975, has made huge career steps since she was leader of the Irkutsk branch of 'Molodyozhnoe Edinstvo' in 2000. She was elected to the State Duma in 2007 and appears to have worked with Anisimov for Putin in 2008. She was appointed to the presidential administration in 2012 to lead a new department on relations with non-systemic opposition (led by Anisimov), and was subsequently moved to oversee regional politics before replacing Oleg Morozov as head of the domestic politics in March 2015. Voronova's rise illustrates again the emergence of a younger generation to influential positions. Maxim Rudnev, born in 1987, was appointed director of the central executive committee of United

Russia in September 2014. Timur Prokopenko, who had served as press secretary first to deputy speaker of the Duma Vladimir Pekhtin and then as press secretary to Boris Gryzlov (2009–2011), was appointed to the domestic politics department of the presidential administration in October 2012, overseeing the information policy division, then, from December deputy head of the department and responsible for youth and information policy. Like Voronova, Rudnev and Prokopenko have emerged from systemic party youth organisations – in their cases, UR's 'Molodaya Gvardia' (MG), in which they played prominent roles since its formation in 2005.[46]

Russia beyond Putin?

Much is made in the Western discussion of Russia about the centrality of Vladimir Putin, his popularity ratings, and his use of patriotic, even nationalist rhetoric to boost this popularity. Similarly, much is made of the non-transparency of Russian decision-making and the relationships between clans and networks. Both of these points have some merit. Undoubtedly, Vladimir Putin is popular: since March 2014, polls conducted by the Levada Centre have suggested that support for him has exceeded 75 per cent. All other political figures, including Zyuganov, receive support of less than 10 per cent.[47] Putin is also undoubtedly a central figure in Russian politics, often personally taking decisions on matters of strategic import (such as those taken regarding the situation in Ukraine in 2014) at the summit of the vertical of power and at the heart of a system that he has adapted and tailored – and much of that system is non-transparent.

With this in mind, it is important to look beyond Putin to attempt to interpret Russia and how it is changing, including how teams take shape and individuals are promoted. The team surrounding Putin is made up of groups of individuals with whom he has worked for many years, a largely stable one comprised of trusted associates, professionals, and a regional elite. This leadership team has taken shape over a considerable time frame, and stretches deep and wide into Russian business, administration and politics. If the core leadership team consists of trusted and proven long-term associates of Putin, a poll conducted in February 2015 suggests that a majority sees that Putin's wider team consists of those of a 'like mind' ('edinomyshlenniki' – in other words who share Putin's views) and professionals. Sixty-one per cent thought that there should be more of those who share Putin's views in the team, and a decreasing number of people think there should be a radical change in the team – from 47 in 2012, to 21 per cent in 2015. A majority (54 per cent) thought that the team should remain broadly as it is.[48]

Beyond the core leadership team, however, the professionals and regional elites who play important roles both implementing the decisions of the top leadership team, and even being involved in decision-making on non-strategic matters, should be an increasing focus of attention as individuals are brought into the wider team, tested and promoted. Those who succeed are likely to have considerable experience across business, state administration and regional politics, and will have developed networks accordingly. To understand better the ongoing rotation, and unavoidable retirements and replacements, and the elections in 2016, 2018 and 2024, observers will benefit from having much greater familiarity with the inner workings of Russian politics, having watched promotions and being aware of who is considered loyal and effective (and who are in their networks); and an awareness of those who have risen in administrative positions. Similarly, organisations such as the ONF, the ASI and youth party organisations appear to be serving as platforms for both the co-option of individuals into the system, and the emergence of new figures, including a younger generation who are playing an increasing role in running Russia.

Indeed, this is becoming increasingly necessary, since retirements, illness and deaths begin to oblige the leadership team to evolve as it seeks effective managers: Vladimir Yakunin, long-term head of Russian Railways and a member of the leadership team, in effect took retirement in August 2015 (though in October it was reported in Russian media that he was dismissed); and in January 2016, General Igor Sergun, head of Russian military intelligence, passed away aged 58. Other prominent individuals are close to retirement age – Secretary of the Security Council Nikolai Patrushev is 64, for instance, and Foreign Minister Sergei Lavrov is 65. This adds emphasis to the Russian observer's point above about teamwork taking shape among a new generation of upwardly mobile individuals and networks.

Notes

1 'Splits emerging in Putin's Russia: oligarchs vs. hardliners', *Daily Telegraph* (27 July 2014); 'The chilly fallout between Putin and his oligarch pals', *Bloomberg* (22 January 2015).

2 This has been a regular feature of the mainstream Western discussion of Russia for some years. See discussion in Chapter 3, and B. Judah, 'The end of Vladimir Putin', *Politico Magazine* (31 July 2014); B. Whitmore, 'The warlord checkmates the Tsar?', *The Power Vertical*, RFE/RL (18 March 2015); A. Motyl, 'Goodbye, Putin: why the President's days are numbered', *Foreign Affairs* (5 February 2015).

3 L. Shevtsova, 'Has the Russian system's agony begun?', *The American Interest* (17 March 2015).

4 Cited in M. Schrad, 'Putin has Aspergers? Don't flatter him', *Politico* (6 February 2015).

5 Volodin's phrase was part of an answer to a question about Western sanctions on Russia. Though the aphorism has been widely reported, the transcript of the session is unavailable to offer a more precise quote or to check the context and other points he made during the session. '"No Putin, no Russia" says Kremlin deputy chief of staff', *Moscow Times* (23 October 2014), www.themoscowtimes.com/news/article/no-putin-no-russia-says-kremlin-deputy-chief-of-staff/509981.html. See also 'Est Putin – est Rossia, Nyet Putina – Nyet Rossii' [There is Putin – there is Russia, no Putin – no Russia], *Izvestiya* (22 October 2014).

6 'Morgan Stanley preduprezhdaet: glava gosudarstva uidyot' [Morgan Stanley warns: the head of state will go], *Nezavisimaya Gazeta* (12 January 2005), www.ng.ru/politics/2005-01-12/1_revolution.html.

7 See, for instance, 'Russian hearts, minds and refrigerators', *Financial Times* (16 February 2015). This is the 'battle for Russian minds' between the agenda on Russian state television of a glorious Russia in a patriotic struggle against Ukraine and the West and the imposition of sanctions having a negative impact on living standards, leading to the increasingly sparse and expensive contents of the fridge at home – thus undermining Russian support for Putin's policies in Ukraine.

8 V. Ryzhkov, 'Putin must change direction or face coup', *Moscow Times* (1 December 2014), www.themoscowtimes.com/opinion/article/putin-must-change-direction-or-face-a-coup/512204.html; D. Jensen, 'A coup against Putin?', Institute of Modern Russia (4 February 2015), http://imrussia.org/en/analysis/politics/2166-a-coup-against-putin; P. Goble, 'Interest in a palace coup against Putin said growing among Russian elites', *The Interpreter Magazine* (8 March 2015), www.interpretermag.com/interest-in-a-palace-coup-against-putin-said-growing-among-russian-elites/.

9 Correspondence with Jacob Kipp, May 2015.

10 R. Sakwa, *The Crisis of Russian Democracy: The Dual State, Factionalism and the Medvedev Succession* (Cambridge: Cambridge University Press, 2011).

11 An article central to this thesis is O. Kryshtanovskaya and S. White, 'Putin's militocracy', *Post-Soviet Affairs*, 19:4 (2003). B. Rentz, 'Putin's militocracy? An alternative interpretation of siloviki in contemporary Russian politics', *Europe-Asia Studies*, 58:6 (September 2006),

pp. 903–924, provides a stimulating critique of the thesis. Other articles include I. Bremmer and S. Charap, 'The siloviki in Putin's Russia: who they are and what they want', *The Washington Quarterly*, 30:1 (winter 2006–2007); D. Rivera and S. Werning Rivera, 'Is Russia a militocracy? Conceptual issues and extant findings regarding elite militarization', *Post-Soviet Affairs*, 30:1 (2014), p. 28. This latter article provides a good overview of the debate.

12 Though the two teams of officials had considerable crossover in membership, Kryshtanovskaya and White suggested that only Dmitri Medvedev and Sergei Ivanov were common to all three groups. O. Kryshtanovskaya and S. White, 'Inside the Putin court: a research note', *Europe-Asia Studies*, 57:7 (November 2005), p. 1069.

13 Kryshtanovskaya and White, 'Inside the Putin court'.

14 V. Pribylovsky, 'Power struggles inside the Kremlin', *Open Democracy* (31 December 2014); Y. Felshtinsky and V. Pribylovsky, *The Corporation. Russia and the KGB in the Age of President Putin* (London: Encounter Books, 2008).

15 A. Ledeneva, *Can Russia Modernise? Sistema, Power Networks and Informal Governance* (Cambridge: Cambridge University Press, 2013), pp. 55–61; N. Petrov, 'The nomenclatura and the elite', in M. Lipman and N. Petrov (eds), *Russia in 2020: Scenarios for the Future* (Washington, DC: Carnegie Endowment for International Peace, 2011), pp. 516–520.

16 E. Minchenko, *Problema 2012 i politburo* [The 2012 Problem and the Politburo] (9 December 2010), http://minchenko.ru/blog/ruspolitics/2010/12/09/ruspolitics_468.html; http://minchenko.ru/blog/ruspolitics/20122, October 2014.

17 Here is not the place to list everyone. Minchenko's 'Candidate members' list, as framed in 'Politburo 2.0' i postkrymskaya Rossia' [Politburo 2.0 and post-Crimea Russia] gives a good list that is largely compatible with the other models.

18 Kryshtanovskaya and White, 'Inside the Putin court', p. 1069; Ledeneva, *Can Russia Modernise?*, pp. 77–78.

19 For a good, brief overview, D. Jensen, 'Russian clans' ongoing feud', Institute of Modern Russia (12 June 2013), http://imrussia.org/en/analysis/politics/489-russian-clans-ongoing-feud.

20 Ledeneva, *Can Russia Modernise?*, p. 77.

21 O. Ptashkin, 'Zakon o bespredele' [Law on lawlessness], gazeta.ru (18 June 2010).

22 V. Putin, 'Pochemu trudno uvolit cheloveka' [Why it is hard to fire a person], *Russkiy Pioner* (16 June 2009), http://ruspioner.ru/cool/m/single/1999. There was some suggestion that Putin himself did not write the article. Nevertheless, his name is attached to it, and thus commentators agreed that it would have been edited and censored by Putin and his assistants. Others, including Medvedev, have voiced similar views.

23 He is now a KPRF deputy in the Federation Council, the upper house of parliament.

24 'Zasedanie nabludatenlovo soveta Agentstva strategicheskikh init-siativ' [Meeting of the Supervisory board of the Agency for Strategic Initiatives] (14 November 2013), http://kremlin.ru/transcripts/19625.

25 Kudrin had voiced his opposition publicly in the USA. Cited in 'Russian finance chief ousted in power struggle', Reuters (26 September 2011), www.reuters.com/article/2011/09/26/us-russia-idUSTRE78P3JR20110926.

26 'Soveshchanie o khode ispolnenia ukazov prezidenta ot 7 Maya 2012 goda' [Meeting about the implementation of presidential decrees of 7 May 2012] (7 May 2013), www.kremlin.ru/news/18039; 'Surkov uvo-len s dolzhnosti vitze-prem'era' [Surkov fired as deputy prime minis-ter], lenta.ru (8 May 2013), http://lenta.ru/news/2013/05/08/surkov/; 'Ot redaktsii: pravitel'stvo otvechaet pered prezidentom, a president ne otvechaet ni pered kem' [Editorial: the government is responsible to the president, while the president is responsible to nobody], Vedomosti (8 May 2013).

27 He was replaced as Minister of the Interior by Vladimir Kolokoltsev, a career policeman and Moscow Police Commissioner from 2009 to 2012.

28 Medvedev fired numerous governors during his term in office, and some senior figures such as Yuri Luzhkov, long-term mayor of Moscow, in September 2010. Though he had been co-opted into United Russia, he was not a member of the inner circle. T. Stanovaya, 'Ot bitvy Moskvui k bitve za Moskvu' [From the battle of Moscow to the battle for Moscow], politcom.ru (16 September 2010); T. Stanovaya, 'Moskovskaya sdelka tandema' [Tandem's Moscow deal], politcom.ru (4 October 2010). Several governors have been fired since 2012, including Sergei Bozhenov, governor of Volgograd, and Alexander Khoroshavin, Sakhalin governor. It is worth noting that the ONF appears to have played an important role in the monitoring of these governors and requesting their removal. Governors have not, by contrast, been voted out by the populations in the yearly regional elections.

29 See discussion in F. Hill and C. Gaddy, Mr Putin: Operative in the Kremlin (Washington, DC: Brookings Institute Press, 2013), p. 237; A. Ledeneva, Can Russia Modernise? Sistema, Power Networks and Informal Governance (Cambridge: Cambridge University Press, 2013).

30 A. Ledeneva, How Russia Really Works: The Informal Practices that Shape Post-Soviet Politics and Business (London: Cornell University Press, 2006). For discussion of the historical background of this col-lective approach, see E. Keenan, 'Muscovite political folkways', The Russian Review, 45:2 (April 1986), pp. 115–181.

31 L. Ryazanova-Clarke, 'How upright is the vertical? Ideological norm negotiation in Russian media discourse', in I. Lunde and M. Paulsen (eds),

From Poets to Podonki: Linguistic Authority and Norm Negotiation in Modern Russian Culture (University of Bergen: Department of Foreign Languages, 2009).

32 A. Goltz, 'Putin's power vertical stretches back to Kursk', *Moscow Times* (17 August 2010).

33 See A. Monaghan, *The Russian Vertikal: The Tandem, Power and the Elections*, Chatham House Programme Paper (June 2011); A. Monaghan, *Defibrillating the Vertikal? Putin and Russian Grand Strategy*, Chatham House Research Paper (October 2014).

34 N. Gevorkyan, N. Timakova and A. Kolesnikov, *Ot pervovo litsa. Razgovory s Vladimirom Putinym* [First Person: Conversations with Vladimir Putin] (Moscow: Vagrius, 2000), pp. 181–182.

35 Hill and Gaddy, *Mr. Putin*, p. 237.

36 Cited in Hill and Gaddy, *Mr. Putin*, pp. 350–351.

37 Sechin is mentioned alongside Patrushev, Ivanov, Medvedev and Kudrin.

38 K. Shegolev, *Kto est kto: ispolnitelnaya vlast* [Who is Who: Executive Power] (Moscow: AST Astrel', 2009), p. 461, 'Igor' Sechin perviy vozle Putina' [Igor Sechin first by Putin], *Vedomosti* (22 May 2012).

39 N. Grib, *Gazovyi Imperator* [Gas Emperor] (Moscow: Kommersant/ Eksmo, 2009), p. 160.

40 Putin, speaking on 7 March 2012, www.youtube.com/watch?v=JYr Uos3YyyI.

41 In May 2014, Khloponin was reappointed deputy prime minister, but relieved of his duties as presidential plenipotentiary to the North Caucasus.

42 As noted in Chapter 3, Putin first proposed establishing the ASI in May 2011 at a regional meeting of the ASI, an organisation that would promote new business and act as a 'spring board' for young people – and co-opting them.

43 'Gubernator na kontrole' [Controlling governor], *Rossiiskaya Gazeta* (30 March 2015), www.rg.ru/2015/03/30/gubernatory.html.

44 'Gubernatorov razdelili po effektivnosti' [Governors ranked by effectiveness], *Izvestia* (27 January 2014), http://izvestia.ru/news/564600.

45 In conversation with the author, January 2016.

46 Rudnev was a member of MG's coordination council and was responsible for mobilisation in 2010–2012, and Prokopenko led the group from 2010–2012.

47 Gennadiy Zyuganov received 7 per cent, Alexei Navalniy 1 per cent. 'Reiting Putina upersya v protestniy elektorat' [Putin's rating has run into the protesting electorate], *Nezavisimaya Gazeta* (1 April 2015), www.ng.ru/politics/2015-04-01/1_rating.html.

48 'Komanda Putina: edinomyshlenniki, professionaly, ili lichnye druzya?' [Putin's team: like minds, professionals or personal friends], VTsIOM Press Release 2798 (22 March 2015), http://wciom.ru/index.php?id=268anduid=115188. VTsIOM is widely considered to

be less independent than some polling organisations such as Levada, but nonetheless, the results offer an interesting view into how the leadership team is evolving. 'Badovski: edinomyshlenniki vazhnee professionalov-naemnikov' [Badovski: like minds are more important than professional-journeymen], *Vzglyad* (23 March 2015), http://vz.ru/news/2015/3/23/735875.html.

Conclusion: reinterpreting Russia in the twenty-first century

The war in Ukraine has served to refocus Western political attention on Russia through the lens of the potential threat it poses to the West: Breedlove is one of many senior officials who have emphasised concerns that a 'revanchist' and aggressive Russia poses a challenge that is 'global, not regional, and enduring, not temporary'.[1] British Foreign Secretary Philip Hammond stated that the UK's 'security and that of our neighbours in Eastern Europe is menaced by President Putin's flagrant disregard for international law in Ukraine', even that Russia was the number one threat to the UK. Indeed, Hammond's remarks are illuminating about how Russia has come to be seen in the West, and are worth citing at length:

> Russia's illegal annexation of Crimea and the aggression in Eastern Ukraine are both attacks on the international rules-based system. In the place of partnership, Russia has chosen the role of strategic competitor ... we will maintain our efforts to ensure that the EU remains resolute, robust, united and aligned with the US in the face of this challenge. Because this isn't just about Ukraine, it's about Russia and its future intentions, about its apparent aspiration to exercise control over the former Soviet republics which were liberated by the collapse of the USSR in 1989 – an event we celebrate, but which President Putin describes as the greatest geopolitical catastrophe of the twentieth century.[2]

These observations – an illustrative blend of how the West and Russia disagree, have differing conceptualisations of history and international affairs, and repetitive but misleading clichés about Russia – show how the war has exposed and intensified two important sets of questions that run through this book. First, it has exposed, again, a set of fundamental disagreements between Russia and the West, one that has become increasingly systemic since the mid 2000s. That Russia and the West see the post-Cold War history of European security in very different – and increasingly diametrically opposed – terms is likely to render their positions unacceptable to each other, and truly common *and shared* interests few and far between. Indeed, the war in Ukraine has highlighted conflicts of interest and friction in values, and emphasised a sense of Russian competition with the West. As one Russian observer put it, in 2014, Russia 'broke out of the post-Cold War order and openly challenged the U.S.-led system'. The rivalry between Russia and the West, he suggested, is 'likely to endure for years'.[3]

While there are lobbies in the West who seek a return to a more positive relationship with Russia, and some have suggested that the war in Syria may offer grounds for some form of cooperation between the West and Russia in their opposition to Islamic State, this has yet to flower. Indeed, in many ways, Russia's military deployment and air campaign in Syria has also emphasised the themes running through the book – the sense of surprise in the West when the Russians acted, and the deep disagreements over the nature of the situation in Syria, the root causes and the possible solutions. Moreover, the tensions between the West and Russia appear likely to continue given first the potential for NATO's Warsaw summit, scheduled for July 2016, to emphasise the differences and disagreements between the alliance and Russia, such as enlargement (Montenegro will join), missile defence, and NATO's responses to the war in Ukraine, such as the Readiness Action Plan, and the possibility to enhance partnership measures with states in the post-Soviet space – all of which tread hard on long-term, even chronic, tensions between the West and Russia. Western leaders should not be surprised if Moscow states its disagreement with such measures and statements in vivid terms.

Second, it has exposed problems of how the West has interpreted Russia since the end of the Cold War. The sense of surprise occasioned by the Russian annexation of Crimea, as discussed in Chapter 1, is only underlined by the sense of novelty: that events in 2014 have marked a significant turn, the end of the 'post-Cold War era', and that it is only now that the differences in interest and values have become pertinent. NATO officials have suggested that 'In the course of just a few weeks Russia clearly emerged as a revisionist power'.[4] Other senior Western officials and observers suggest that '*we now know that*' the hoped-for convergence between Russia and the West will not happen while Putin is in charge, that Putin is 'challenging the rules-based order that has kept the continent's peace'.[5] This indicates that important signals that have been increasingly visible for years – at least since 2007 – have been either missed or ignored, even as the sense of dissonance between Russia and the West became more pronounced.

The optimism of the 'end of history' era and the possibility of Russia's progress towards Western-style democracy and partnership with the West has proven remarkably resilient, if increasingly reflexive and automatic. This was reflected in the UK's House of Lords report on EU–Russia relations published in February 2015. 'For too long', it noted, 'the EU's relationship with Russia has been based on the optimistic premise that Russia has been on a trajectory towards becoming a democratic "European" country'.[6] Yet if the refrain that the West 'must see Russia as it is, rather than as the West would like it to be' has been often, even yearly, repeated since the mid 2000s, NATO and many of its member states have largely avoided systematically updating their thinking about Russia and shaping a sophisticated Russia policy – at least until the high drama of 2014. But recalibrating at a time of crisis is hardly likely to provide sober evaluation.

Furthermore, Hammond's comment shows the gaps in perspectives about the post-Cold War era. The frame of reference to describe the relationship is often depicted in terms of a 'return' to a Cold War style confrontation between the West and Russia, a sense of 'déjà vu', emphasised by dogmatic assertions of Putin's attempts to rebuild the USSR. This indicates the linear understanding of Russia's development towards democracy and partnership (or retrogressive, back to the USSR) that has dominated Western understandings of Russia since the early 1990s.

One cause of this is that, until 2014, Russia had largely disappeared from the Western political map. In consequence, there has been a long-term reduction in coordinated specialist capacity to understand Russia, particularly in Western governments and international organisations. Specialist expertise about Russia still exists, but it has diminished as a result of changing priorities and budget cutbacks, especially regarding specific sectors such as the Russian military and security sectors and the economy.

If the wars in Ukraine and Syria have illuminated these limitations, and there have been some hasty attempts to address them, the House of Lords report did not see 'evidence that this uplift is part of a long-term rebuilding of deep knowledge of the political and local context in Russia and the region',[7] a point also emphasised by the discussion in the USA about Russia expertise at the end of 2015.[8] The prolonged discussion has resulted in several reasons for this, including that experts do exist, but that there is a reluctance or inability to hire them, even that a conscious choice has been made at the highest levels that such expertise does not need to be sustained. Whatever the underlying reason, given the pressing nature of other priorities, both domestic and elsewhere in the world, and the likely ongoing nature of budget cuts or limits, it appears unlikely that, for the foreseeable future at least, significant additional resources will be allocated to Russia studies.

But a simple increase in resources and the number of analysts will not necessarily facilitate the correction of analytical mistakes and recognition of warning signs or the better interpretation of Russia and the reduction of surprise in the West about it. There is a need to reassess the conceptual approach. Since 2004, mainstream Western thinking about Russia has been too focused on the 'regime question' and the trajectory of Russia's democracy and transition towards partnership with the West, progressively narrowing and becoming simplified to an increasingly intense focus on Vladimir Putin, his popularity ratings (including using this as an explanatory tool for understanding Russian foreign policy) and civil society and the liberal or radical elements of the anti-Putin non-systemic opposition.

While in different ways these merit attention, too much focus on them distorts our understanding of Russia. This distortion is emphasised by a screen of symbolic and often imprecise language that has contributed to an increasing abstract version of Russia, one that has become further blurred by the extravagant but usually misleading use of analogies, and increasingly partisan and emotional. The frequent references to the Cold War serves to distort understanding of Russia, the references to mid-twentieth-century Nazi Germany, so evident in the wake of the war in Ukraine, even more. They distort the debate by short-circuiting it, silencing dissent through guilt by association, and anchoring the discussion to an increasingly mythical and politicised twentieth century, and facilitating easy assumptions about eternal, 'unchanging' and expansive Russia. In political terms, this is not 'déjà vu', but mental arthritis, and it amplifies the polemic about Russia. In practical terms, it means preparing for a replay of the last war.

But much has changed in the West, in Russia and in the relationship, and a substantial transformation has taken place in the European institutional architecture since 1991. Much of the Western hope for partnership has been based on statements of faith rather than substantive assessment of Russian goals, and they have fallen foul of divergent understandings of post-Cold

War developments, diverging priorities and definitions of how to approach these priorities – and, in consequence, real disagreements about European security and international affairs. The result is that, rather than moving on together, the West and Russia have moved on in different directions, a trend emphasised by a sense of dual – and increasingly contradictory – histories and diverging concepts through which the world is understood. The mainstream Western interpretation of Russia, however, has struggled to move on from the framework approach set in the early 1990s, the linear trajectory depicting Russia as either in transition to the West or heading back to the USSR. Though this approach has produced some fine work, it is also the approach that has underpinned the persistence of the view of 'Russia the West would like to see' at the expense of the Russia 'as it is' – and therefore at the root of the persistent sense of surprise about Russia.

To be sure, there is widespread criticism of Putin, but underpinning this is a persistent hope that he will change or that his departure will be the instigator of systemic change. Of course, there are likely to be retirements of senior personnel – and one day, one way or another, Putin himself will go. But there is already a long track record of failed predictions along these lines, particularly of Putin's departure, and care will need to be taken to avoid broken clock analysis, of repeating it until simply being right by chance and not understanding the reasons for or the implications of the change. Furthermore, if there is recognition that Russia's democratic trajectory is no longer a useful prism for understanding it, and that Russia is 'increasingly defining itself as separate from, and as a rival to, the EU', and that its 'Eurasian identity has come to the fore and ... the model of European "tutelage" of Russia is no longer feasible',[9] correcting the course will prove more difficult.

Indeed, much of the discussion, even in reports that acknowledge this, tends still to focus on the decline in Russia in standards of democracy, corruption and rule of law – in effect, on the often repeated criticisms of 'Putin's Russia' and the assertions that Russia is not monolithic but diverse, including many who regard the West favourably. This may, in parts, be true, but it also implicitly imports the convergence with Europe and transition after Putin approach. It is a continuation of optimistic hope, rather than sober analysis of the diversity within Russia, including many who do not favourably regard the West.

Shaping a more sophisticated understanding of Russia and how it is evolving will require drawing some lessons from the methods that were used to understand the USSR. This is not to suggest a re-invigoration of Soviet studies to understand a backward-looking Russia, but to propose a constructive reflection on what has gone before, what has been useful and what has not. The continued existence of problems that were identified over a decade ago, for instance, should be cause for concern. Leo Labedz's assertion in the 1980s that there is far too much non-scholarly, melodramatic discussion of Soviet politics, one in which observers simplify, stereotype and mythologise through interpretative flights of imagination and the use of historical metaphors, and in which the key to Soviet politics was sought in the writings of avowed enemies of the regime, echoes loud today in the approach to Russian politics. The result, now, as then, leads both more to emotionally exaggerated fiction than sober analysis,[10] and to the wrong frames of reference for the bases of Russian thinking, politics and policy. The war in Ukraine has only heightened this sense of partisanship and the static nature of the debate about Russia in entrenched positions.

Second, a classical area studies approach is one of the skills that must be relearned. Again, this is not to suggest the adoption of some form of Kremlinology – an art that has become widely (mis) understood as the attempt to interpret the order of protocol on the Mausoleum. (The modern version of which was visible when Putin 'disappeared' from public view for a few days in March 2015, and commentators began to pore over his clothing, comparing the ties he was wearing as evidence that photos were being faked.) Instead, it is the serious multi-disciplinary study of Russia that builds an empathetic understanding of Russian history, society and politics, and includes accurate linguistic and conceptual interpretation.

An important element of area studies is also a more sophisticated understanding of the wider Russian political landscape and political culture. This includes an interest in and careful observation of the idiosyncrasies and minutiae that make Russian politics what it is, a deeper knowledge of the main institutions and a much more developed biographical knowledge of established and emergent individuals, their backgrounds, careers, networks and the roles they play – including not only the leadership team and non-systemic opposition, but also in specific sectors (military, energy and so on). Emerging from this will come a more sophisticated grasp of power both in Russia itself, and how the Russian leadership deploys it in its international dealings. This is particularly important given the competition between Russia and the West and Moscow's increasingly obvious attempts to deploy power abroad, as shown by Russian actions in Syria and further afield.

The relearning of these skills is essential to enhance the ability to handle and examine sources more carefully and pose the right questions of Russia – and the ability to distinguish between fact and assumption, knowledge and opinion. Testing the reliability of sources and distinguishing between the signal and the noise, filtering out the important information from the unimportant, is becoming ever harder. But it becomes more important because of the increasing sense in the mainstream Western discussion that almost *all* signals from Russia are to be interpreted as 'Kremlin propaganda' and dismissed as such – unless they come from an opposition figure or group, in which case they are treated as reliable. Though there is undoubtedly propaganda, however, dismissing all evidence as such would be a very misleading and dangerous step – as would largely accepting the opposition's views.

At the same time, the increased ability to look further and deeper into Russian affairs and interpret them accurately is only part of the solution. The positive effect of even a substantial increase in the scale of expertise will remain limited if the coordination of this expertise remains limited. Too often a gap is evident between Russia expertise and public policy. The consequent problem of 'unknown knowns' within the Western system needs to be addressed and reduced. This means that Russia experts will have to shape and deliver a convincing, sophisticated Russia agenda that is relevant and accessible to politicians and officials. It will mean retiring easy but tired metaphors and lazy repetition of superficial points of reference, and mean ensuring that Russia is seen in terms of the twenty-first century, rather than the twentieth. It will also mean reversing the process of separation that has taken place since the 1990s between the Russia expert community and the wider strategic studies community, and establishing more institutionalised and resilient links between Russia experts and public policy officials and politicians, not just those working on the Russia desks, but more broadly. Whatever measures are taken, Russia will continue to surprise Western policy-makers and observers, but these can be mitigated by the development of a more empathetic, sophisticated analysis of Russia that prepares Western politicians and policy-makers for both realistic foreign policy and domestic political developments rather than desirable ones or wishful thinking.

The mainstream view of Russia in the West has on one hand tended to see Russia as an appendage of Europe, one that is bound to Europe, rather than seeing it as a Eurasian state with interests not only in Europe but across the world. On the other hand, the mainstream view has tended either to ignore, or refuse to grasp, many of the concepts that influential Russians have used to organise their experiences and make sense of the world on the international stage, and ignore much of the minutiae of Russian domestic political life. International disagreements are reduced to simple Russian intransigence (even when it is not), foreign policy actions to Russian authoritarianism and the populist requirements of domestic popularity; domestic politics is reduced to Putin and watching his popularity ratings and the growth or decline of civil society and the emergence of potentially anti-Putin figures.

This is the result of an unhappy blend of ethnocentrism and political optimism that has failed to see that although there are common interests, and despite appearances and a certain relief that the Cold War was over, the Russian authorities neither began their post-Cold War journey from the same 'end of history' starting point as Western states, nor wanted to join the West to become 'like the West'. Given the increasing dissonance and competition between the West and Russia, having a clearer interpretation of Russia matters. It is time, belatedly, to move on from the immediate post-Cold War optimism of the end of history and superficial comparisons of Russia with the USSR, and begin to shape an interpretation of Russia in the twenty-first century.

Notes

1 'News article: Breedlove: Russia, violent extremism challenge Europe', *DoD News* (25 February 2015), www.defense.gov/news/newsarticle. aspx?id=128249.

2 'Foreign Secretary speech at the Lord Mayor's Easter Banquet' (26 March 2015), www.gov.uk/government/speeches/foreign-secretary-speech-at-the-lord-mayors-easter-banquet.

3 D. Trenin, *Russia's Breakout from the Post Cold War System: The Drivers of Putin's Course* (Moscow: Carnegie Endowment, December 2014), p. 1, http://carnegieendowment.org/files/CP_Trenin_Putin2014_web_Eng.pdf.

4 M. Rühle, *NATO Enlargement and Russia: Die-Hard Myths and Real Dilemmas*, NDC Research Report (15 May 2014).

5 Sir John Sawers, 'The limits of security', King's College, London (16 February 2015), emphasis added, www.kcl.ac.uk/sspp/departments/warstudies/news/newsrecords/THE-LIMITS-OF-SECURITY.pdf; P. Stephens, 'A short telegram about Vladimir Putin's Russia', *Financial*

Times (19 February 2015); M. McFaul, 'Confronting Putin's Russia', *New York Times* (23 March 2014).

6 *The European Union and Russia: Before and Beyond the Crisis in Ukraine*, European Union Committee, House of Lords, 6th Report of Session 2014–2015 (London: The Stationery Office, February 2015), p. 23.

7 *The European Union and Russia: Before and Beyond the Crisis in Ukraine*, p. 26.

8 'Lack of Russia experts has some in US worried', *Washington Post* (30 December 2015), www.washingtonpost.com/news/powerpost/wp/2015/12/30/lack-of-russia-experts-has-the-u-s-playing-catch-up/.

9 *The European Union and Russia: Before and Beyond the Crisis in Ukraine*, p. 22.

10 'The use and abuse of Sovietology: essays, critical and polemic by Leopold Labedz' (Special Anthology), *Survey*, 30:1/2 (March 1988).

Epilogue

The new politics of Russia: Interpreting change was written in the shadows of Vladimir Putin's return to the Russian presidency in 2012 – and the opposition protests that accompanied it – and the worsening in relations between Russia and the Euro-Atlantic community caused by Moscow's annexation of Crimea in 2014. Although relations had long been tense and difficult, full of frustration and disagreements, the annexation had come as a surprise to many in the Euro-Atlantic community, a 'rude awakening'. Some Western officials and observers depicted the annexation as an 'Anschluss of our times': historical analogies of Germany's annexation of the Sudetenland in 1938 coloured the policy and media debate about Russia, with discussion of Munich-type appeasement and President Putin as the Adolf Hitler of the day. A debate ensued about whether there was a return to Cold War with Russia. Equally, many thought that a 'new era' was beginning, and the contours of a new world order were taking shape.[1]

In the book, I sought to examine both the evolving domestic situation in Russia and Moscow's relationship with the Euro-Atlantic community in a longer-term context. I also wanted to inject an important undercurrent into the analysis by examining how we in the Euro-Atlantic community think about Russia. What were the recurring themes and questions? Why were we so persistently surprised by Russia? As the book went into the copy-editing process, Moscow intervened militarily in the Syrian civil war in 2015 (another surprise for many), precipitating a further sharp deterioration in relations between Moscow and the Euro-Atlantic community. Each side imposed sanctions on the other,[2] and all but closed off channels for diplomacy. So, the book concluded by emphasising the long-term and systemic character of the dissonance in relations, the intensified antagonism and rivalry – and Russia's emergence as a strategic competitor challenging the international rules-based system.

As I prepare the second edition, Europe faces an even deeper crisis. Moscow has launched a renewed assault on Ukraine, and explicitly points to a wider contest with the Euro-Atlantic community. While specific numbers and details on illustrative metrics are disputed, they offer some indication of the scale of the tragedy that is unfolding. In March 2023, just over one year after Moscow launched its assault on Ukraine, the United Nations High Commissioner for Refugees estimated that more than eight million Ukrainian refugees are displaced across Europe and nearly six million more displaced within Ukraine. Some 17 million people in Ukraine are in need of humanitarian assistance.[3]

The economic consequences of the war, including the destruction of much civilian transport and energy infrastructure, are devastating for Ukraine. The International Monetary Fund estimated in October 2022 that Kyiv needed between three and four billion dollars each month in external assistance simply to keep Ukraine's government operating, and by December the governor of Ukraine's Central Bank estimated that the economy would lose at least one third of its GDP in 2022.[4] The economic consequences have rippled out further afield into Europe and beyond as supply chains are disrupted and commodity prices rise.[5]

And worse still is the appalling price in human life. The total number of casualties suffered by both sides in what began as a war of movement but which quickly became attritional are, at the time of writing, unclear and disputed. But estimates in late January 2023 suggested perhaps an overall figure of a quarter of a million killed and wounded in the fighting.[6] Since then, heavy fighting has continued, particularly around and in the cities of Bakhmut and Avdiivka, and in June Kyiv launched a major offensive. Even if a ceasefire brought a swift end to the current fighting, the structural socio-economic devastation being wrought on both Ukraine and Russia will have many and varied long-term consequences, whether in terms of the scale of practical reconstruction required or of reintegrating thousands of veterans, many with post-traumatic stress, into societies in which economic prospects are limited.

The eruption of a major conventional war in Europe has come as a deep shock. Russian forces stand accused of atrocities and violations of human rights law, 'many of which amount to war crimes', according to the UN Commission of Inquiry on Ukraine, both by perpetrating massacres and by targeting civilian infrastructure.[7] In March 2023, the International Criminal Court issued a warrant for the arrest of Putin himself on charges of war crimes in Ukraine, including the 'unlawful deportation of children'.[8] Indeed, many are debating whether Russia is waging a genocidal war against Ukraine.[9]

Moreover, the industrial character, scale and duration of the attritional fighting – reflected not only in terms of lives lost but also the ammunition and equipment consumed by both sides – sits very uncomfortably alongside concerns among officials and observers in the Euro-Atlantic community about the sustainability of their effort to support Ukraine and the potential for an escalation in the fighting and the spread of the war.[10]

Each side is daily firing thousands, and in some periods, even tens of thousands, of artillery rounds.[11] Thousands of pieces of military equipment lie destroyed in the fields. And specific episodes in the war – a missile falling on Poland in November 2022 and explosions on the Nord Stream pipelines, for instance – only serve to highlight the dangers of the war spilling beyond Ukraine,[12] and that this is a war being fought under a nuclear umbrella. Indeed, since Moscow launched its assault, and especially when Russian forces have suffered setbacks, there has been recurring and persistent debate about whether, facing conventional defeat, Moscow might resort to using nuclear weapons.[13]

Even in conventional warfare terms, though, there are concerns about Iranian and North Korean support for Russia, and even more so about Chinese support. In October 2022, the USA assessed that Iranian troops were in Crimea to assist Russia with drone operations in the war.[14] And in January 2023, the USA imposed sanctions on a Chinese firm for providing support to Russian forces.[15] In sum, the war has raised the spectre of the eruption of World War III.

Observers have (rightly) pointed to the renewed and intensified assault being 'another rude awakening' for the West, and the start of another 'new era'.[16] Substantial shifts with long-term practical consequences are already underway in the Euro-Atlantic security architecture. In February 2023, Moscow suspended its participation in the new START treaty, the last remaining nuclear arms control agreement between the USA and Russia, raising questions more generally about the future of arms control. Equally, the European Union has made Ukraine a candidate country for membership, and at NATO's Madrid summit in June 2022 Sweden and Finland were invited to join NATO.[17]

NATO is strengthening its presence in eastern Europe, establishing new battlegroups and substantially increasing high-readiness forces.[18] At the time of writing, the Euro-Atlantic community's relations with Moscow have been essentially frozen for over a year. Though stopping short of actively joining Ukraine fighting against Russia, the Euro-Atlantic community has provided Kyiv with extensive political, economic and military support. Many Western observers and officials have expressed their view that there can be no peace on Putin's terms, even that Russia should be weakened and unable to recover quickly, if not strategically defeated and humbled, such that it cannot wage such a war again.[19] Even so, senior Western officials point to the need to be able to support Ukraine in what is likely to be a long, attritional war.[20] On 4 November 2022, the USA established the Security Assistance Group Ukraine, to 'posture' the USA to support Ukraine's 'short term' battlefield needs, as well as its 'long-term requirements to deter and defend against future Russian aggression'.[21]

Russia's relationship with the Euro-Atlantic community: from 'systemic dissonance' to 'strategic contest'

In the first edition, I sought to frame and to reflect on the Euro-Atlantic community's relationship with Russia more specifically, rather than broader Russian foreign policy. I argued against the persistent depictions both that the deterioration in the relationship was caused simply or even largely by Putin's return to the Kremlin in 2012 and that this was tantamount to a 'return to Cold War'. Depicting the relationship in this way allowed for thinking about the challenge to slip into comfortable mental furniture when assessing the problem. Too often the emphasis on 'Putin's Russia' facilitated wishful thinking about the problem being solely with one man and the prospects for change following his departure; too often the words 'Russian' and 'Soviet' were seen as synonymous or interchangeable. The shorthand of 'Putin's Russia' and 'return to Cold War' eclipsed too much: they masked the complexities of Russian politics, and they masked change within Russia and more broadly in international affairs. Not only had the wider world changed so much but the direct challenge in the bilateral relationship was in too many ways different to what had taken place in the second half of the twentieth century for the analogy to be really useful. Indeed, it was serving to obscure the evolving – and deteriorating – dynamics of the relationship, since the term 'new Cold War' had been in frequent (and repetitive) use since 2007. Undoubtedly, relations worsened after 2012, but this represented an intensification of a longer-term dissonance that had taken shape in the early 2000s.

This dissonance, I argued, built on a blend of long-standing frustration on both sides at failed attempts to develop partnership and a series of substantive policy and value disagreements on a wide range of questions. By 2013 this dissonance was already becoming structural and systemic: the first years of the 2010s saw spy scandals, for example, and substantive disagreements over Libya and the character of the so-called 'Arab Spring'. Common ground was very limited, and genuinely shared interests all the more so. Each side was explicit that they understood each other's positions but disagreed with them.

Since then, the dissonance has intensified through a number of well-known crises, from Turkey shooting down a Russian jet in November 2015 (which then Russian Prime Minister Dmitry Medvedev stated gave grounds for war)[22] to the many allegations (by both sides) of interference in domestic politics – most notably by Russia in the US elections in 2016 and in the UK's Brexit referendum and the attempted murder of Sergei Skripal and his daughter, Yulia, in the UK in 2018. These regular (not to say frequent) crises, among numerous others, such as Moscow's withdrawal from the Intermediate-Range Nuclear Forces Treaty in 2019 and the poisoning (in 2020) and then jailing (in 2021) of Alexei Navalniy (which occasioned another round of Western sanctions on Russia and mutual diplomatic criticisms), contributed by the late 2010s to the relationship becoming widely described as part of a 'Great Power Competition'.

With Moscow's military invasion and naval blockade of Ukraine in 2022, this has intensified into what I now call a structural contest, one yet further solidified almost day to day by developments such as the arrest of *Wall Street Journal* reporter Evan Gershkovich in March 2023 on charges of espionage for the USA – the first such accusation made against a foreign journalist in Russia since 1986. Even if some suggest that thought should be given to how negotiations to secure a ceasefire in the war might take shape,[23] therefore, it is very hard to see how the wider Euro-Atlantic community and Russia even begin to alleviate this wider contest, let alone resolve it. Any serious attempt to do so will require a familiarity with the character and depth of the roots of the dissonance described in this book.

From regional challenge to global contest

The book originally focused specifically on the bilateral relationship between the Euro-Atlantic community and Russia. It deliberately did not look at wider aspects of Russian foreign policy, such as Moscow's relationship with China or, more broadly, with the Middle East and North Africa or what the Russian leadership still calls the Asia-Pacific region. This would have called for a different kind of book.

But these are now undoubtedly central aspects of Russia's world view and activity, as reflected in Moscow's strategic assumptions and planning and its actions. Indeed, the struggle with Ukraine has emphasised this attempt to shift attention to what Russian officials call the 'post-West World' and even an attempt to 'defend multipolarity'.[24] Sanctions imposed after the annexation of Crimea, and then much more substantially in 2022, have driven Moscow to accelerate and intensify its plans to develop diplomatic and economic relations with non-Western states and multilateral organisations, such as OPEC+. This approach is codified in Russian strategic planning concepts, including in the updated Foreign Policy Concept, published in March 2023.[25] Russian foreign policy is no longer Western-centric.

I have examined in depth the implications of this shift elsewhere,[26] but here it is worth noting two points. First, the foundations of Moscow's approach are set out in its strategic forecasting and planning, which are largely pessimistic about what changes in the world order mean for Russia. The Russian state invests substantial effort into foresight, and the primary entity for this at the national level is the Security Council, which has adopted a significant role in coordinating forecasting and strategic planning. Nikolai Patrushev, the secretary of the Security Council, has given an indication of the sorts of scenarios envisaged in the official *Strategic Forecast of the Russian Federation to 2035*. These include a shift to a polycentric world order; the USA continuing to seek to maintain its unipolar domination of international affairs; the emergence of a US–China bipolar world model; and a strengthening of regionalisation processes.[27] It is this view of international affairs, one that is in many ways based on a geopolitical and geo-economic view of international affairs, that serves as the foundation for Russian activity.

Moscow concluded that a 'Great Power Competition' was emerging about a decade before the Euro-Atlantic community did,[28] and even before the annexation of Crimea in 2014 there was a broad consensus that international affairs were entering a systemic crisis. Many in the Russian policy community saw geopolitical and technological changes leading inexorably to war. This view crystallised during the 2010s. Prominent Russian observers, for instance, suggested in 2016 and 2017 that 'the reconstruction of the world order that began at the beginning of this decade will continue with increasing speed and on an ever larger scale', that a revolutionary situation was emerging in international affairs.[29] Such views were shared by senior officials, including Putin, Lavrov and Valeriy Gerasimov, who all pointed to the world entering a period of transition with sustained turbulence and competition – even conflict – over resources, transit routes and access to markets.[30]

These assumptions shape Moscow's international activity and are likely to continue to do so for the foreseeable future. Any consideration of the bilateral relationship between the Euro-Atlantic community and Russia must be global in context and outlook, and based on an understanding that Moscow sees a long-term shift underway in international affairs through to 2030 and beyond. Certainly, Moscow's renewed and intensified invasion reflects unresolved policy clashes between Kyiv and Moscow – it may even be seen as the ongoing consequences of the dissolution of the Soviet Union. Moreover, it reflects the Russian leadership's view of the Euro-Atlantic community in the region: senior officials often refer to the support of the USA and its allies for Kyiv in facilitating attacks against Russia and Washington's desire to extend the conflict.[31]

But it is also taking place in a broader context. For Moscow, the fighting is not a localised war in (eastern) Ukraine with some regional effects rippling out to other regions. It is part of a global contest, with some fighting currently in Ukraine. The Russian leadership points, for example, both to the efforts by the USA to maintain its global dominance and the 'unipolar moment' and to the destabilising and threatening actions of the USA and its allies in other regions, including in the Arctic, Central Asia and the Asia Pacific region.[32] For Moscow, then, this is the first real salvo in a long-term global struggle that may well last through the decade.

The values gap, democracy and Russia's domestic politics

The first edition of the book also examined the mechanics of Russian domestic politics and power – particularly elections and protests, as well as political culture – but it did not focus explicitly on examining whether Russia was a democracy. Partly, this was because this issue had already been very thoroughly examined. Indeed, as I argued, by the mid-2010s, whether or not Russia was a democracy had long been the central guiding question of Russia studies – and I sought to offer a critique of the persistent hopeful search for democratic change in Russia, reflected in the subtitle 'interpreting change', a reference to historian Herbert Butterfield's book *The Whig Interpretation of History*.

Although I did not directly and explicitly address the question of whether Russia was democratic, therefore, the point I was making was that it was by then already clear that Russia was *not* a democracy by, for instance, British or EU standards, and had not been for some time – and nor was it (then) likely to become so in the short term or the foreseeable future. Moreover, it was also very clear that alongside the various policy disagreements, a values gap had emerged between the Euro-Atlantic community and Russia. Much of this, I think, still stands, especially for the situation at the time.

Since then, though, the relationship has evolved. It has shifted in terms of the content of the disagreements over time. But it has also changed in terms of the balance of emphasis between policy disagreements and the values gap as reasons for the systemic dissonance. Values have become the central point of dissonance. Indeed, the 'values gap' has evolved into a 'values clash'.

This evolution can be traced on two connected threads. The first is in the way that the values gap between the Euro-Atlantic community and Russia has now come to the forefront of the relationship. One of the most prominent features of the debate about Russia in the last few years is that Russia is part of an authoritarian challenge to international democracy. This point was made by Joseph Biden in late 2017. He emphasised that 'the Russian government is brazenly assaulting the foundations of Western Democracy around the world'. Moscow had launched, he stated, 'a coordinated attack across many domains', seeking to 'weaken and subvert Western democracies from the inside' because the Russian leadership saw Western democracy as the greatest threat to its survival. In so doing,

Moscow sought to shift attention 'away from corruption and economic malaise at home', activate 'nationalist passions to stifle internal dissent', and 'consolidate its power'.[33]

This view is now central to the public and policy debate about Russia. Although the extensive range of policy disputes remains – the list has even grown – it is too often boiled down to simply being a dispute over whether or not Moscow really opposed NATO enlargement and whether NATO enlargement provoked the invasion of Ukraine or was simply a pretext. Instead, the clash of values now dominates debate and policy thinking, with authoritarian Russia seen to be challenging democracies and the international rules-based order.[34] For many, the assault on Ukraine reflects Moscow's authoritarian and imperialist tendencies.

The second thread is in Russian domestic politics. Since the first edition was published, Russia has gone through two parliamentary (2016 and 2021) and one presidential (2018) electoral cycles; another presidential election looms in 2024. There was also a referendum held in 2020 on amendments to the constitution. These changes formalised longer-term, pre-existing legislative trends and consolidated the formal power of the president.[35] They comprised a range of measures including placing the Russian constitution above international law and enshrined a number of policy measures, such as pension and welfare reform, and also patriotic education. Importantly, the changes also nullified two points regarding presidential terms, removing the 'in a row' clause that regulates the maximum number of terms, and annulling the number of previous terms served by either Putin or Dmitry Medvedev.

But this change really serves to highlight a form of continuity: since the first edition was written and published, there has been considerable political continuity. In the wake of numerous amendments to electoral legislation, the United Russia party, having performed poorly in 2011 (as described in the first edition), went on to win overwhelming victories in 2016 (winning 353 of 450 seats) and again in 2021 (324 of 450 seats). The opposition, such as it is, is still reflected mainly in the Communist Party and the Liberal Democratic Party of Russia (LDPR).[36] Both parties remain as 'systemic' opposition, but even so they struggle to play substantive roles, only occasionally challenging United Russia in regional elections. The arrest in 2020 of the LDPR's Sergei Furgal, who had two years previously defeated a United Russia candidate to become governor of Khabarovsk region, illustrates some of the challenges that even systemic opposition faces in Russia. Furgal and his supporters claimed that the arrest and trial were politically motivated, but in February 2023 he was sentenced to 22 years imprisonment for murder and attempted murder.

Nor has the 'non-systemic' opposition been able to play a major role. Certainly, it has faced serious obstacles from the authorities – Alexei Navalniy's political movement, including his Anti-Corruption Foundation, was designated an 'extremist' organisation in 2021 and was ordered to suspend its activities. As noted above, Navalniy himself was poisoned, and then imprisoned in 2021. In May 2022, the courts extended his sentence by a further nine years. But, as described in the first edition, the different sections of the non-systemic opposition have often been fragmented in their purpose and have remained unable to coordinate their activities to secure electoral success,[37] or even build wider popular support. Navalniy has remained the main point of focus for Western analysis of Russia's opposition. But the growth during the 2010s of Russian public awareness of Navalniy's activities not only led to a small increase in approval in polling but also to much higher numbers of disapproval.[38]

This is not to suggest that there is no change at all. Indeed, there is a constant undercurrent of evolution, whether it be legislative, as the leadership shapes the electoral environment, or in terms of the landscape and organisations, and in individuals. In terms of the landscape, for instance, the roles of some organisations have changed. The All-Russian Popular Front (ONF), for instance, discussed in the first edition, has evolved substantially, growing to become much more prominent and active. It has taken on not only a greater role in policy formation and oversight, but has even adopted an active role in supporting the 'special military operation' in its project 'Everything for Victory'.[39] Moreover, the establishment in the second half of the 2010s of the National Guard (also known as Rosgvardia) reflects Moscow's intent to control dissent and especially protest – to prevent a 'maidan type' situation emerging in Russia.[40] Alongside the smearing of opposition political figures and the introduction of ever tighter legislation on public gatherings, this shift in law enforcement structures further contributes to limiting public protest in Russia. Protest on the streets, therefore, has remained very much weaker than virtual protest.

And in terms of people, while the overall picture of the political landscape is one of longevity – senior individuals often remain in position for many years – there is also an ongoing process of what I described in the first edition as a 'refreshment of the system', with a younger generation emerging into senior positions. This dual process continues, with both long-term members of the team and younger individuals being promoted. In February 2023, this was illustrated by the promotions of Rashid Nurgaliev (born in 1956), Mikhail Kovalchuk (born in 1946), and Alexei Shevtsov (born in 1979) to positions in the Security Council.

Indeed, the emergence of a new generation to prominent positions – a process that might be called 'omolozhenie' or 'youthification' – deserves more analytical attention. Parliamentary elections in 2016 brought many younger members of parliament, for example. But this is especially visible in 2023, as younger individuals are appointed to important positions in the Russian system, overseeing parts of the war effort. Deputy Prime Minister Dmitry Grigorenko (born in 1978) appears to be Prime Minister Mikhail Mishustin's right-hand man and occupies a number of important positions in government structures, including chief of government staff and membership of several commissions and councils, such as the Government Coordination Council for the Support of the Russian Armed Forces, Other Troops Military Units and Agencies, where he oversees the working group on financial matters and normative regulation. Oleg Gorshenin (born in 1978) took command of the National Defence Management Centre for some months from late 2022 to spring 2023. And Kirill Lysogorsky (born in 1986), Deputy Minister of Industry and Trade, was appointed in 2022 to direct and coordinate work on financing the tasks of the state defence order and planning and implementing budgetary support for the development of the Russian military-industrial complex, among a wide range of other tasks.

These complexities and dualities of Russian politics deserve continued attention. Putin's personal popularity and the leadership's careful attention to the mood of the population goes hand in hand with manipulation of the electoral process. Putin wins, as one observer has correctly put it, on a playing field that is far from level.[41] But specifically in terms of Russian democracy, the overall conclusion has only become clearer and more obvious: the values gap grows and has evolved into a clash, and democracy recedes ever further.

On one hand, Russian officials have become increasingly explicit about their rejection of European values and liberalism. In 2019,

Putin stated that liberalism had 'outlived its purpose',[42] and he has only become more vivid in his criticism of Western 'neo-colonial' and 'neo-liberal and essentially totalitarian' politics since then.[43] On the other, in Russia ever tighter foreign-agent laws, combined with increased controls on media and speech and the arrests of journalists (such as Ivan Golunov in 2019, Ivan Safronov and Taisa Bekbulatova in 2020) and protesters all point to a much harsher political climate.[44] This accelerated significantly after March 2022, with the introduction of new legislation criminalising criticism of the invasion and the Russian armed forces, and even the activities of the Wagner Private Military Company.

In fact, the situation has evolved such that the wider conversation is no longer about whether Russia is a *democracy* but about whether Russia is, as *The Economist* put it, 'in the grip of fascism'.[45] The assertion that Russia under Putin is fascist has featured on the fringes of debate since the mid-2000s, with observers comparing Putin to Adolf Hitler or Benito Mussolini. This was partly because of the debate about the interpretation of the origins of and responsibility for World War II. On one hand, Russians pointed the finger at those who collaborated with Nazi Germany; on the other, some, particularly in Central and Eastern Europe, pointed the finger at Russia and the Soviet role in the Molotov–Ribbentrop Pact. This developed further after 2014, with Russian and Ukrainian officials and commentators each accusing the other of fascism,[46] and has become particularly prominent after Moscow launched its renewed assault in February 2022.[47]

But this debate is misleading. While it offers a satisfyingly accusatory moral shorthand, the epithet 'fascism' has long been little more than a widely used term of abuse, a synonym for something undesirable. But fascism is not a synonym for something bad or authoritarian nationalism or a 'dictatorship'. It is – was – a very specific political ideology, one with particular characteristics and representing a particular set of circumstances, even located in a certain time in history (the 1920s to the 1940s). Real fascism was a revolutionary ideology, one that rejected both communism and institutional Christian norms and heralded a national rebirth and a new kind of human being.[48] While some features of Fascist parties of the 1920s and 1930s are visible in Russia – a leader presenting himself as the embodiment of the state and the nation, the blend of the past (including myths) and the future, the idea of a collective national identity, and a degree of violence in society, including a paramilitary subculture – neither Putin nor United Russia represent a radical revolutionary ideology, let alone a utopian one.

Moreover, if, as the first edition of *The new politics of Russia* discussed, Russian society more broadly is left-leaning, even socialist, there are other countervailing arguments. The Russian leadership does not, for instance, oppose institutional Christianity – indeed, it actively supports the Russian Orthodox Church. The leadership also has a mixed relationship with right-wing movements in Russia, using groups such as Russkii Obraz to its advantage against the radical right wing of the political spectrum, but then turning and applying pressure and even punitive measures against those groups. Russia is not, therefore, fascist in its classical definition. The terms 'illiberal', 'authoritarian' or 'autocratic' may not satisfy at an emotional level, but they offer a more accurate description of Russian politics.[49] This returns us to the question of how we think about Russia.

Interpreting change

The character of expertise on Russia in the Euro-Atlantic community was an important underlying theme of the first edition. I traced the evolution of expertise from the 1990s, underlining the decline of resources dedicated to the study of Russia, the narrowing scope of study and the often-attenuated connections between expertise and policy making such that even that expertise which did exist did not influence policy making or the public debate as much as it could or should have. There were not only significant gaps in analysis, therefore, but also 'unknown knowns'. Since then, the context has evolved considerably: Russia's return to the headlines since 2014, and all the more so since 2016 with the charges of interference in the US elections, has led to a huge increase in attention and discussion. Many more voices became involved in the debate about Russia. Two related points echo from the arguments I made in the first edition.

The first relates to the 'health' of Russia studies. A broad debate about this rumbled on for the remainder of the decade. Some prominent specialists emphasised that in the second half of the 2010s Russia studies was enjoying a revival, even a 'golden era', because of access to sources and a lack of ideology. There was, according to one, 'an abundance of knowledge about Russia and the region for those willing to listen'. This work was primarily in the political science field, focusing on political behaviour and public opinion, democracy and protest, and property rights.[50]

Even so, by the end of the 2010s, a number of eminent research or university centres that focused on the study of Russia, Eastern Europe and Eurasia had either been much reduced in scale or hollowed out. Moreover, prominent observers noted that Russia's 'ubiquity in US politics is not the same as being known', and US academic work on Russia was still steadily diminishing, with few Americans now learning Russian or studying Russian history, and lacking in cross-disciplinary dialogue. Much the same held true in the UK, including in policy-making circles.[51] Moreover, some of those who argued that Russia studies was thriving also accepted that this expertise was not well translated into public or policy debate.[52] These problems directly echo the arguments I made in the book.

Since February 2022, however, the debate has taken another noteworthy turn. The shock of war is driving a self-reflective and very critical reassessment of Russia studies. This is happening at two levels. First, there is a vigorous debate about the validity of academic theories, particularly questioning realism, or more specifically often against individual realists such as John Mearsheimer, seeking to emphasise why his argument that NATO enlargement caused the war is wrong.[53] Within this, there is some criticism of Western Russia-watchers – particularly military analysts – for failing to predict how poorly the Russian military would perform (and how strategic studies and former Western practitioners were more accurate in their predictions).[54]

A second critical thread is emerging from within the discipline of Slavic and Russia studies itself. Indeed, for some in wider Russia or Slavic studies, the events of 2022 have served as a 'major exogenous shock, which greatly affected the field of Russian studies'. Some analytical approaches and theoretical lenses became 'outdated', and the 'intellectual and institutional infrastructure of scholarship in the field' faced 'major challenges', with a need for new scholarly solutions.[55] Far from Russia studies 'thriving' just a few years ago, therefore, some have pointed to 'the sorry state of the discipline problematically known as Slavic Studies', and the need for 'collective reflection on the field's systemic failures ... and blind spots'.[56]

This discussion has tended to focus on the need for change in Russia studies, particularly its 'decolonisation'. Some emphasise that Western academia has 'overlooked to a large extent the trauma caused by Russian imperialism' and ask why it has taken a war of conquest for experts to recognise Russia's imperial and colonialist nature. Others emphasise that Western academia needs to 'decentre' Russia, and especially the state (St Petersburg and Moscow), instead focusing more attention on including voices from colonised nations, regions and groups, especially Ukraine, Central Asia and the Caucasus, and ethnic minorities within Russia.

For such observers, it was just such an over-focus on Russia – the dominance of 'Russia firsters' in the Western academic community and the ways in which apparently the Russian state's point of view was taken as a default starting point – that led to the misjudgement of both Moscow's strength and Ukraine's resilience in the war. The discipline suffered from a 'distinctly Euro-centric character of theorising' and a relative ignorance of eastern European insights and the validity of their experiences'. Indeed, some have pointed to the relatively small scale of Ukraine studies before the war, and the difficulty of securing tenure track positions in that field. All told, such 'decolonisation' would be a 'profoundly political act of re-evaluating long established and often internalised hierarchies, of relinquishing and taking back power'.[57]

As a result, at one level, some point to a slump in student interest in studying Russian, the language of Tolstoy but also of Putin, at university, and as an ethical choice turning instead to studying Ukrainian or Polish.[58] On another, though, these critiques are leading to re-evaluations of approaches to examining Russia, with discourses on 'getting Russia right', lecture series on 'rethinking Slavonic studies' emphasising diversity and even the launch of a 'novel research ecosystem that renews our methodological toolkit, creates new knowledge commons and focuses on key research questions'.[59] This will all doubtless introduce and produce a wide range of interesting work.

Nonetheless, it is perhaps worth examining these critiques a little more closely. Let us say first that if prediction becomes the basis for judging expertise, then yet more trouble looms for the discipline. Prediction, to paraphrase the scientist Niels Bohr, is difficult, particularly about the future: it is more the realm of 'seers and prophets'.[60] It is often subject to wishful thinking and subjectivity, and as we have seen, anticipating the future and mapping its complexities has not been a strength of Russia studies. (There is, however, much to be said for foresight thinking and the attempt to conduct methodologically rigorous approaches to thinking about the future, identifying the full range of possibilities and mapping uncertainty, though this has not yet featured substantially in the debate.)

And as for the critique of realism, this is part of a wider debate that should continue. Realists in the wider International Relations discipline certainly face questions. But too often this has become a narrow debate focused on a blame game – essentially a denial that the USA or NATO are to blame for the war because of NATO enlargement. This can become overemphasised, even with the suggestion that Moscow did not even really oppose NATO enlargement.

Moscow launched the invasion, so carries responsibility for it. To turn this into a debate about NATO enlargement into Ukraine, however, is to miss the much wider and deeper nature of the challenge Moscow poses: this is not a war solely or specifically about NATO enlargement, or even European security. As discussed above, it is about what the Russian leadership sees as the shape of the future international environment and a global geo-economic competition. This means that there are also questions to be posed of those who advocate liberalism, including those who have argued that geopolitics is an illusion and that economic realities would compel Russia to compliance with the Western order.[61]

The two lines of Russia-specific critique bear more detailed reflection. In fact, the very small group of (pre-2022) Western analysts of Russia's military spent much of the 2010s pointing to the shortcomings of the Russian military – not just the reforms and modernisation processes that were clearly underway but also the problems that Moscow was having in implementing them and the distance still to go before they were complete. Furthermore, it was largely this group that sought to emphasise not only that the Russian leadership continued to use military firepower as a tool of policy but also in late 2021 and early 2022 that an actual war loomed.

Indeed, this rather small group of specialists spent much of the decade arguing against an orthodoxy that prevailed across the wider analytical and policy community from 2014 that Moscow favoured 'measures short of war', even that the Russian military now *eschewed* firepower. This orthodoxy was framed in numerous neologisms – 'hybrid warfare', 'grey zone warfare', 'liminal warfare' and so on – few of which bore any connection to how Moscow saw either international affairs or the role of the military.[62]

Certainly, few – including Western officials and experts on the Russian military – expected that Moscow would decide to deploy a 'special military operation', and thereby not conform to the way they had trained and exercised, or even, apparently, to some traditional tenets of Russian military strategy.[63] So, there is a valid call for more nuanced and sophisticated study of the Russian armed forces and Russian military power more broadly, and the study of this war and its consequences will hopefully contribute to that. Including a more nuanced view of history in the debate would have perhaps mitigated the sense of surprise among many observers that the Russian armed forces have throughout the campaign suffered from highly problematic command and control and logistics: these have been features of almost every occasion where Moscow has gone to war since the Napoleonic wars (and they are not characteristics limited to Russia).

But if there are questions of analytical accountability to be posed, they should go first to those who have long advocated that Moscow had invented a new form of warfare, waged with non-military tools and eschewing firepower, and to those many specialists who argued that conventional warfare had fallen out of fashion and that grey zone aggression and hybrid warfare should be the points of focus. Such assertions continued even as the Russian military built up its forces around Ukraine in 2021.

Within Russia studies more narrowly, there is also much to discuss. The decolonisation agenda is one that fits into a wider debate in Western societies about imperialism and decolonisation, both in universities and in the wider public and political context. But those who argue that it has taken this war for Western observers to notice that Russia is an imperial power will benefit greatly from doing some background reading, because this is simply untrue. Moscow has long been widely recognised (and criticised) for being an imperial power. And those arguing for a 'decentralisation' of attention to non-Russian ethnicities and nations in the region will surely also want to look deeper into the wider extant literature on these very themes, especially from the 1990s and 2000s. So, the foundations of this discussion already exist and do not need to be reinvented: good historiography will contribute to the sophisticated development of the discipline, and – hopefully – greater cooperation between disciplines.

Importantly though, while it may correctly encourage a wider analytical horizon, the war also *obliges* a yet more sophisticated and multifaceted examination of the Russian *state*, how it works (and does not work) and its policies. To study the full range of actors and listen to the many voices of the region is valuable; to be able to interpret Moscow's intentions and activities is now *essential*. For Russia experts in the Western academic and analytical world to turn away from the questions relating to the power of the Russian state now is to invite more very unpleasant surprises. The Russian leadership is explicit about contesting the Euro-Atlantic community, and a complex and nuanced interpretation of this challenge is necessary.

Any new approach for the discipline will have at least two sets of significant implications for those involved. First, whether Russia studies was thriving or not in political science in 2017, the research lens was too narrow: large gaps remained. Through the 2010s, in contrast to the burgeoning number of people examining themes such as Russian media, propaganda, disinformation and the like, there were few genuine experts (as opposed to fly-by-night commentators) on Russian military strategy. And, with a couple of honourable exceptions, there were even fewer on Russian naval or maritime power or Russian intelligence and security capabilities (as was made explicit when Sergei and Yulia Skripal were poisoned), or on the Russian defence industry, as is now being made explicit as the fighting has become attritional.

Consequently, there were very few substantive reports available for consultation in March 2022, for example, on Russian military logistics or the Russian defence industry – and as a result much ill-informed speculation characterises the discussion. Furthermore, this created a context in which anecdotal evidence quickly becomes recycled and laundered into the debate as fact. An illustration of this is the repeated assertions about Russia taking microchips from washing machines and inserting them into weapons as an example of the success of sanctions against Russia and difficulties faced by the Russian defence industry. This claim appears to have originated in a remark by US Commerce Secretary Gina Raimondo following a conversation with the Ukrainian Prime Minister.[64] However, while fairly simple microchips similar to those installed in domestic appliances are indeed inserted into weapons, such simple microchips do not have to be taken from domestic appliances because they are not covered by sanctions and can easily be bought.[65] These problems in many ways echo and extend those prevailing in 2014, as described in the first edition.

There is no doubt that it is valuable to study the dynamics of society, protest and property rights. But the evolving character of the power of the state also requires attention. For much of the Western Russia-watching community in the post-Cold War era, 'mobilisation' has been considered to be an act of the political opposition against the authorities. Despite obvious and explicit efforts by the state to rehearse mobilisation as a preparation for – and an act of – war, especially from the mid-2010s onwards, this was more or less missed by much of the Russia-watching community. Given the 'partial' mobilisation in September and the shift of Russia onto a war footing in October, how state mobilisation functions should become a subject of interest – the various actors involved and their responsibilities; the problems the authorities face and the solutions they find, including, apparently, altering legislation to suit the state's requirements; the digitalisation of the draft-summons process; and a version of public–private partnership in the management and implementation of the mobilisation process.

The second set of implications relates to the practical approach to Russia studies, in terms of methodology and the vexed and perennial question of connecting expertise, including in academia, to public policy and wider debate. Those who study Russia face a shifting context, which emphasises a reliance on method to shape substantive, original contributions that add to and develop the wider debate, rather than telling us more and more about less and less. For many established Western experts, travel to Russia, especially to conduct interviews or substantive research, will likely be much more limited, if at all possible, for the foreseeable future. Russia increasingly appears closed as Russian journalists are silenced and foreigners leave.[66] In some senses, this may be offset both by information available online and by the arrival into the Euro-Atlantic community of many Russian and Ukrainian political scientists, economists and journalists, who are actively contributing to the debate.

But experts will be aware now not just of disinformation but increasingly of availability bias in their access to information and sources: reliable and accurate information is that much harder to find. There is both a moral hazard in working with Russian state sources and an access question, given Moscow's classification of much data. So, there is now a premium on shaping productive and fruitful questions, accessing and handling sources, and having a command of historiography and the evolution of the debate. To cope with this context and remain in some way connected to what is happening in Russia, there is a growing requirement for a strong grasp of the relevant languages, for working across disciplines (including familiarity with their different methodologies) and, ideally, for a linguistic and political horizon that is broader still. The more that Russian strategy and international activity is 'post-Western', reaching out to other parts of the world, the more beneficial it will be for researchers to study the relevant languages and politics of these other regions.

While conducting and promoting their research, experts will also have to contribute to a debate that remains awash with the same superficial and apparently cyclical readings of Russia that characterised the debate in 2014 and 2015, as discussed in the first edition: the emotive analogies with the 1930s, the speculation about 'coups', 'purges' and apparat struggles, the 'Putinology', including his rationality and health, and assertions of the 'end of the Putin era' and Russia's imminent disintegration. All these have persisted since 2015 and they have become particularly prevalent since February 2022 and were again given renewed energy during PMC Wagner's abortive mutiny in June 2023. They are likely to continue as the fortunes of war roll back and forth and as presidential elections loom in 2024. Balancing an understanding of change with continuity will be important, as will methodological rigour in shaping forecasting and scenarios; as noted above, wishful thinking should not be confused with foresight.

At the time of writing, the implications of the abortive mutiny in June for Putin's authority and the balance of the Russian political landscape remain very unclear. Likewise, the implications of Ukraine's renewed offensive in summer 2023 and the question of whether Moscow is able to achieve its goals in Ukraine or will be obliged either to seek terms or to escalate the war to a 'counter-terrorist operation' or even declare 'war' and what this means in practical terms – for instance in another round of mobilisation – are similarly unclear. But we have a longer-term context and some structural navigational points from which to work.

Putin emphasised in February 2023 in his speech to the Federal Assembly that the presidential elections scheduled for 2024 would take place in strict adherence to the law and in 'observance of all democratic, constitutional provisions'. Elections, he continued, 'always reveal different approaches to resolving social and economic goals. That said, the leading political forces are consolidated and united in the main idea – the security and wellbeing of the people, our sovereignty and our national interests override everything else for us'.[67] Of course, the Constitution, especially after the amendments in 2020, gives the President considerable powers, but at the time of writing, we should expect them to go ahead. Although he has still not yet announced his intention to stand, Russian media indicates that the preparations are underway and that the 'basic scenario in preparing for the elections is his participation', and that public support for him is 'high'.[68]

This is an important question and one that will feature prominently in the Western discussion about Russia through the autumn and into the spring of 2024. But there is a much more substantive agenda about change and continuity in Russia. How does the collective leadership, including in the military, evolve and change, and to what end? What does the 'youthification' process mean for the political landscape through the mid-2020s? Although there has been much discussion of 'purges' and firings of senior commanders since February 2022, the evidence for this remains slim. Some, such as Dmitry Bulgakov do appear to have been fired, others rotated to other positions. Some, perhaps, have resigned. But more broadly, the defence and security leadership remains in post: despite some shifts, the majority of the Defence Ministry and General Staff senior command continue in jobs they have held for years. Is this same group of people capable of radical change?

Two questions do nevertheless emerge. First, rather than taking place during a crisis, major personnel changes more often take place after it. It may well be, therefore, that we see personnel changes when the fighting stops (this is known euphemistically in Russian as 'orgvyvody' or 'organisational conclusions'). Will those of the younger generation who are in key positions be promoted to top jobs?

Second, related to this, in the military more specifically, will a group of 'Young Turks' begin to emerge in the officer corps to contest the views of the senior military leadership – and what effect might this have on military reform and culture? If they did, would they prove to be 'critics' or 'builders'? This will be particularly important given the announced major changes planned in the structure and scale of the armed forces to be implemented first by 2026 and then by 2030. What are the real, practical implications of the eventual replacement of Shoigu and Gerasimov (which has been so often rumoured since early 2022) – would this substantially change Russian military culture, which has evolved over decades? What would be the implications for the Russian armed forces for the remainder of the 2020s – would plans for the development be substantively altered?

More broadly, the effects of the war on politics and society are combining with state initiatives to cause important changes. War appears to be becoming 'normalised' in society, reaching a wider number of families and homes. What will be the effects on society of large numbers of young men being killed, and the maimed and traumatised returning home? The authorities have stated their intent to establish substantial financial support mechanisms for veterans and bereaved families. But the consequences of the fighting are likely to have a coarsening effect on society, with violence more prominent. The Russian Prosecutor's Office recorded a 4 per cent rise in murder and attempted murder in Russia in 2022;[69] and there have been attacks in Russian cities, such as the explosion that killed the military blogger Vladlen Tatarsky.[70] And how do those returning from the front reintegrate into society – what will be their employment prospects? The partial mobilisation in autumn resulted in many fleeing the country; what are the long-term effects of this? To what extent is it permanent, or is it simply temporary to avoid mobilisation? To what extent does this affect the economy – are those who have migrated essentially living abroad but 'working from (a different) home'? What effects will this migration have on the host countries and their relations with Moscow? Less commonly observed, though, is that there was also a 38 per cent increase in the consumption of antidepressants in Russia.[71] Does this too have long-term effects? If some parts of society face more violence or are increasingly medicated, what of the impact of other problems such as homelessness and suicide that often beset de-mobilised troops?

And what of the roles of organisations such as Yunarmiya and the ONF that have played a growing role in the patriotic education of Russian youth and society? Organisations such as this may begin to provide a growing percentage of a cadre for rebuilding the armed forces, sewing a form of active patriotism into the fabric of a military that the authorities seek significantly to expand in size. To what extent could this mean society evolving from one which reflects paramilitary characteristics to one that is militarised? Likewise, the Russian Orthodox Church is playing an ever more important role in society and education, including in higher education.

If the state emphasises patriotism and Russian civilisation, even introducing courses on the 'fundamentals of Russian statehood',[72] does this begin to become a state ideology? And if one may ask whether Russian society is becoming intoxicated by this Russian civilisation agenda, we can also wonder whether a society in which teachers report schoolchildren to the authorities, leading to the arrest of their parents, is not already toxic.[73]

Finally, at another, broader level, there are questions that relate to the shifting nature and characteristics of Russian power on the international stage. How does Moscow respond to the new waves of sanctions? In the wake of the first substantive sanctions in 2014 and 2015, the Russian leadership responded by imposing counter-sanctions, which had consequences for European economies. More importantly, though, it invested in 'import substitution' measures. While there were problems with this, these measures served to build up Russian agriculture such that Russia became one of the world's leading grain exporters by the end of the decade. What will characterise the new approach, and how will this affect the economy through the rest of the decade?

Related to this, what about Russian diplomacy, and how Moscow attempts to sustain support across the globe as the Euro-Atlantic community seeks to ensure Russia's isolation? Much attention focuses on the Russo-Chinese relationship. But what about Russia's developing partnership with Iran? What do the long-term results of initiatives in Africa and the Middle East look like? And with states in the Indian Ocean?

And there are questions about the evolving character of Russia's power. Traditionally, Russia is seen as a continental, land power. But the war is accelerating Moscow's emphasis on developing power at sea. If one of the key underlying reasons for the ongoing war against Ukraine is the effort to control the Sea of Azov and the Black Sea, an important consequence of the war is the growing dependence of the Russian economy on seaborne trade.

Looking ahead, therefore, there are many questions about the future, certainly more questions than answers. How the contest between the Euro-Atlantic community and Russia evolves and what are the possible shifts in the Russian political landscape through the mid-2020s are only the most prominent and obvious. But there are others – to what extent can shifts in the political landscape lead to real, substantive change? Would a different leader change Moscow's intent to develop the Northern Sea Route, for instance, or move

Russia's economy away from its core characteristics of focusing on strategically important goods and attempting to develop wider economic relationships across different regions of the globe? In many ways, as the author William Gibson suggests, the future is already here, it is just not very evenly distributed. Interpreting it requires a knowledge of where we have come from: the backstory. From this basis, we can try to peer into the fog of the future.

Notes

1 N. Granholm, J. Malminen and G. Persson (eds), *A Rude Awakening: Ramifications of Russian Aggression Towards Ukraine* (Stockholm: FOI, 2014); 'Ukraine: a rude awakening to a new world order', *Financial Times* (6 April 2014), www.ft.com/content/86d07e5c-bb28-11e3-b2b7-00144feabdc0.

2 R. Connolly, *Russia's Response to Sanctions: How Western Economic Statecraft is Reshaping Political Economy in Russia* (Cambridge: Cambridge University Press, 2018).

3 'Situations: Ukraine refugee situation' (28 March 2023), https://data.unhcr.org/en/situations/ukraine; 'Ukraine emergency: aid, statistics and news', *USAforUNHCR* (n.d.), www.unrefugees.org/emergencies/ukraine/.

4 'IMF estimates Ukraine needs $4 billion a month to keep government operating', *The Hill* (12 October 2022), https://thehill.com/policy/3685408-imf-estimates-ukraine-needs-4-billion-a-month-to-keep-government-operating/; International Monetary Fund, 'How Ukraine is managing a war economy', (22 December 2022), www.imf.org/en/News/Articles/2022/12/20/cf-how-ukraine-is-managing-a-war-economy.

5 UK government, *Integrated Review Refresh 2023: Responding to a More Contested and Volatile World* (London: HMSO, 2023), https://assets.publishing.service.gov.uk/government/uploads/system/uploads/attachment_data/file/1145586/11857435_NS_IR_Refresh_2023_Supply_AllPages_Revision_7_WEB_PDF.pdf. p. 10.

6 For overviews giving a range of estimates and some of the challenges, see 'What's the truth about casualty numbers in Ukraine?', *Unherd* (25 January 2023), https://unherd.com/thepost/whats-the-truth-about-casualty-numbers-in-ukraine/; 'Military casualties in Russia–Ukraine war are likely less than commonly stated', *Forbes* (5 March 2023), www.forbes.com/sites/vikrammittal/2023/03/05/military-casualties-in-russia-ukraine-war-are-likely-less-than-commonly-stated/.

7 'War crimes, indiscriminate attacks on infrastructure, systematic and widespread torture show disregard for civilians, says UN Commissioner of Inquiry on Ukraine', Office of the High Commissioner for Human

Rights (16 March 2023), www.ohchr.org/en/press-releases/2023/03/war-crimes-indiscriminate-attacks-infrastructure-systematic-and-widespread. There is much discussion of specific aspects of these charges. See, for just one instance, 'Caught on camera, traced by phone: the Russian military unit that killed dozens in Bucha', *New York Times* (22 December 2022), www.nytimes.com/2022/12/22/video/russia-ukraine-bucha-massacre-takeaways.html. The Ukrainian government says that tens of thousands of war crimes have been committed since February 2022. Ukrainian courts have charged 135 suspected of war crimes and already prosecuted and jailed 21-year-old Vadim Shishimarin for the murder of Oleksander Shelipov. 'Ukraine conflict: what war crimes is Russia accused of?', *BBC News* (17 March 2023), www.bbc.co.uk/news/world-60690688.

8 'Situation in Ukraine: ICC judges issue arrest warrants against Vladimir Vladimirovich Putin and Maria Alekseyevna Lvova-Belova', International Criminal Court (17 March 2023), www.icc-cpi.int/news/situation-ukraine-icc-judges-issue-arrest-warrants-against-vladimir-vladimirovich-putin-and.

9 'Is Russia committing genocide in Ukraine', United States Institute of Peace (21 September 2022), www.usip.org/publications/2022/09/russia-committing-genocide-ukraine; 'Is Russia committing genocide in Ukraine? What experts say', *Time* (15 March 2023), https://time.com/6262903/russia-ukraine-genocide-war-crimes/.

10 'West risks running out of ammunition, warns NATO Chief Jens Stoltenberg', *The Times* (14 February 2023), www.thetimes.co.uk/article/west-must-stock-up-as-putin-prepares-for-more-war-nato-chief-warns-gnfqb976d; 'NATO's Secretary General warns of 'full-blown war' with Russia', *New York Times* (9 December 2022), www.nytimes.com/2022/12/09/world/europe/russia-ukraine-nato-stoltenberg.html#:~:text=Putin%20of%20Russia%20could%20pose,was%20a%20%E2%80%9Creal%20possibility.%E2%80%9D.

11 A. Vershinin, 'The return of industrial war', *RUSI Commentary* (17 June 2022), www.rusi.org/explore-our-research/publications/commentary/return-industrial-warfare.

12 Moscow accused the Royal Navy of this attack. 'Russia accuses British Navy of blowing up Nord Stream gas pipelines in North Sea', *The Independent* (29 October 2022), www.independent.co.uk/news/uk/home-news/nord-stream-gas-ukraine-russia-b2213368.html.

13 J.A. Gannon, 'If Russia goes nuclear: three scenarios for the Ukraine war', Council on Foreign Relations (9 November 2022), www.cfr.org/article/if-russia-goes-nuclear-three-scenarios-ukraine-war; K. ven Bruusgaard, 'How Russia decides to go nuclear', *Foreign Affairs* (6 February 2023), www.foreignaffairs.com/ukraine/how-russia-decides-go-nuclear.

14 UK government, *Integrated Review Refresh 2023*, p. 8; US department of defense, 'General says Iranian drones, troops operating in

Ukraine', (22 October 2022), www.defense.gov/News/News-Stories/
Article/Article/3195380/general-says-iranian-drones-troops-operating-
in-ukraine.

15 'US sanctions Chinese satellite firm for allegedly supplying SAR imagery
to Russia's Wagner Group', *SpaceNews* (27 January 2023), https://
spacenews.com/u-s-sanctions-chinese-satellite-firm-for-allegedly-
supplying-sar-imagery-to-russias-wagner-group; 'US hits Chinese,
Russian firms for aiding Russian military', *Reuters* (24 February 2023),
www.reuters.com/world/us-commerce-targets-entities-china-other-
countries-latest-russia-action-2023-02-24.

16 J. Lunden et al. (eds), *Another Rude Awakening: Making Sense of
Russia's War Against Ukraine* (Stockholm: FOI, 2022); O. Scholz,
'The global Zeitenwende', *Foreign Affairs* (January/February 2023),
www.foreignaffairs.com/germany/olaf-scholz-global-zeitenwende-
how-avoid-new-cold-war; European parliament, 'The Russian attack
on Ukraine marks a new era for Europe, MEPs say' (1 March 2022),
www.europarl.europa.eu/news/en/press-room/20220227IPR24204/
the-russian-attack-on-ukraine-marks-a-new-era-for-europe-meps-say.

17 Finland formally joined in March 2023 and will be officially welcomed
at the NATO summit in July, but, at the time of writing, Sweden's membership remains delayed.

18 NATO, 'Madrid summit ends with far-reaching decisions to transform
NATO' (30 June 2022), www.nato.int/cps/en/natohq/news_197574.htm.

19 K. Kallas, 'No peace on Putin's terms', *Foreign Affairs* (8 December
2022), www.foreignaffairs.com/russian-federation/no-peace-putins-
terms; 'Pentagon chief's remarks show shift in US's declared aims
in Ukraine', *The Guardian* (25 April 2022), www.theguardian.
com/world/2022/apr/25/russia-weakedend-lloyd-austin-ukraine;
J. Rostowski, 'Russia must be humbled', *Project Syndicate* (25
October 2022), www.project-syndicate.org/commentary/russia-putin-
humiliation-in-war-often-drives-progress-by-jacek-rostowski-2022-10.

20 'NATO chief: west must brace to support Ukraine in a long war',
The Guardian (22 March 2023), www.theguardian.com/world/2023/
mar/22/jens-stoltenberg-nato-chief-west-support-ukraine-for-
long-war.

21 'Press release: US Department of Defense establishes Security Assistance
Group-Ukraine in Wiesbaden', US Army Europe and Africa 16 November
2022), www.europeafrica.army.mil/ArticleViewPressRelease/Article/
3219717/press-release-us-department-of-defense-establishes-security-
assistance-group-uk.

22 'NATO and UN seek calm over Turkish downing of Russian jet', *The
Guardian* (24 November 2015), www.theguardian.com/world/2015/
nov/24/nato-and-un-seek-calm-over-turkish-downing-of-russian-jet;

'Russia Prime Minister Dmitry Medvedev says Turkey's downing of Su-24 gave grounds for war', *The Independent* (9 December 2015), www.independent.co.uk/news/world/europe/russia-prime-minister-dmitry-medvedev-says-turkey-s-downing-of-su24-gave-grounds-for-war-a6767011.html.

23 See, for instance, J. Powell, 'Ukraine must fight the war but plan for peace', *Prospect* (25 January 2023), www.prospectmagazine.co.uk/essays/ukraine-fight-war-russia-plan-peace.

24 'Lavrov calls for a post-West world order', *Deutsche Welle* (18 February 2017), www.dw.com/en/lavrov-calls-for-post-west-world-order-dismisses-nato-as-cold-war-relic/a-37614099; 'Russia creating genuine never-before-seen multipolar world, says foreign intelligence chief', *Tass* (7 April 2022), https://tass.com/politics/1434003.

25 *Kontseptsiya vneshnei politikii Rossiiskoi Federatsii* [Foreign policy concept of the Russian Federation], no. 229 (31 March 2023), Ministry of Foreign Affairs, https://mid.ru/ru/foreign_policy/official_documents/1860586/

26 A. Monaghan, *Power in Modern Russia: Strategy and Mobilisation* (Manchester: Manchester University Press, 2017); A. Monaghan, (ed.) *Russian Grand Strategy in the Era of Global Power Competition* (Manchester: Manchester University Press, 2022); A. Monaghan, and R. Connolly (eds) *The Sea in Russian Strategy* (Manchester: Manchester University Press, 2023).

27 'Statya Sekretarya Soveta Bezopasnosti Rossiiskoi Federatsii v "Rossiiskoi gazete"' [Article by the Secretary of the Security Council of the Russian Federation in 'Rossiiskaya Gazeta'], Security Council of the Russian Federation (12 November 2019), www.scrf.gov.ru/news/allnews/2677/.

28 'Vystuplenie i diskussiya na Myunkhenskoi konferentsii po voprosam politiki bezopasnosti' [Presentation and discussion at the Munich Conference on Politics and Security] (10 February 2007), http://kremlin.ru/events/president/transcripts/24034.

29 F. Lukyanov, 'Raspad ili pereustroistvo?' [Collapse or rebuilding?], *Rossiya v Globalnoi Politike* (1 January-February 2016), https://globalaffairs.ru/articles/raspad-ili-pereustrojstvo/; O. Barabanov et al., *Global Revolt and Global Order: The Revolutionary Situation in Condition of the World and What to Do About It,* (Moscow: Valdai, 2017), https://valdaiclub.com/files/13306/.

30 Monaghan, *Power in Modern Russia*.

31 'Kommentarii Nikolaiya Patrysheva po itogam zasedaniya Soveta Bezopasnosti' [Nikolai Patrushev's commentary on the Security Council meeting] (5 April 2023), http://kremlin.ru/events/security-council/70872.

32 'Nachalnik Generalnovo shtaba VS RF general armii Valerii Gerasimov provyol brifing dlya voennykh attashe inostrannykh gosudarstv' [Chief of the General Staff of the Russian Armed Forces, General Valerii Gerasimov, gave a briefing for defence attaches of foreign states], Russian Defence Ministry (22 December 2023), https://function.mil.ru/news_page/country/more.htm?id=12449283@egNews.

33 J. Biden and M. Carpenter, 'How Joe Biden would stand up to Putin and Russia', *Foreign Affairs* (5 December 2017), www.foreignaffairs.com/articles/russia-fsu/2017-12-05/how-stand-kremlin.

34 *National Security Strategy* (October 2022), White House, www.whitehouse.gov/wp-content/uploads/2022/10/Biden-Harris-Administrations-National-Security-Strategy-10.2022.pdf, p. 2; NATO 2022 Strategic Concept (29 June 2022), www.nato.int/strategic-concept, p. 3.

35 W. Partlett, 'Russia's 2020 constitutional amendments: a comparative analysis', *Cambridge Yearbook of European Legal Studies*, vol. 23 (December 2021), pp. 311–342.

36 The Communist Party is the largest nationwide opposition force in what is essentially a left-leaning society and tends to come second in most elections. The LDPR is a nationalist party.

37 'Infighting erupts in Russia's anti-Kremlin opposition over Alexei Navalny', *Reuters* (10 February 2021), www.reuters.com/article/us-russia-politics-navalny-opposition-idUSKBN2AA2EK; 'Russia's "last liberal party" cuts ties with Navalniy supporters', *Moscow Times* (18 October 2021), www.themoscowtimes.com/2021/10/18/russias-last-liberal-party-cuts-ties-with-navalny-supporters-a75327.

38 Disapproval of Navalniy among those polled grew from 35 per cent in 2013 to 50 per cent in 2020 and 60 per cent in February 2022. 'Alexei Navalny: otnoshenie k politike i evo ugolovnomu presledovaniyu' [Alexei Navalny: attitudes towards the politician and his criminal prosecution], Levada Centre (8 February 2023), www.levada.ru/2023/02/08/aleksej-navalnyj-otnoshenie-k-politiku-i-ego-ugolovnomu-presledovaniyu.

39 'Narodniy front: Otpravil podarki Rossiiskim voennym v zone SVO' [The Popular Front: sent gifts to Russian troops in the zone of the SMO], *RIA Novosti* (19 February 2023), https://ria.ru/20230219/podarki-1852965285.html.

40 For discussion of Rosgvardia, see Monaghan, *Power in Modern Russia*.

41 T. Frye, *Weak Strongman: The Limits of Power in Putin's Russia* (Princeton: Princeton University Press, 2021).

42 'Vladimir Putin: liberalism has "outlived its purpose"', *Financial Times* (17 September 2019), www.ft.com/content/2880c762-98c2-11e9-8cfb-30c211dcd229.

43 'Podpisanie dogovorov o prinyatii DNR, LNR, Zaporozhskoi i Khersonskoi oblastei v sostav Rossii' [Signing of the agreements about the accession of the DNR, LNR, Zaporizhia and Kherson regions into Russia] (30 September 2022), http://kremlin.ru/events/president/news/69465; 'Poslanie Prezidenta Federalnomu Sobraniyu' [Presidential address to the Federal Assembly] (21 February 2023), http://kremlin.ru/events/president/news/70565.

44 Golunov was released and cleared after a public outcry that the arrest was based on fabricated evidence. Bekbulatova has since been labelled a foreign agent and moved abroad. Safronov was convicted on charges of treason and in 2022 was sentenced to 22 years' imprisonment.

45 'Vladimir Putin is in thrall to a distinctive brand of Russian fascism', *The Economist* (28 July 2022), http://economist.com/briefing/2022/07/28/vladimir-putin-is-in-thrall-to-a-distinctive-brand-of-russian-fascism.

46 For detailed and extended discussion, see M. Laruelle, *Is Russia Fascist? Unravelling Propaganda East and West* (Ithaca: Cornell University Press, 2021).

47 A. Motyl, 'Yes, Putin and Russia are fascist – a political scientist shows how they meet the textbook definition', *The Conversation* (30 March 2022), https://theconversation.com/yes-putin-and-russia-are-fascist-a-political-scientist-shows-how-they-meet-the-textbook-definition-179063.

48 For discursive overviews defining 'classical' fascism, see R. Griffin, Fascism (Cambridge: Polity Press, 2018); 'Fascism', *The Rest is History* (25 January 2021), https://play.acast.com/s/the-rest-is-history-podcast/17.fascism.

49 Laruelle, *Is Russia Fascist?* describes Russia as 'illiberal' with some Russia-specific aspects of fascism; R. Horvath, *Putin's Fascists: Russkii Obraz and the Politics of Managed Nationalism in Russia* (London: Routledge, 2022).

50 T. Frye, 'Russian studies is thriving, not dying', *National Interest* (3 October 2017), https://nationalinterest.org/feature/russian-studies-thriving-not-dying-22547; S. Wilson Sokhey, 'Russian studies is thriving at ASEEES', PONARS (20 November 2017), www.ponarseurasia.org/russian-studies-is-thriving-at-aseees; 'Interview with Sean Guillory, part I', NYU Jordan Centre (25 March 2019), https://jordanrussiacenter.org/news/sean-guillory-interview/#.ZCr31uzMKcI.

51 M. Kimmage, 'The wily country', *Foreign Affairs* (March/April 2020), www.foreignaffairs.com/reviews/review-essay/2020-02-11/wily-country; M. Laruelle, 'Russian studies' moment of self-reflection', *Russian Analytical Digest*, no. 293 (3 March 2023), p. 2. In terms of

policy circles, one report found that in the UK (despite promises to increase resources dedicated to the region), the number of staff who could speak Russian to an advanced level fell by nearly 30 per cent over five years from 2017 to 2022. T. Durrant, and J. Urban, *How Should the Foreign Office Change Now?*, Institute for Government (28 July 2022), www.instituteforgovernment.org.uk/publication/report/how-should-foreign-office-change-now.

52 T. Frye, 'Why IR theory gets russia wrong', *Foreign Affairs* (23 May 2016), www.foreignaffairs.com/russian-federation/why-ir-theory-gets-russia-wrong; T. Frye, 'The Mueller Report: the silence of the experts', *Moscow Times* (24 July 2019), www.themoscowtimes.com/2019/07/24/the-mueller-report-and-the-silence-of-the-experts-a66552.

53 F. Kostelka, 'John Mearsheimer's lecture on Ukraine: why he is wrong and what are the consequences', EU Ideas (11 July 2022), https://euideas.eui.eu/2022/07/11/john-mearsheimers-lecture-on-ukraine-why-he-is-wrong-and-what-are-the-consequences/; G. Rachman, 'It makes no sense to blame the West for the Ukraine war', *Financial Times* (13 February 2023), www.ft.com/content/2d65c763-c36f-4507-8a7d-13517032aa22.

54 See J. Edmonds, 'Start with the political', *War on the Rocks* (28 April 2022), https://warontherocks.com/2022/04/start-with-the-political-explaining-russias-bungled-invasion-of-ukraine.

55 V. Gelman, 'Exogenous shock and Russian studies', *Post-Soviet Affairs*, 39:1–2 (2023), pp. 1–9.

56 V. Donovan, 'The (sorry) state of the field or why Western humanists need to listen in silence and solidarity', *ASEEES NewsNet* (January 2023), https://issuu.com/aseees/docs/2023_jan_nn_final/s/17941107; Laruelle, 'Russian studies' moment of self-reflection', p. 2.

57 Decolonisation will be the core theme for the Association of Slavic, East European and Eurasian Studies annual convention in 2023, www.aseees.org/convention/2023-aseees-convention-theme#:~:text=The%202023%20ASEEES%20convention%20invites,historical%20force%20within%20the%20region. A. Shaipov and Y. Shaipova, 'It's high time to decolonise Western Russia studies', *Foreign Policy* (11 February 2023), https://foreignpolicy.com/2023/02/11/russia-studies-war-ukraine-decolonize-imperialism-western-academics-soviet-empire-eurasia-eastern-europe-university; 'Moscow's invasion of Ukraine triggers soul searching at Western universities as scholars rethink Russian studies', Radio Free Europe/Radio Liberty (1 January 2023), www.rferl.org/a/russia-war-ukraine-western-academia/32201630.html; M. Mälksoo, 'The postcolonial moment in Russia's war against Ukraine', *Journal of Genocide Research* (11 May 2022), www.tandfonline.com/doi/full/10.1080/14623528.2022.2074947.

58 'Student interest in studying Russian slumps', *Times Higher Education* (13 September 2022), www.timeshighereducation.com/news/student-interest-studying-russian-slumps-ukrainian-surges.

59 'How to study Russia', *Russian Analytical Digest*, no. 293 (3 March 2023). The Russia Program at the Elliott School of International Affairs, George Washington University, launched on 10 March 2023: https://therussiaprogram.org. The Slavonic Studies Section at the University of Cambridge presented the 'Rethinking Slavonic Studies' seminar series, www.mmll.cam.ac.uk/news/slavonic-section-presents-rethinking-slavonic-lecture-series-2022-23.

60 P. Saffo, 'Six rules for effective forecasting', *Harvard Business Review* (July-August 2007), https://hbr.org/2007/07/six-rules-for-effective-forecasting.

61 G. J. Ikenberry, 'The illusion of geopolitics. the enduring power of the liberal order', *Foreign Affairs* (May/June 2014). For discussion, see P. Porter, 'Russia and Ukraine', presentation at International Studies Association Conference, 13 May 2023.

62 This includes both Russia watchers and security and international relations specialists, and a huge industry has been built on this theme since 2014. H. Reisinger and A. Goltz, *Russia's Hybrid Warfare: Waging War Below the Radar of Traditional Collective Defence*, NDC Research Paper (November 2014); R. Thornton, 'The Russian military's 'new main emphasis', *RUSI Journal*, 162:4 (2017), www.tandfonline.com/doi/abs/10.1080/03071847.2017.1381401; D. Kilcullen, *The Dragons and the Snakes: How the Rest Learned to Fight the West* (London: Hurst & Co, 2020); E, Braw, 'Conventional Wars have fallen out of fashion: grey zone aggression is the new thing', ICDS Commentary (23 November 2021), https://icds.ee/en/conventional-wars-have-fallen-out-of-fashion-grey-zone-aggression-is-the-new-thing. For robust discussion of this through the lens of international relations and strategy rather than Russia studies specifically, see P. Porter, 'Out of the shadows: Ukraine and the shock of non-hybrid war', *Journal of Global Security Studies*, 8:3 (2023) .

63 C. Dougherty et al., 'What the experts got wrong (and right) about Russian military power', *War on the Rocks* (30 May 2022), https://warontherocks.com/2022/05/what-the-experts-got-wrong-and-right-about-russian-military-power.

64 'Sanctions force Russia to use appliance parts in military gear, US says', *The Washington Post* (11 May 2022), www.washingtonpost.com/technology/2022/05/11/russia-sanctions-effect-military.

65 Author's correspondence with Julian Cooper, April 2023.

66 In September 2022, the US State Department advised US citizens to not travel to Russia and those residing in or travelling to Russia to leave. On 13 February 2023, this advice was repeated, given an increased risk of detention. 'Russia travel advisory', US State Department (13 February 2023), https://travel.state.gov/content/travel/en/traveladvisories/travel advisories/russia-travel-advisory.html.

67 'Poslanie Prezidenta Federalnomy Sobraniyu' [Presidential address to the Federal Assembly], (21 February 2023), http://kremlin.ru/events/president/news/70565.

68 'V Kremle obsudili orientir dlya prezidentskykh vyborov 2024 goda' [In the Kremlin they have discussed the orientation for the presidential elections in 2024], *RBK* (6 March 2023), www.rbc.ru/politics/06/03/2023/6404e1a79a794715eaa85883.

69 'Stress-test' [Stress test], *Kommersant* (28 March 2023), www.kommersant.ru/doc/5900685.

70 Tatarsky's real name was Maxim Fomin. His funeral was attended by hundreds of mourners and a military band. 'Kuvalda ot boitsov ChVK "Vagner" i venok ot Margarity Simonyan: Vladlena Tatarskovo pokhoronili na Troekurovskom kladbishche' [A sledgehammer from the warriors of PMC Wagner and a wreath from Margarita Simonyan: Vladlen Tatarsky was buried in the Troekurovsky cemetery], *MoscowOnline* (8 April 2023), https://msk1.ru/text/world/2023/04/08/72201425.

71 'Rossiyane s momenta nachala mobilizatsii aktivno ckupayut uspokoitelnie sredstva' [Since the beginning of the mobilization, Russians have actively bought sedatives], *Vedomosti* (28 September 2022), www.vedomosti.ru/society/articles/2022/09/28/942835-rossiyane-aktivno-skupayut-uspokoitelnie.

72 'Rossiiskoi tsivilizatsii ishchut podkhodyashchee napolnenie' [Russian civilisation is looking for suitable content], *Kommersant* (1 April 2023), https://kommersant.ru/doc/5912304?from=glavnoe_4.

73 'Urok SIZO. Kak antivoenniy risunok shkolnitsy iz Tulskoi oblasti obernulsya ugolovnym delom protiv ee otsa' [Lesson from the pre-trial detention centre: How a schoolgirl from Tula's anti-war drawing became a criminal case against her father], *Mediazone* (2 March 2023), https://zona.media/article/2023/03/02/masha; 'Otsa shkolnitsi s antivoennym risunkom otpravili pod domashnii arest' [The father of a schoolgirl with an anti-war drawing has been put under house arrest], *Vedomosti* (3 March 2023), www.vedomosti.ru/politics/news/2023/03/03/965102-ottsa-shestiklassnitsi-s-antivoennim-risunkom-otpravili-pod-domashnii-arest.

Index

Notes are indicated by the letter n. appearing after the page number, followed by the note number. For example 87n.11 refers to note number 11 on page 87.

UR *see* United Russia (UR) party
'USSR 2.0' 6

Vaino, Anton 136
values gap 85, 86, 161–2, 164–5
vertical of power 39, 45,
    113, 131–6
Vigilant Skies 66
violence 175
Vladivostok 98, 100
Volgograd, terrorist attacks 42
Volodin, Vyacheslav 104, 105, 107,
    126, 131, 137
Voronova, Tatiana 137–8

Wagner Private Military Company
    165, 173
war crimes 155–6, 177n.7
war
    in Ukraine 2, 5–8, 26, 28, 31,
        82–6, 145–6, 155–7,
        167–73
    measures short of 169–70
West
    cooperation *see* cooperation
        with the West
    interventionism 68, 77, 82, 84
    relationship with Russia
        'common' but not 'shared'
            agenda 75–8
        compounding of 67–71
        conceptual gaps 1–2, 7–9,
            18–19
        different approaches to
            common histories 61–3
        different conclusions 72–5
        European security 76–8
        international affairs 2–6
    threat of democracies 161–2

understanding of Russia
    clarification 19
    clichés and stereotypes 3–6
    exchanges of opinion 51
    flawed and distorted 16–21
    ideological 38–9
    interpretation 27–8
    linguistic dissonance 9–12,
        18–19, 23n.26, 80–1
    post-Cold War 6–9, 60–3
    problems with 3–6, 145–152
    protest demonstrations 91–3
    Putinology 17–18, 44–6,
        122–4, 152
    speculation and
        insinuation 41–8
    state of surprise 3, 28–9,
        48–52
    support for liberal
        opposition 37
    see also Euro-Atlantic
        community
World Trade Organization (WTO),
    Russia entry into 66
'wrong side of history,' Russia
    on 13–14

Yabloko party 37, 96, 106
Yakunin, Vladimir 139
Yeltsin, Boris 5
'youthification' ('omolozhenie')
    164, 174
Yunarmiya 175

Zhirinovsky, Vladimir 103, 128
Zolotov, Viktor 122, 123, 126
Zubkov, Viktor 107
Zyuganov, Gennadiy 103, 105,
    113, 127, 128, 138